FLEEING FUNDAMENTALISM

Also by CARLENE CROSS

The Undying West: A Chronicle of Montana's Camas Prairie

Fleeing Fundamentalism

A Minister's Wife
Examines Faith

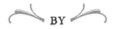 BY

Carlene Cross

```
BR1725.C755 A3 2006
Cross, Carlene.
Fleeing fundamentalism : a
minister's wife examines
faith
Chapel Hill, N.C. :
Algonquin Books of Chapel
```

ALGONQUIN BOOKS OF CHAPEL HILL 2006

Published by

ALGONQUIN BOOKS OF CHAPEL HILL

Post Office Box 2225

Chapel Hill, North Carolina 27515-2225

a division of

WORKMAN PUBLISHING

225 Varick Street

New York, New York 10014

Library of Congress Cataloging-in-Publication Data
Cross, Carlene.
    Fleeing fundamentalism : a minister's wife examines faith / by Carlene Cross.
        p. cm.
    ISBN-13: 978-1-56512-498-1; ISBN-10: 1-56512-498-7
    1. Cross, Carlene.   2. Christian biography.   3. Spiritual biography.
4. Fundamentalist churches.   5. Fundamentalism.   6. Religious right.
7. Christian conservatism.   I. Title.
BR1725.C755A3 2006
277.3'0825'092—dc22
[B]   2006046544

10 9 8 7 6 5 4 3 2 1

First Edition

All the events in *Fleeing Fundamentalism* are true.
Only the names have been changed.

Contents

Preface

AT THE DAWN of the twenty-first century, religious Fundamentalism has emerged as one of the most powerful forces at work in America. Contesting modern secular values, it threatens scientific advances such as stem cell research, the separation of church and state, and the civil liberties of many. Yet for all its visibility, the Religious Right remains incomprehensible to a large number of people.

For years, as a minister's wife in the Fundamentalist movement, I embraced its ideology—one that measured all moral choice against the dictates of an error-free Bible and then set out to force that intrepretation upon America. *Fleeing Fundamentalism* is the story of my conversion as a child to this often airtight system, as well as my later escape, taking my own children with me. Alongside my story, I have tried to show how and why Fundamentalist groups came into existence, and what motivates their startling and troubling worldview.

In telling my story, I hope to examine this modern phenomenon and challenge its notions, those both individually inhumane and universally grandiose. I hope to remind people of the warning Thomas Jefferson gave us: that when government teams up with religion, it creates a "formidable engine against the civil rights of man."

The Religious Right's biblical creed translates into a frightening sacrifice of societal and personal freedom. Nationally, this loss of liberty is encroaching upon our political system. Privately, it is being played out between individuals and families in homes across America. *Fleeing Fundamentalism* is one such story.

One

The Farm

I WAS SEVENTEEN on the day my destiny came to claim me. That evening in 1975, I sat in the kitchen of our old farmhouse and listened to the rainsquall move over the Rockies and into our valley. I felt the air grow heavy and oppressive, almost purple, as off to the east leaped platinum branches of lightning, momentarily suspended in silence until thunder shook the windowpanes with a great crash. A second lightning bolt flickered in the alfalfa field outside, illuminating the page open before me: "And I stood upon the sand of the sea, and saw a beast rise up out of the sea, having seven heads and ten horns, and upon his horns ten crowns, and upon his heads the name of blasphemy."

I looked up as torrents of water slammed against the windows like buckets of silver paint, and I imagined the awful Beast of Revelation rising out of the firmament, his seven heads leering toward the shore. Twisted bone like ram's horn grew from each skull, and every mouth gave the roar of an enraged lion, his huge yellowed canines gleaming in the moonlight. His bellowing heads swept from side to side, sending a fearsome echo through the mountains, and pendant loops of slaver whipping the air. I pictured the Devil standing on the white beach calling out to the creature at sea, "I give you authority over all tribes, tongues, and nations. Everyone whose name is not written in the Book of Life will follow you."

"I will burn my mark into their foreheads," the Beast screamed back. "No one will buy or sell without it."

"Six … six … six," Satan cried, with a howling laugh.

Closing Mom's Bible, I shivered as goose bumps sprang up on my arms. How, I wondered, were Satan and his hideous Beast planning to sear 666 into people's skins? Would they be like the calves we branded in the spring, bawling pitifully as the white smoke and the stench of burning animal flesh filled the sky? I could just see the heavenly angels of Revelation crying, "Woe to the inhabitants of the Earth," as they opened the scrolls of judgment, releasing hail and fire down upon mankind, and locusts and scorpions to torment all who were left behind. I thought about the desperate future of the world and how Mom said that Jesus was coming back to rapture all the faithful Christians to heaven and leave all the unsaved behind to live through the Great Tribulation and wear the Beast's brand. It was in that moment that I stepped from the pathway of my normal life and detoured into another world — that of serving God rather than indulging my own sinful flesh, which, until that instant, I had always been happy to do.

IN THE YEARS before this epiphany, I grew up in a farmhouse at the far corner of a valley in a far corner of Montana, itself a far corner of the world. Who could tell why I was embarrassed to be from the country, so unlike the seemingly contented folks around me? While others confined their dreams to the Sears catalog, I squandered long winter evenings in front of the crackling fire, dreaming about the outside world, where fine folks shopped in grand department stores and slick-shoed salesmen with immaculate fingernails asked if they might be of some assistance. I had been cheated. I knew that everything in the city was exciting, even thrilling, because I saw the evidence every night on the *CBS Evening News with Walter Cronkite,* or in the glossy magazines I pored over in the back of the school library.

I was mesmerized by the modern world, and the only place within less than two days' drive that it could be found was in the pages of *McCall's, Life, Look,* and *Harper's.* Thankfully, these treasures were kept in the library's alcove, where a person could find some privacy and dream uninterrupted about becoming as beautiful as movie star Faye Dunaway or skating heroine Peggy Fleming.

These magazines never came to our house. We got only the pictureless, brown-papered *Farmer's Journal,* which detailed some boring new farm bill Senator Mansfield had introduced to Congress. I knew that people in New York debated sophisticated notions like high fashion and romance; they never worried about the depressed future of livestock. Instead of boots caked with cow manure, they wore gleaming cordovan Florsheims and rode up the elevators of sparkling glass skyscrapers that looked out across endless miles of a tempestuous sea. Back here on the farm, people kept both feet — and their imaginations — firmly planted on the ground. But in the city people were masters of their own destinies.

In the January 5, 1968, issue of *Life,* I read about a confident actress named Katharine Hepburn, who never let anyone tell her what to do. When Ms. Hepburn was acting in *Guess Who's Coming to Dinner?* she had the guts to tell Stanley Kramer, the director, how to perform his job. It made him pretty mad, but he forgave her, and they won two Oscars for the movie that year. I wanted to be like Katharine Hepburn, self-assured and witty — not plain and coarse like the people who lived in my stifling world, people who didn't enunciate their words or finish their sentences.

Our kitchen table collected these characters like hogs collect

lice. On winter afternoons when northers rolled down from Canada, chilling the valley so fast you could watch the mercury fall, my
father and his friends gathered in our kitchen to tell stories. They
would come in from the blizzard, fumbling out of their leather
jackets and stomping the snow from their boots, while the blaze in
the river-rock fireplace spread its heat throughout the house. Mom
moved quietly through the kitchen, plugging in the percolator and
putting huckleberry pie in the oven. As the smell of warm berries
and tamarack fir scented the room, the grown-ups hardly noticed
my skinny frame, wedged into the corner. There I fantasized that I
was a visiting anthropologist recently arrived to study the language
and ways of a primitive tribe. I knew I could gather all I needed to
understand them from the stories they were about to tell. Anecdotes
forged in raw, abbreviated sentences — the bones of a tale without
a morsel of flesh.

My father loved these hours of yarn spinning. He would stretch
back from the table, his head of curly black hair resting back on
calloused hands the size of dinner plates. He had a handsome face,
with boyish dimples and the dark eyes of his Slavic ancestry. But
his brow, lined with furrows like a new-plowed wheat field — *that*
marred his looks. Only during these unguarded moments of storytelling would the worries fade and his expression melt into a roguish
grin, hinting that another man, less anxious and more playful, hid
inside that powerful frame. I suspected that he kept himself reined
in for fear that a lapse of his stern vigilance would allow the whole
farm to slide into hell — or worse, foreclosure.

Dad's Bohemian parents immigrated to America in 1910, moving west to homestead in Montana. I figured his seriousness came
mostly from a devastating experience he had as a small boy. When
he told the story, I could tell it had changed his life. "Mom was in

town for supplies, and Dad and me was just standin' there lookin' at the hay crop, when all of a sudden he collapsed. I started pushin' his chest to get his heart goin' again, but he was cold as a stone. It was thirty-six — the dark days of the depression ... thought we was gonna starve that winter for sure."

I shifted in my little corner of the kitchen, telling myself that all such misfortune could be avoided if one lived in the city, where people didn't have to wage war against the elements of nature and spoke with proper English. I made a pact with myself to talk like my mother and my teachers in town, who never confused *was* and *were*, or dropped the *g* in *looking*. With my speech straightened out, I might even be able to move to California and make it in the movies, and no one would ever know I came from the farm.

But I had more flaws than country speech: number one was my limp hair. I knew that the whole world admired luxuriant hair, because women who made it in Hollywood always had plenty of it. My teeth were a mess too, and I had a bad premonition that given my reedy frame, the voluptuousness that my chosen future required might make success a real long shot.

Thank God Mom was proactive in my self-improvement. Although she teased me about my wispy hair, I knew we were secret accomplices in my eventual escape from the farm. Every Tuesday morning we'd jump into the brown '54 Fairlane and head off on an extravagant eighty-mile adventure into Missoula for dance lessons. As I grew older, the trips would expand to include appointments for braces and piano lessons. Gliding along over the county road, I would glance at my mother, with her soft brown eyes, shining hair, and thousand-kilowatt smile. It didn't surprise me she understood the importance of such cultural refinements, because she came not from hardscrabble immigrants but from an impressive lineage of French sea captains, Revolutionary War heroes, and poets. And Mom, too, was accomplished far beyond your typical Montana farmwife. After graduating from high school, she had left the valley and earned her RN at Holy Rosary School of Nursing in Missoula.

I looked out the car window and up onto the hillside at the homesteads dotting the desolate prairie like ships wrecked on a vast shoal. *Mom doesn't belong here, either,* I thought, in this place where cows drooled along the roadside, and dilapidated homesteads buckled and warped, their rafters finally tumbling into their cellars. This was no place for a woman who loved to read, to bask in a heavenly reprieve from raking second-cutting alfalfa and immerse herself in Jane Austen. Most farm women came back from the harvest to happily put on their aprons and sprinkle flour, sift icing sugar, and dream of a new stove so they could bake more blue-ribbon pies. But not Mom. Mom shucked off her boots and coveralls and started another book or a more complicated piano piece, or grabbed up my brother, Dan, my sister, Melanie, or me and read to us. Her proper English had a different rhythm to it than Dad's or any of his friends'. I wondered why she had ever consented to live in such a harsh place with winter snowdrifts the size of school buses and dust that swirled through the valley all summer long. I dreamed about coming back to rescue Mom after I got my big break in Hollywood. Then she could live the life I thought she deserved. I soon learned that someone else had that same notion long before me.

It was a hot August afternoon when Mrs. Goodman drove up our dirt road, followed by a plume of dust that filled my mouth and eyes as I jumped into her car. The Goodmans owned the farm at the far end of the valley, and their daughter, Sally, was my best friend since third grade. Mrs. Goodman baked a lot of pies, cakes, and buttery pastries, and she and Sally were heading into town to pick up next week's supplies. She had called Mom to see if I wanted to come along for the ride. As the hot westerly wind blew over the prairie, sending rippling green waves across the wheat field, we stuck our heads out the window and let the scorching breeze hit our faces.

Then all of a sudden, Mrs. Goodman said right out of the blue, "Ya know your mama nearly married another man."

"She did?"

"Yep, when she was in nurses' training, she fell madly in love with an Air Force pilot named George Johnson. Some say he looked like James Dean no less, 'cept in a officer's uniform. Real handsome fella, he was — serious career man too, with all them stripes and stars on his sleeve. He gave her a big diamond ring and asked her to marry him and move away with him to Spokane — big city and all. Your mama was mad about him. And he was crazy as a loon for her too, him makin' that four-hour drive all the way from Washington State and all, even in real bad weather."

I sat silently, unsure whether I wanted Mrs. Goodman to go on. I looked into the glaring sun and imagined my mother living on a tree shaded lane, surrounded by manicured lawns and free from the dust that swirled off the dirt road and settled like a thin sheet over her furniture. I pictured refined Air Force officers and their wives coming to dinner and saying things like "What did you think about that new Faulkner novel, Mary Lou?"

Mrs. Goodman interrupted my thoughts by saying, "Then one night George come into town during a bad storm, took your mum out for a fancy dinner. When she came back that night, she was gigglin' and carryin' on, tellin' all the girls about the new house George wanted to put a down payment on."

I imagined Mom bursting into the nurses' dormitory that night, describing the lovely stucco bungalow in Spokane and the girls staying up to chatter about the upcoming wedding. Affected by the great joy in the room, even the nuns were probably swept up in the moment and got out some wine they had hidden away for special occasions.

"Saddest thing," Mrs. Goodman went on. "George headed back out in the blizzard to get himself home safe. Then right outside Missoula his car hit an icy patch on that old bridge — you know that death-trap overpass near Lolo?"

"No."

"Threw him right over the cliff and killed him. Your mum took it real hard, just wouldn't stop crying."

I sat motionless on the brown vinyl seat while the summer sun beat onto my pale stick legs, causing little rivulets of sweat and pasting me to the seat. Mrs. Goodman continued: "You know, yer dad, who folks say always loved yer mama, bless his soul, drove into Missoula that night and took her back to her family out here. She married him . . . 'bout a year later."

In my mind I heard the phone ringing as the young nurses and nuns poured more wine and clicked their glasses together, until one of the nuns picked up the phone and handed it to Mom. After listening a moment, she cried a terrible scream and collapsed onto the floor. All I could think about for days was how Mom had buried the life that might have been. She never gave so much as a wistful hint of it as she tugged on long underwear, jeans, rubber boots, plaid flannel wool jacket, and mismatched mittens to go out into twenty-below winter weather to wrestle breech calves from their mothers' wombs. Dad never talked about such subjects either — he was too focused on keeping the ranch alive, and maybe on trying to prove to Mom that he could make a go of it on this unforgiving patch of land.

Besides working with tireless devotion, Dad also pinched every penny he could. When we went into Missoula, we ate at the Oxford

Café, where a dollar fifty could buy you ham hocks and lima beans or cow brains and eggs. On the way home Dad invariably stopped at a scrap-metal depot called Pacific Hide and Fur, where elk heads, deer hides, greasy machinery parts, and rusty beaver traps hung from the walls. In the dog days of summer the sluggish air in the old wooden building reeked of 90-weight oil and rancid animal flesh as my father rummaged through the scrap piles, filling a box to the brim with spare parts and then paying three cents a pound for them. He took the rusting steel home to mend or build farm equipment with, welding and pounding it into rakes and plows and harrow disks and teeth. One of the contraptions Dad made from the scrap metal he bought there was what we called the hoopie. Instead of acknowledging his ingenuity, I rolled my eyes at the rattletrap Frankenstein as it bounced across the field scooping up hay, and prayed that my friends from town wouldn't drive by and see it.

Even as a snobbish child, however, I had to admit that my father did possess talents. He could read my face like a Las Vegas cardsharp, which meant that he knew I considered him a common farmer and that being his daughter was like being dealt a bad hand at blackjack. I might have been spared a whipping or two if my rebellion had ended with merely thinking disrespectful thoughts rather than acting on them as well: sassing him or rolling my eyes when I felt he was being particularly farmerlike. Such acts of defiance always brought on sound spankings, which I considered a moral outrage and thus, during their administration, refused to shed a single tear, sparking a titanic clash of wills between my father and me. I told myself that no matter how long it took to wear him down, I would not weep.

As he got the wooden paddle down from the top of the refrigerator, he would say, "You're like a wild horse, Carlene — one that needs broke."

We'll see, I thought. As the paddle came down on my bottom, *whap ... whap ... whap ... whap ...* , I bit my lip, or sometimes even laughed at him. To me it was like winning a chess tournament; as the paddle vibrated my father's arthritic hand, I told myself, *It's simply a matter of the mind.*

After these conflicts I often ran out into the vast grassland to feel the pure, wide emptiness of its silence. The rolling hills enfolded me with warmth and the fragrance of sage as I stood and gazed at the distant granite peaks, purple on the horizon. In these silent moments I wondered about God. Did He live in the enormous sky and visit only when the clouds broke and His finger traced the meadow floor? Or did He really want more to do with the world and so hid Himself in unexpected things like the killdeer and the cottontail? I knew that a great deal of human energy, mine included, was spent trying to figure out how God acted and why some people got help from Him and others didn't, like the ones who got thrown from cars and broke their necks or were killed in weird wheat-threshing accidents. Did it help if you joined the right church or said complicated prayers? Did these appeals put you at the head of His priority list? I thought a lot about how God kept track of things, but mostly I kept these wonderings secret.

The only people who seemed unembarrassed to talk about such things were the teachers at Vacation Bible School who came to our valley each summer. Rocky Mountain Bible Mission, an organization that took on the task of bringing the gospel to rural areas in Montana, sponsored the Bible school. They started out by sending missionaries to the homes of farm families in the valley, encouraging them to let their children attend the weeklong event. One spring day in 1963, a pleasant, slow-talking, born-again cowboy arrived at our ranch. He pulled up in a brand-new red pickup, got out, and leaned himself against the door of his shiny rig. As I watched from the bedroom window, I knew immediately that this guy was in deep trouble. He wore a big, wide cowboy hat and drove a four-wheel-drive — both things that Dad called "overkill." He introduced himself to my father as Sam Guptal, a minister from the Rocky Mountain Bible Mission, and said, "I wanted to invite your children to the Vacation Bible School we're sponsoring."

Dad told him he had thirty seconds to get off our property. My father mistrusted preachers of any persuasion. When he was a young man, his mother, a devout Catholic, was diagnosed with cancer. The doctor told him, his brothers, and Grandma's priest, but did not tell her. The brothers, grown and with ranches of their own, were fiercely protective of their mother and still carried the pain of the sudden loss of their father. As they were gathered in Grandma's kitchen to decide what to do while she lay resting in the back room, Father Connelly appeared at the door.

"I'm needin' to speak with yer mum, boys."

"We will deal with this our own way," my father answered.

"Aye, t'would be a mortal sin keepin' her from preparin' her soul for final unction. 'Tis a mortal sin — an unpardonable one."

"Get out," one of Dad's brothers told Father Connelly.

The priest returned to his car, pulled out of the driveway, and hid down the road. When he saw the brothers leave, he sneaked back to the house and told Grandma she was dying of cancer. My father saw the priest's car from the ridge and came barreling back to the house, but it was too late. Livid, he ran Father Connelly off the property. Fifteen years later he did the same to the Rocky Mountain Bible preacher.

Eventually Mom convinced Dad that Sam Guptal was different from Father Connelly (her great-grandfather had been a Protestant minister), and Dad let us go to Vacation Bible School. I knew the only reason he budged on the issue was because he loved Mom so much. But he did warn her, "I'll tell ya, Mary Lou, you're gonna have to keep an eye on them people. I don't trust 'em, not one damned bit." To my astonishment, he even let Sam Guptal talk to Mom about religion. The preacher began dropping by to discuss the mysteries of God and leave religious books for her to read. She loved the company and the conversation on philosophical subjects — more compelling than hog futures and wheat prices. That my father was leery of him made me even more curious about what the preacher had to say.

After that first summer, each June the mission sent four college students to stay with families in the valley and teach Bible school. We always boarded two of them in our bunkhouse. They were from towns with fascinating names like Edmonton, Toronto, and Kamloops, also in the foreign country of Canada. I worried that these students would feel like purebred champion show dogs thrown into a pack of junkyard mutts, but they actually seemed charmed with farm life, wanting us to drive them out in the fields to see the cows, asking questions about the upcoming harvest season, and even volunteering to help my Dad change sprinkler pipes — offers that utterly bewildered me.

During that week, to the delight of the valley's farm kids, the Bible college students set up class in the nearby two-room schoolhouse. Lined up in ragamuffin rows, we sat at our wooden desks, listening raptly to exotic stories about the Holy Land and a loving man with flowing brown hair and piercing eyes named Jesus. I liked it most when the teachers pinned pictures of him on the bul-

letin board: the Savior holding a tiny lamb or, with his hands out-
stretched, feeding the five thousand. The Lord's hair waved in long,
soft curls, like no man I'd ever seen, and his face looked peaceful,
calm, and sophisticated — a guy who wouldn't holler or cuss about
anything.

We'd spend the week covered in paste, glue, and felt, construct-
ing colorful art projects from Popsicle sticks, colored yarn, and paper plates. We'd learn serious Christian choruses that seemed far
more cultured than the Hank Williams songs I heard on the radio.
"Onward, Christian so-o-oldiers, Marching as to war, With the
cross of Jee-sus Going on before . . . ," cried our little militia as we
marched in formation. Each Bible verse we memorized earned us
a gold star, placed in a column above our names, and I delighted
in stacking them up like shining stepping-stones to heaven. We'd
quiz each other until we could rattle off the words without a stutter.
Standing proud, we'd recite, "I beseech ye therefore, brethren, by the
mercies of God, to present your bodies as a living sacrifice." Biblical
words seemed superior to plain country talk, and I loved to wrap my
tongue around the sonorous phrases. Our teachers told us that the
object of memorization wasn't just to win prizes, but to come to the
point where you knew you were a sinner and needed Jesus in your
heart. The concept seemed logical to me. I did have to admit that I
had a hard time doing what I was told. So at age eight I asked the
Lord to come into my heart and clean it up. In return I promised to
serve him forever.

But even my pledge to God didn't diminish my romantic fantasies. At age thirteen, my braces came off and I began studying *Seventeen* magazine for tips on how to look like a New York model. Next to
the bathroom sink lay a dog-eared copy of the magazine, and strewn
across the counter was a rainbow arsenal of shadows, mascaras,

and blushes that I needed to help me make the transformation. But when my father saw the effects of my efforts, he said, "Wash your face." In keeping with my general attitude toward obedience to him, I acquiesced, then sneaked my makeup onto the school bus and put it on during the long ride into town. By the time I entered my freshmen year I had decided that if I was going to take LA by storm I'd better do a test run in my high school. I became a varsity cheerleader; then that year and each one following, I became a class officer, which in a student body of a hundred wasn't exactly like being elected to Congress, but I imagined it was.

My sophomore year I discovered Ernest Hemingway and, with his stories, a new world of carnal sensations. When our teacher, Mr. Davis, assigned *For Whom the Bell Tolls,* I instantly fell in love with Robert Jordan, the young American in the International Brigade who had gone to Spain to fight the fascists. When Hemingway described Jordan's love for his compatriot Maria, odd things awakened inside my body, forcing my heart to speed up, and a strange catch to rise in my throat. Reading "He put his lips behind her ear and moved them up along her neck, feeling the smooth skin and the soft touch of her hair on them," I felt a delicious sensation rustle in places hitherto undiscovered. I finished the book early and checked out every novel the library had by Ernest Hemingway. His muscular sentences and virile characters filled me with a new, curious energy. Then I turned my imagination from Hemingway's characters to the man himself: robust and rosy cheeked, brimming with passion. I wished I could have been his expatriate lover in the 1920s, gone to Paris to live with him in the Latin Quarter overlooking the Seine. Hemingway and his sensual words only heightened my wanderlust dreams.

Late at night, as a pale sickle moon rose over the mountains,

I'd lie in bed, press my new transistor radio hard against my ear, and slowly turn the volume up. Like a prisoner of war, I'd strain to hear informed voices from the outside world, roaming the dial for distant echoes, strange whisperings and hissings, the rise and fall of the signal sounding lonely and searching — an adventure companion. In my imagination I thought of all the faraway places in the world. I pictured English royal guardsmen and Scottish pipers, the drums of Africa, boatmen riding the Nile, French stone cottages with thatched roofs, and bedouins in the Sahara, olive gardens in Greece, wine sippers chatting in a Paris café. There was a great big world out there, and I would see it all. Starting in Los Angeles, I would get a degree in art, and then travel to all the exotic places I'd dreamed about. I ordered a catalog from the California Art Institute, careful to abbreviate my return address from County Road 382 to CR 382, so the admissions counselors wouldn't suspect my lack of worldliness. Only twenty-four months to go until graduation — even I could put up with chasing cows that long.

Then in 1973 the Rocky Mountain Bible Mission started a year-round church in our local town of Hot Springs, preaching that the Bible represented the exact words of God. Mom began attending and even convinced Dad to join her when there were no pressing needs on the ranch. Although he came along, he seemed uncomfortable, keeping to the edge of the crowd, hands in his pockets, like an ill at ease schoolboy. Mom was glad to see the church open its doors, because over the years she had put away her books on literature and increased her study of the Bible. No one in the valley wanted to talk about *Little Women* or *Under the Lilacs*. On the other hand, Sam Guptal was stopping by more often, giving her books on end-time prophecy. Her favorite author was no longer Louisa May Alcott but Hal Lindsey.

Lindsey taught that Jesus was coming back to "rapture" all the faithful Christians to heaven and leave all the unsaved behind to live through the Great Tribulation, a time when the Antichrist, the Beast, would rise from the sea and become the leader of the European Common Market. The Beast would make everyone take his 666 mark and then would cause the armies of the world to enter into the great and awful battle of Armageddon, the most hideous war ever imagined, when blood would run so high that it flowed like a river, reaching the horses' bridles. Many Christian scholars were writing that the Bible declared the timetable for this heart-stopping event had already begun. In Matthew 24, Jesus said that once the Jewish people came back into the Holy Land, as they did in 1948, he would return before a single generation had passed away. *Oh, my God,* I thought, counting forward, *I only have a few years left.*

Suddenly instead of dreaming about faraway places, I conjured up visions of the Beast and the heavenly angels of Revelation crying, "Woe, to the inhabitants of the Earth," as they opened the scrolls of judgment to torment all who were left behind. In my nightmares I saw celestial beings tearing the fifth seal, which opened the bottomless pit. The sea became blood, and the fifth angel prophesied, "Men will seek death and will not find it." Some nights these visions would be so real I would sit bolt upright in bed, my cotton nightgown drenched with sweat. My attraction to Fundamentalism was not out of quiet reflection but cold fear.

Dan, who was a year ahead of me in high school, also got caught up in the end-time fever and left for Big Sky Bible College in 1974. He started writing home about his prophecy classes and other fascinating courses like Christology, pneumatology, and hermeneutics. One night at the dinner table Mom quietly suggested that I follow him the next year. Although I didn't want to be left out of all the exciting temptations in New York and California, I certainly wasn't keen to miss the Rapture and be left to endure the Tribulation. With blood flowing in the streets, even Los Angeles lost its allure. Considering the upcoming evil, my worldly fantasies were both petty and futile — how attractive could a young woman be with 666 burned into her forehead?

Two

Big Sky Bible College

O N A SCORCHING SEPTEMBER day in 1975, Dan and I drove Highway 200, a road that snaked through the Rocky Mountains and flattened out across the patchwork wheat and cornfields of eastern Montana, true as a surveyor's line. As we barreled over the narrow two-lane black-top toward an empty horizon, Dan described the new world that I was about to enter. I leaned against the window and gazed at the abandoned homesteads, their slats and rafters twisted into violin curves littering the desolate grassland.

I studied Dan's wide-open face as he drove. He was every inch a farm boy, with his heart in the usual place: on his sleeve, in plain view. A year older than me, he had been generous and easy to get along with over the long eternity of our childhood, and we had developed a deep, comfortable friendship. Changing sprinkler pipes in the sticky gumbo clay or baling hay on hundred-degree afternoons, we had worked together, tugging, sweating, feeling the muscles in our arms and shoulders turn sore, the searing Montana sun on our backs. I respected Dan for bearing his farm responsibilities with dignity, working twelve-hour days in the field without complaint (unlike me), driving enormous tractors, hay rakes, and combines at the age of ten. But Dan admired my streak of independence, and I knew he wished he could say the kinds of things that had earned me whippings more than once. Such disrespectful talk would never have fought its way across his lips. Yet even though we came from opposite poles of temperament, we never disagreed on anything important. While bucking hundred-pound bales into huge rectangular pyramids, we discussed our devotion to Eric Clapton, the Doors, and now, speeding off to Bible College, we forged a new and exciting common bond — Fundamentalist religion.

"The campus is an old army base," Dan told me, "sold to the school when the military moved out in the early seventies. President Longston has a great vision from God that the college will grow from 250 to over a thousand by the end of the decade — won't that be cool?"

He went on to say that the administration was trying to get accreditation status for the school, but it was difficult because national education requirements mandated that they have more PhDs on the faculty (they had only one) and build a much better library (which then housed only twenty thousand books). Dan added that I should take Mr. Harmon's Old Testament survey class but avoid Mr. Johnson's Christian Education. As far as the dress code went, women had to wear skirts unless the temperature dropped below zero, but I shouldn't worry about that, because once winter hit I could wear pants most days.

"Your roommate, Jean, is *really* smart," he said. "She's the only woman in Greek class and the best exegete in the room on top of that. She's a straight-A student in every class and is very dedicated to the Lord."

A mixture of anticipation and anxiety made my stomach churn. I knew that Dan had flourished at Big Sky Bible College, as he had in high school, where he was an honor student and athlete — a typical firstborn: eager, serious, scholarly, an overachiever on all counts. It was nerve-racking to think that everyone might be expecting the same from me — especially my new roommate, Jean. Just thinking about how easy it would be for me to become a blight on the family name made me feel even more nauseated.

It was midafternoon when we arrived, sweaty and sticky from our five-hundred-mile drive. The cowpoke community of Lewistown stretched before us, its main street lined with antique brick buildings bearing bleached and forgotten hand-painted ads: Marlboro, the girl with the Coca-Cola bottle cap on her head, LIVE BAIT — all faded and crumbling under the relentless Big Sky sun. Cowboys walked bowlegged down the dusty Wild West streets, in search of feed or tractor parts or Calamine lotion from the Rexall Drug.

The college was tucked away in the mountains fifteen miles north of town, so we turned onto Highway 81 and drove the last leg in silence, winding deep into the Judith Range and pulling a horsetail of dust behind us like a burning fuse. The road narrowed, and dirt clods thudded on the floorboard beneath our feet. At a switchback in the mountain road, a group of concrete buildings emerged — identical box houses standing at the entrance of the compound like soldiers at attention. The Quonset huts that once held army officers now housed the college's faculty and staff. Disguised in great semicircular steel mounds stood a gym, post office, and mess hall, and, farther up, olive-drab barracks melted into the tree line like a camouflaged tank battalion. It felt like arriving at boot camp on the backside of the moon.

I peered out the window as the car slowed and we passed the guard shack. Dan waved to a clean-cut couple strolling down the sidewalk. "That's Pete O'Neill and Jane Parks — very spiritual people. You'll like them a lot." I wanted to ask Dan what it took to be a "spiritual person," but since I wouldn't have confessed under torture that I didn't already know, I simply said, "I can't wait to meet them." As I watched young people laughing and hugging one another, the feeling that I was in a strange and foreign place began to ease. It was obvious that a strong camaraderie united the students at Big Sky Bible College as they exchanged greetings of "Praise the Lord" and "God is faithful" like secret handshakes. Dan wheeled into a parking space next to a group of students unloading bags and boxes, pole lamps, and pictures. In the open plaza a crowd was gathered around a young woman who, Dan told me, had recently returned from a summer mission in Africa. "It was miraculous . . . ," she was saying with tears in her eyes.

I stepped out of the car, and a late summer breeze wafted the smells of fried food from the cafeteria, newly cut grass, and Johnson's Floor Wax from the propped-open dormitory door — the exciting aroma of college life. As I took my boxes up to the second floor and looked for room 214, I had a strong sense that a chapter of my life was ending and another about to begin. I poked my head through the door, and sitting at her desk waiting for me was my new roommate, Jean. Jean had a somber, makeup-free face and long, straight auburn hair. She stood up and held out her hand. "Nice to meet you," she said, surveying me with no-nonsense intensity. "Hey, let me help you with those bags."

I could see her scrutinizing my belongings as we unpacked them: Avon Skin So Soft lotions and mango moisturizing shampoo, lavender body powder and lacy underwear. I started to feel nervous, because by looking at Jean, I could tell that my things were probably too girlie for her — maybe even unspiritual. She was more the sportswoman type: thin but broadly built, with an athletic, unthinking vigor. I spotted on Jean's desk a picture of her sitting on a huge boulder with the Cascade Mountains jutting white and ragged

behind her, and a handsome sandy-haired man in khaki shorts and
heavy-soled hiking boots with his arms around her shoulders. It
looked like a great opportunity to divert her attention from my
oversize makeup bag, which she was about to discover. "Wow, that's
sure a great-looking guy; is he your boyfriend?"

"Used to be, but I broke up with him last spring. I'm headed for
the mission field, and he doesn't feel the Lord's calling to go. So I've
decided there just isn't any future for us. There is no doubt in my
mind that God wants me to be a missionary."

Wow, I thought, *Dan was right.* Jean must be the ultimate in
Christian dedication: a woman who could spend her life in a tropical forest, translating the Bible into obscure languages and dodging
tarantulas — a real Jane Goodall type, only motivated by religious
enthusiasm.

Once we hung my last floral dress in the closet, Jean said, "Great,
all done — just in time for services." We changed into our best skirts
and headed across the road to the enormous administration building, where the college chapel was located. When you're in a new
world and you don't know what to do, the best tactic is to follow
people who have the routine down — people like Jean. So I noticed
her every move and let each one make an imprint on me. She sat
silently and watched the front row of professors assemble near the
huge pipe organ, which was sounding out in glorious unison with the
gleaming grand piano. I did the same. The handsome president, Mr.
Longston, charged up to the podium, and everyone fell into silence.
He lifted his hands high into the air, looked right and then left, at
the piano and organ, and in a magnificent baritone voice boomed,
"A mighty fo-ortress i-is our God." As if pulled by a strong magnet,
the audience snapped into place. "A bu-ulwark never fa-a-ailing,"
they shouted with gusto. I felt a magnificent vibration elevate me

above the vale of this present world, permeating the sanctuary and shaking the windowpanes next to me, drawing the flesh on my arms into goose bumps. It was as though I had been transported to the very gates of heaven. My insides warmed, and I knew that sitting beside Jean, before a company of a thousand heavenly angels, was right where I belonged, with sacred music booming off the rafters and people swaying in place, closed-eyed and euphoric in the spirit, of like minds — brothers and sisters all.

That first week Jean and I attended all the welcome-to-campus socials, and she introduced me to everyone she knew. We'd laugh our way back to the dorm and throw ourselves on the bed, where she'd whisper, "Jan Hanford is still in love with Greg Palmer even though he broke up with her last year; he, on the other hand, is mad about Patti Schroder, but she thinks he's pret-ty creepy." Then, after the valuable social update, I'd climb into my top bunk and drift into a deep sleep while Jean stayed up into the early morning hours, her tiny desk lamp pressing down onto her huge Greek lexicon, whispering to herself, "*Lambano* — present, active, indicative — meaning 'to take'; *gnorisas* — aorist, active, nominative, singular — meaning 'to know.'"

While Jean earned perfect scores in all her classes, I adapted to my new life as a student. Each day was filled with classes, chapel, devotional hours, and church services. When we weren't occupied with scheduled events, Jean and I spent our time reading and talking about the meaning of the universe, which made me realize that I didn't miss the conversations I might be having in Los Angeles or New York. This was the *real* world, not the carnal one that existed in large cities where people didn't acknowledge Jesus as God or realize that He would soon return to rapture the faithful to heaven. I knew I'd chosen the right path, although, mind you, not necessarily an easy one. Following God would save me from the great judgment to come, but I knew it would also throw me into a battle against a treacherous adversary known by many names: the Prince of Darkness, Beelzebub, the Father of Lies, the Old Serpent, the Great Red Dragon.

In our classes and daily chapel messages we learned that Satan traveled to and fro throughout the world looking for unwitting sinners to devour. Whenever temptation struck, the Devil and his legion of spirits caused the enticement. The horned Beast reared his ugly head in the form of humanism, liberalism, socialism, and the theory of evolution — to name a few. Those who succumbed to his philosophies and temptations not only sinned on earth, but also were headed for an eternity in hell. When I thought about hell, just as when I thought about the Great Tribulation, I was entirely relieved that I had been snatched from the jaws of death, and my feet planted safely on the path of righteousness. It was exciting to be inducted into this new family that had taken the mantle of "true defender of the faith," standing firm on the fundamentals of Christianity, leading the fight against the Catholics, who worshipped icons, the Jews, who didn't believe Jesus was God, and the liberals, who didn't acknowledge the Bible as inerrant. Those poor souls would find out that hell was not only a bonfire for the lost, but also a burning camp for those who perverted the real teachings of the Bible. I was beginning to understand God's exciting timetable for the whole human race.

My favorite class by far was on the Book of Revelation. The first day, our teacher, Dr. Harvey, strode across the freshly waxed floor of the lecture hall, grabbed the long pointer stick that sat in the corner and began poking it into the air toward us: "The foremost lesson in Bible interpretation is that *every* word of Scripture is inspired. Not some of it, not parts of it, but *every* letter." He paced across the front of the room, surveying the crowd with a steely glare that made us know he was talking about matters of extreme spiritual importance. "That means that every detail of history, every doctrine, every word of prophecy is without error and must be taken in its literal sense." Then he stopped dead in his tracks and looked each student in the eye. "These are God's very words here, young people. Don't ever let me hear you say differently!"

The whole faculty considered Dr. Harvey our school patriarch, a distinguished man with white hair that he carefully slicked back from his small forehead, making his pensive, ice blue eyes look as though they could cut through steel in a heartbeat. He was tiny of stature but had an electric frame that radiated energy through every seam of his slightly oversize suit. When he was a young man, he had attended Dallas Theological Seminary, America's stronghold of Fundamentalism, along with the famous Christian thinker Hal Lindsey. The seminary had been formed in 1924 to combat the popular teachings of higher criticism (applying techniques of literary analysis, archeology, and comparative linguistics to Scripture) — in other words, liberalism. The alumni of Dallas Theological Seminary took seriously their mission to champion orthodox Bible interpretation and defeat theological lenience.

"When the Bible speaks of a millennium, it means ten centuries. The seven-day creation is precisely that. When the author of Revelation talks about a battle between Jesus and Satan on the plain of Armageddon outside Jerusalem, that is exactly what will happen." His tiny body shot up as if it had been zapped with a cattle prod. "Biblical inerrancy," he shouted, "is the doctrine that separates us from the liberals, who are heretics of the worst measure!"

The whole class gaped at him, their young faces expectant and credulous. *What an exciting quarter this was going to be!* I thought, my palms sweating, my shirt sticking to my back, the bottoms of my feet tingling — learning from a man considered to be one of the founding fathers of American Fundamentalism. Knowing God's mind on all those tantalizing end-time prophecies, I would devour this class like a starving woman swallowing crumbs off a plate.

After months of note-taking, the scenario looked like this: God divided history into seven epochs, and according to the Bible we were presently in the sixth — the Church Age; anything after Jesus' crucifixion was the Church Age. The Rapture would mark the end of the Church Age and thrust the world into the Great Tribulation, which would last for seven years. In the first half of the Tribulation, the Antichrist would rise from the sea and make a pact with Israel, and together they would rebuild the Jewish temple on Mount Moriah. Now the Muslim Dome of the Rock rested there, but an earthquake or some natural disaster could easily burst it asunder and leave room for the Jews to reconstruct their own holy site. Once the temple was built, the Antichrist would betray Israel, declare himself God, and set up his own worship in the temple. In the meantime 144,000 Jews would acknowledge Jesus as the Messiah, get saved, and begin preaching the gospel across the world, which would make the Antichrist furious and prompt him to unleash a great persecution upon them. A helper of the Antichrist, called the False Prophet or the Beast (probably the pope), would appear and make everyone take the 666 mark in order to buy or sell anything. After this the wars would begin. The Beast's alliance with Israel would trigger an Arab alliance to attack Israel, which would prompt a Russian-African alliance to counterattack the Arabs by sea. This event would signal the Beast to spring into action, uniting with Red China and sending two hundred million soldiers into the Middle East for a terrible fight that would plunge the world into Armageddon, the final Great

War. Then a heavenly trumpet would sound, and Christ would return in the clouds to set up his kingdom on earth, which would last for a thousand years.

It was thrilling to see how the Old Testament books of Ezekiel, Daniel, and Isaiah agreed with the New Testament books of Matthew, Thessalonians, and Revelation, describing exactly what was in store for the human race, like a divine jigsaw puzzle. My appreciation for Scripture was growing each day: it could predict the future, give an accurate account of history, and guide Christians along the path of right living. Now I understood why students on campus memorized entire chapters of the Bible so that they would know what to do and how to act each moment of the day. Once a person realized what God's Word said about any particular topic (and it had something to say about every imaginable human action), there was no excuse for disobedience. I did notice, however, that some sins were counted more seriously than others; even though the Bible did say that all sins were equal in the eyes of God and under the blood of Jesus, a few transgressions made everyone more nervous than the normal ones of lying, cheating, and gossiping.

For example, there was the relationship between our school nurse, Diane, and her friend Evie. One day someone walked into Diane's dorm room, and the women were lying next to each other in bed — under the covers. After that the faculty started monitoring their every move. At a closed staff meeting the professors discussed the shocking event and ended up suspecting that abhorrent acts, worse than the average sins, were being performed. I was embarrassed to admit that I didn't know anything about people who were attracted to their own sex, so I waited because I knew Jean would have a decided opinion on the matter. "It's depraved," she stated flatly. "The apostle Paul has made the issue clear. The Letter to the

Romans states that homosexuals have given themselves over to a reprobate mind." That sounded pretty awful to me. I decided that it probably meant they were demon possessed or at least heavily influenced by demons.

One day I was in a bathroom stall when Diane and Evie burst into the lavatory. Thinking they were alone, Evie broke into tears. As I peeked through a crack in the hinge, a fugitive flush raced over my cheekbones, and stitches of fright seized my limbs. What unpredictable lasciviousness was I about to witness? Evie was a big girl with a serious face and thick brown hair that hung in her eyes. That day her bangs were wet and stuck together like fringe, as if she had been crying for a long time. She collapsed around the sink to give her shaking legs support and wept in long, quiet waves. Diane tried to get Evie to stop crying, and when she couldn't, she grabbed her and said in a gentle but stern whisper, "Get ahold of yourself!" Diane's arms looked strong like a wrestler's, and I wondered if women who liked each other naturally had more muscle than those who didn't. As she pleaded with Evie, I could see sadness in her eyes, and all of a sudden, without the crucial time I needed to let the Holy Spirit take over, I felt sorry for her and Evie and wondered why God found it necessary to be so strict on the subject.

I thought the two women had enough problems fighting depravity, so I didn't tell Jean what I had seen. Even so, later that winter when I had the flu and made an appointment to see Diane, Jean declared, "I'm not letting you see the *school nurse* alone!" We entered the old army base infirmary, and Diane checked my throat in a professional manner. Jean was afraid Diane was going to make me take off my shirt just to look at my breasts, but she didn't. As Diane examined my swollen glands, our dorm counselor stopped in for an unexpected visit. I darted a glance at Jean, who, I realized, must have requested that she stop by. Diane didn't act as if she suspected anything, and prescribed antibiotics to clear up my infection. It wasn't long before Diane and Evie left Big Sky Bible College. A professor told Jean that the administration had requested that they go.

Besides homosexuality, demons persuaded people to do all kinds of evil things. The Prince of Darkness caused great havoc in this world and interfered with almost all the church's perfectly laid plans. I didn't want to be on the wrong side of the eternity coin, so I decided to take the Bible seriously right from the start and follow its teachings to the letter. Doing that seemed uncomplicated to me: just believe every word of the Scripture and listen to what the professors said that it meant. It came to my great amazement, however, that one stubborn student named Odhran Welch refused to follow this simple formula. Whenever Odhran opened his mouth, I mentally slapped my palm to my forehead and thought, *What is he thinking?*

Odhran was a gangly lad from Ireland, with thick glasses and lazy Dublin-looking eyes. Sarcasm tinged his oddly syllabled accent, and wild mahogany ringlets, as nonconformist as his attitude, fell around his eyes. He seemed determined to submit Christianity to the iron logic of broad daylight, even when it butted up against the college's view of things. Didn't he realize that the mysteries of God were matters of faith and not reason? Most incredible about Odhran's rebellion was that it usually surfaced in Mr. Foreman's classes — the most conservative, ill-tempered professor on campus.

Foreman's angry face moved like a hatchet, chopping out the words of his lecture. He was a stout, heavy-jowled man with black horn-rimmed glasses that rode low on his broad nose, matching perfectly his crew cut and 1950s wardrobe. He didn't teach in a normal voice like most of the professors, but shouted as if he were Jonathan

Edwards delivering a sermon — which had the effect of making you feel like a sinner in the hands of an angry God rather then a simple college student.

"And what does God say your sin does to Him in chapter 13 of Jeremiah? It makes Him weep because you are like the Israelites worshipping the golden calf. He weeps when He looks down on the long, dismal span of history and beholds in horror the spectacle of the world, His people creating other gods, taken in indulgence, intemperance, and debauchery, abusing their bodies. God weeps over these abominations, knowing that every time you refuse to surrender to Him, you nail Jesus to the cross anew; that once more you hammer into His precious head the sharp crown of thorns, and the blood drips down His divine forehead in sheets. Think of the spikes tearing at the flesh of His hands, His feet. Think of the torment, and ask yourself if you could be responsible for it. When you refuse to surrender to the will of the Lord, you place Jesus back on the cross again."

When Mr. Foreman wasn't preaching his lectures in class, he was scouring the campus with a gaze as merciless as the sun, looking for students who had not yet surrendered to the will of the Lord. He never had to look far. When he did observe someone doing anything that he felt was a bad testimony, he called the quaking religious novice into his office for a hearing. The entire student body feared Mr. Foreman and walked far out of the way to avoid any chance of a face-to-face encounter with him. Odhran was the only student I knew who actually challenged the grouchy professor.

One morning the young Irishman confronted Mr. Foreman in a class we both attended, one on the Gospels. The professor had worked himself up to a good sweat twenty minutes into his lecture when he proclaimed that in Mark, chapter 10, verse 1, when Jesus arose from Capernaum and traveled to the coast of Judea, he actually levitated and flew. Odhran sat straight up in his chair. The professor went on, reinforcing his argument with the use of Greek, a common practice among Bible teachers. "The Greek word *arose* can more precisely be interpreted *levitated*," he declared. "The fact that Jesus traveled from Capernaum to Judea — by the farther side of the Jordan — is a sure sign that the trip was too far to go on foot."

Odhran wasn't about to let Foreman's flying Jesus go uncontested. He raised his hand and said, "That don't seem in keepin' with the Lord's usual form o' transportation."

Everyone froze. Mr. Foreman hesitated, focused his eyes over the top of his horned spectacles, and growled low, like a dog awakened by a prowler. "My exegesis is sound. Are you challenging that?"

Since Odhran hadn't studied Greek, he was left to appeal to common sense, which Mr. Foreman insisted had nothing to do with things. Once the debate ended, a smile crossed the professor's face, and I knew that the foolish young Odhran had ruined his grade again.

What bothered me was how Odhran could dive headfirst into a hornet nest, foolish enough to sacrifice his GPA in order to disagree with Mr. Foreman. Didn't he realize that the school posted our grades in the college newsletter, and that those on the honor roll were considered the best Christians on campus? Honor students became class officers and always won the religious service awards. Odhran needed to stop kicking against the goads, as God warned about in Acts 9, and take a cue from David Brant, "the impeccable Christian scholar," as Jean called him.

David was student body president, with a 4.0 grade point average and a famous memory, which allowed him to quote much of the Bible from recall. He was not only smart, but he could preach like the legendary evangelist Billy Sunday, so much so that the faculty had granted him its top preaching award for 1975. Plenty of the girls on campus agreed with Jean when she said, "He's also the most eligible man on campus." David had soft black hair that curled gently in waves, its color matching his large, round and mysterious eyes, which seemed aloof until you spoke to him, and then they became warm and intent, like those of an understanding counselor. He discussed important theology with women in the same way he did with men. Unlike some of the guys on campus, who had a hard time taking the girls seriously, David treated them with respect and didn't seem to entertain the idea that they weren't equal when it came to intelligence. I knew that Jean liked this best about him. And if brains and sensitivity were not enough, he was six feet tall and broad shouldered and the best forward on the intramural basketball team. I loved to sneak into the gymnasium and watch him dribble gracefully past the other boys, his body twisting into the air in a perfect layup. David also kept himself neat and never came out of the dorm looking ragged or unkempt, but as impeccably dressed as a Wall Street stockbroker. All these good traits aside, everyone admired David for yet another reason — unlike most of the students, who were farm kids or had grown up in the church and never experienced real debauchery, David had been wild before his conversion. When he gave his testimony about how he and his family had been saved from alcoholism, everyone listened openmouthed.

The story began when David's father, a chronically inebriated logger, found the Lord. At the time, David too was generally drunk or hungover. Although he had been a fine athelete in high school, David had spent much of that time drinking and shoplifting clothing from the local department store. By the time he enrolled at a community college, he was staggering through most of his classes, intoxicated. Then suddenly one day David watched his father magically transform from a violent man into a zealous teetotaler, preaching salvation to all who would listen. After the miracle had continued for six months, David dedicated his own life to God and became a brand-new person, leaving for Bible college within a month. That had been three years ago. Now he held the distinction of being the most esteemed spiritual leader on campus.

I'd seen David speak once in chapel. You can tell a lot about a preacher by the way he approaches the pulpit: some swagger up, while others, self-conscious and shy, fairly tiptoe; some glide; some hop, bursting with excitement; while others are so lethargic that you know you'll be in a virtual coma before the hour is out. David Brant was the gliding kind; his graceful limbs moved nimbly and naturally. He flowed up to the podium with his head slightly cocked to the right, playful and confident, the full wattage of his astonishingly dark-eyed gaze beaming out into the crowd. In the manner of all charismatic pastors, David held his Bible loose yet firm, letting everyone know he would use it as a sword to "rightly divide the Word of Truth." David's meticulously knotted silk necktie lay perfectly against a dazzling starched white shirt that hugged his olive skin, making his complexion look creamy and refined — more like a dangerous young Turk than a simple preacher. After adjusting the microphone close to his lips, he laid his hand on the podium and tilted almost imperceptibly back on his heels before pulling himself forward into the pulpit and plunging into his sermon.

Like the first strides out of the blocks in a hundred-meter sprint, the first blast from the pulpit reveals how the sermon will go. "The story of Joseph has everything," his sturdy voice rang into the hush, "jealousy, violence, sex, power, money, suspense — and a poignant lesson for all Christians." Thus began David's rousing oration. He implored, whispered, and laughed out loud, told jokes and quoted poems, beseeched, entreated, and even sang a chorus or two as he moved across the stage, bringing his mesmerized audience along with him on a spellbinding adventure packed full of anecdotes, challenges, and nuggets of wisdom.

Intelligence radiated from David like rings on a pond's broken surface. I took my notebook and a pen and quickly wrote down all the astonishing phrases and new religious vocabulary he was using: complicated words like *Eucharist, soteriology,* and *Septuagint.* He had a genius for language, and it occurred to me that he sounded worlds apart from the Montana cowhands I'd grown up listening to. He understood the importance of words and gave them the respect a well-educated scholar could. His vivid verbal illustrations made me want to savor each tidbit of wisdom, each turn of phrase or clever saying, and hoard them for later, stockpiling them until back in my room I could read them over and over. And with Jean scribbling notes furiously next to me, I could tell that I wasn't the only woman on campus impressed with David's oratorical skill.

The next week offered a perfect afternoon for the fall social, a late autumn day when golden leaves fell one by one from the trees, dropping through the air and sticking to car windshields, landing beneath our feet and smelling of dried apples and warm earth. Jean and I pulled on our heavy sweaters and dashed across the road to the administration building. I felt the day's soft light against my skin, glad that the steam-oven heat of summer was surrendering to the fragrances of pumpkin and bracing autumn air. Jean flung open the heavy door, and there stood David Brant, like a Greek god sculpted in alabaster.

"Oh, hello, David," Jean gasped, stepping back bumping into me.

"Hello, Jean," David said, his voice low and playful. "Are you having a good quarter?"

"Good!" Jean blurted out, flushed and short of breath. "I mean, *the Lord* is good this quarter. Well, we know the Lord is always good, but what I really mean to say is that God is being especially good this quarter!" Jean paused in her stammering, and we stood in silence, looking at one another. "Oh — I'm sorry," she said. "This is my new roommate, Carlene."

"Carlene, I've heard about you," David said, turning his hot-house smile in my direction.

My heart leaped. What did he mean by that? Maybe someone had done me the favor of a lifetime and told him they thought I was pretty or smart, or maybe — to God be the glory — pretty *and* smart.

"You're Dan's sister," he finished his sentence.

My heart sank. So that was it. The only notable thing about me was that I was Dan's sister.

"Yes, Dan's sister," I managed to reply, glancing toward the carpet, afraid that he would see the red blush blazing across my cheeks as I thought of his sleek body moving down the basketball court. I was thankful when Jean rescued us both by saying, "We promised Janice Forsberg we'd help her serve punch, so we'd better get going. Nice to see you, David." I knew that Jean was as anxious to make a run for it as I — like two junior bishops unexpectedly meeting Pope Paul in the Vatican hallway. As we sped away, I could still feel the energy that David radiated, hitting my bare skin and giving me goose bumps. There was something intense and mysterious about the guy that worked like an irresistibly strong magnet. Looking at David Brant made me wish that Jesus would postpone the Rapture for a while.

David's story of radical conversion only added to his physical allure. He was a perfect example of the life-changing power of salvation, the kind of transformation that Christians were most proud of — a real catch for the team, like acquiring a Heisman Trophy

winner during the first round of a pro football draft. David's untamed life and his addictions were legendary, but they were behind
him now; as Corinthians stated, "If anyone is in Christ, he is a
new creature, the old things have passed away." It was exciting to
know that whatever happened in a person's life before the religious
transformation didn't matter, because Jesus had covered it with his
blood. Everyone knew that part of David's success came from his
conscientious life of prayer — rising at 5:00 a.m. and praying for all
his unsaved relatives and friends back home, as well as for President
Carter, the earthquake survivors in Uzbekistan, our country in its
bicentennial year, and for continued success in his daily battle resisting Satan and his legion of demons.

The morning after I met David, I slipped out of my bunk precisely at 5:00 and sneaked down the hallway. If I were going to be the
kind of Christian that David Brant was, and find the discipline not
to have inappropriate thoughts about his strong, virile body, I would
have to work on my prayer life. I opened the door to the janitor's
closet, pushed aside the mop smelling of Lysol Pine and mildew, and
knelt on the green linoleum floor. "God, help me possess the gifts
of the spirit: kindness, meekness, gentleness, temperance — yes,
God, mostly temperance concerning my wayward thoughts." Then
I started down a mental list of my unsaved relatives — which was
dauntingly long — asking God to save them from the judgment to
come. Within ten minutes my legs began to shiver, making it hard to
concentrate on my ever-growing inventory of personal offenses and
potential converts, so I decided to think about the sufferings of our
Lord: the crown of thorns gashing His head, the lance wound in
his side, his hands and feet ripped by the rusty spikes. Cold limbs
were nothing to complain about, I told myself. Another ten minutes
passed. Even considering the far worse agonies of Christ, I was still
sorely tempted to save my throbbing knees, so I started to concen-

trate on the torments of the martyrs, which Jean loved to read to me from her thick hardback entitled *Fox's Book of Martyrs*.

Jean would read excerpts out loud while I lay on my bunk. "Hey, listen to this one: 'When Saturnius, the bishop of Toulouse, refused to sacrifice to idols, he was fastened by the feet to the tail of a bull, and the enraged animal was driven down the steps of the temple, bashing the worthy martyr's brains out.' Whew!" Jean would flip the pages until she found another particularly gruesome section. "Diocletian, condemned for his faith at Antioch, was scourged, put to the rack, torn with hooks, cut with knives, his face slashed, and his teeth beaten from their sockets." I put my pillow over my head and imagined what it would be like to have hooks tearing at my flesh, and my teeth beaten out. My God, being a Christian in the first century had to be worse than living through the coming Tribulation! Jean flipped furiously. "Peter, a pious eunuch, was laid on a gridiron and broiled over a slow fire until he expired. . . . Timothy, a deacon of Mauritania, was burnt, his eyes were put out, and then he was crucified upside down."

"Stop, stop!" I'd holler out from the top bunk.

But now, months later, thinking about those poor abused martyrs helped me stick with my prayers each morning. Not to mention the suffering of Jesus with his flesh torn out and the crown of thorns pushed into his head — all of this pain for the sake of my salvation. Thinking about the suffering of Jesus gave me a strange peace, knowing that God would leave heaven and come to earth in the form of a man to endure such agony for me. Instead of being repulsed by such torment, I knew that I needed to consider it, ponder it, and even bask in it. If Jesus and the early saints could face this unbelievable persecution, I could certainly pray for an hour each morning in the janitor's closet, I told myself as I heard people turning on the hot showers in the lavatory next door. So I stayed on my knees and thought about warm, soothing water running over my skin.

Three

The Lord's Work

WITH MY RESOLVE to serve God now in full swing, I determined to find a Christian service assignment the second semester, something that would be truly remarkable, something out of the ordinary. I read down the list of new opportunities posted in the student union building: kindergarten Sunday school teacher at Bible Baptist Church . . . organ player at the Christian Alliance Church . . . assistant to Mrs. Robins's Sunday school class at Temple Baptist Church. But it was the nearly illegible handwritten note at the bottom of the board that sounded the most intriguing of all:

NEEDED: BIBLE TEACHERS FOR THE HUTTERITE COLONY OUTSIDE GRASS RANGE. THIS ASSIGNMENT IS HIGHLY SENSITIVE. PLEASE SHOW UP IN ROOM 213 ON FRIDAY AT 3:30 FOR DETAILS.

Don Jones, the man coordinating the program, was a lumbering giant who peppered his sentences with questionable language like "Jeez" and "Holy Toledo," and belly-laughed at all the wrong times. Each semester he put together unconventional Christian service teams like the one that preached outside cowboy bars in Great Falls or the group that traveled to Deer Lodge to teach Bible classes to convicts at the state penitentiary. His plan to take a team into

Montana's isolated Hutterite colony was just as eccentric. Although Don was friendly, people thought he was an oddball, a verbal stumblebum not cut out for the ministry. He lived in a messy shack in the mountains, wore wrinkled T-shirts, and had decaying teeth. They said his personal hygiene alone would disqualify him for anything other than a tiny rural church. Beyond his lack of physical and spiritual decorum, however, no one knew much about him; he never mentioned having a family, only that he had grown up in Chicago and in his personal life he was something of a loner.

I arrived in room 213 with a scattering of people seated in front. Jones waved his enormous hamlike arm and yelled, "Come on in and sit yourself down." When everyone was seated, he continued, "This is a touchy situation. The Hutterites have never let outsiders in to teach religion. They aren't officially asking us either. It's an interesting deal. I met our host, Samuel, at a revival meeting — you know, a Holy Roller, speakin' in tongues kind of meeting — and by golly, I talked him into letting us teach a study at his house. At the colony, no less!"

"Do the Hutterite elders know we're coming?" someone asked.

"No, that's why it's so sensitive," Don answered. "You gotta be serious about this if you're going. I'm not exactly sure what'll happen."

The assignment sounded more exciting than assisting Mrs. Robins with her Sunday school class, so I told Don I was in. It was early on a chilly, wet January morning when I set out to learn more about these Hutterites. The mountain ash trees above me were bare of leaves as I jumped a narrow ditch filled with ivy and took a shortcut to the library. Inside I thumbed through the card catalog, finding the library's only book on Hutterite history. I took it and nestled into a corner chair under a tall window of a dozen panes. There I learned that the original Hutterian Brethren had been Anabaptist refugees from Switzerland, Germany, and Italy. In 1528 they assembled near the present-day Czech Republic and, following the apostles' example in the Book of Acts, combined all they owned and vowed to live communally. Apparently the Hutterite lifestyle has remained the same since then, for almost five hundred years, making them one of the oldest surviving religious communes in the world. They still live in settlements of 80 to 130 people, and when their numbers approach 150, they split off into a new colony. Although their collective living has always attracted suspicion, over the centuries their refusal to serve in the military, to vote, or to participate in any outside social interaction has brought them even more trouble. In 1536, German religious leaders burned their founder, Jakob Hutter, at the stake. Because Protestants and Catholics alike believed that baptism by submersion was heresy, during the sixteenth and seventeenth centuries, they offered a bounty on every Anabaptist seized. Governments tortured and killed them, setting in motion a legacy of constant persecution and flight. Finally, in 1864, they fled from Russia to the plains of America in search of a secluded haven. Although they had not experienced physical persecution in Montana, they were often treated with disdain and labeled as "Hoots" or "Blackbirds." The local farmers there resented their puritan efficiency, which gave them a corner on 60 percent of the state's pig market, half its egg production, and 17 percent of its dairy sales.

To my astonishment, the book told me that the Hutterite colony we were about to visit outside Grass Range was the oldest in Montana, and it stated that they had maintained a more reclusive lifestyle than almost any sect in North America. They operated their own schools, raised their own food, and made their own clothing. Their elders forbade televisions, radios, cars, and musical instruments, along with dancing, jewelry, eye makeup, and even photography, which was considered a show of vainglory and a violation of the second commandment, in which God prohibited man from making any graven images. The colony still spoke German except in rare interactions with outsiders; their religious texts and schoolbooks were written in German; they wrote, prayed, and sang in German.

The women followed the apostle Paul's dictates to keep their attire simple and wore dark floor-length dresses with long sleeves and aprons and no lace, ruffles, trim, or embroidery — garments made for hundreds of years from the same patterns. The Grass Range Hutterite women did not cut or style their hair but parted their bangs down the middle and rolled them into cylindrical sections, which were wrapped around the head, secured to the back of the neck, and then covered with a scarf, with only the tubular bangs showing. Women had no vote in colony decision making, which was the exclusive right of baptized men over the age of twenty-five. Reading all this, I wiggled excitedly in my chair; entering the Grass Range colony would be like traveling back in time to sixteenth-century Europe.

At our next meeting, Don told me I'd be teaching young women, ages twelve to twenty-two. As I prepared lessons from the Gospel of John, I wondered what Hutterite girls my age would be like. Finally, on a wintry Wednesday afternoon, six of us piled into Don's rattletrap Ford Falcon and ventured out from the campus over the icy two-lane back road. Watching the orange sun shed the day's last ragged light across an empty ocean of snow waves, I decided that if the Hutterites had wanted to flee civilization they had made a brilliant choice in eastern Montana. I was thankful that Don chattered through the space and solitude, interrupting himself with his own laughter.

"I'll be a son of a gun!" he snorted with excitement. "Can ya believe the snowbanks we're pushin' through? White as a polar bear lost in a blizzard." Then he'd laugh and whistle contentedly, tunelessly, something he did all the way to the little burg of Grass Range. Once we approached the colony, however, he quieted. His manner turned apprehensive as we entered the grounds, bracketed by long barns and winter-harrowed gardens, past the huge communal dining hall, homestead-era schoolhouse, and church. The ice packed dirt road wound through a cluster of simple wooden houses to Samuel's cottage. The moment the engine stopped, our host appeared and whisked the six of us inside, like Joshua sneaking spies into the Promised Land.

We crossed a rough enclosed porch, passing between a row of muddy overshoes and a couple of days' worth of split wood, entering a simple room with bare walls, utilitarian handmade furniture, and wood floors where the pine had worn darker where it got the most traffic. There, packed into simple straight-backed chairs and numbering almost forty, sat a group of somberly dressed Hutterites. It was one thing to read about these people; it was another entirely to see them in the flesh. They were the most austere creatures I'd ever laid eyes on. The men's stark black clothing, stiff and unyielding, made them seem as rigid as statues. And the women, wearing scarves and grave expressions, were buttoned down in cotton that covered every square inch of their bodies except for a small opening that allowed the face to peek through. The strictest order of nuns would have seemed positively libertine beside them. Only the smells of the room were recognizable: farmhouse baking and dirt caked boots, cattle salves and wet hounds — staples of Montana farm life.

Don nervously opened the meeting with a prayer and a Bible verse, his voice shaking. "We are here to share in the fellowship of our

Christian brothers and sisters. As it states in Hebrews 10, verse 25: 'Do not forsake the assembling of ourselves together.'"

The Hutterites must have realized that we were as nervous as they, and after Don led a few verses from "Blessed Lord Jesus," I began to see timid smiles peeking out from under their snug head coverings. I took a breath and smiled back. Once Don finished the song, he introduced us to the crowd and dismissed everyone to their classes. Rachael, a twenty-two-year-old beauty with dark eyes and full lips, approached me and said she would take me to our classroom. She was graceful and slight, with delicate features and olive skin. When we arrived in the upstairs bedroom, ten other lovely women, seated around a table, introduced themselves in a whisper; I noted only two last names among them: Stahl and Wollman. They huddled together, a flock of tiny sparrows, timid and dressed in black. And yet their eyes betrayed fascination as they stared at me, silent and direct, while their lips bit back amazement so as not to frighten me away. After I finished my lesson in the Gospel of John, I asked a question to spark discussion. No one said a word. I asked a second . . . still silence. It never occurred to me that the Socratic form of teaching was completely foreign to them. It was unlikely that they had ever been asked their opinion of the Bible — or of much else, for that matter — or that they had ever engaged in conversation with an outsider.

For the first two weeks these young women studied me without making a sound. I worried all the way back to college about how I would ever be able to communicate with my new class. My curled, long blond hair, eye makeup, and blue jeans seemed to generate an unbridgeable chasm between us. Then I thought about their faces, filled with anticipation, playfulness, an eagerness to experience new things, and suddenly, as I looked out of the frosted car window, I wondered if we might not be more alike than I'd imagined.

The next week instead of teaching them John, I said, "Your hair is just beautiful. How do you get it to look so cute?"

They all giggled with delight.

"Can we fix yours like it?" Rachael asked.

They touched my hair gently, with cautious merriment, as though it might burst into a thousand tiny lights — or snakes. Rachael bent down, eyes wide, her face in mine, and whispered, "We love your black eyelashes."

Each of them held my hair and let it fall through their fingers.

"It's the color of wheat!" whispered Mary Ellen, Rachael's sister.

They stood, hands cupped over their mouths, gasping with disbelief as they took turns rolling my bangs. As they lost the battle to contain themselves, their small bodies and long skirts began bouncing around me. At the end of the transformation, for the final step in our secret initiation rite, Rachael's cousin, Sarah, took her scarf off and tied it around my head. At that, they all squealed, and Sarah's sister, Miriam, proclaimed, "Now you are one of us." By complete accident we had discovered the intimacy women can know, across worlds of difference and language — the union that as teenagers we were only beginning to see as possible.

After that, for the first few weeks anyway, we didn't get much Bible studying done. Sometimes I'd feel guilty and wonder if Don would be mad if he knew we weren't discussing John, but I suspected that he would probably just shake his head and say, "Well, for Chrissakes . . ." My apprehension completely vanished when I thought about the anticipation alive in the faces of these women as I told them stories about my life and, in return, they whispered their stories to me. Edna, the older cousin, had left the colony and was working at the hospital in Lewistown, Rachael said speaking softly while the others looked on, wide-eyed as though they were sharing top secret government information, the kind that would get you in deep trouble with the authorities. "No one is supposed to talk about it, though."

Before long Wednesday night became the highlight of everyone's week. Even though Don heard that the elders were unhappy with our presence, we never considered ending our visits. We'd arrive at Samuel's to find a houseful of joyful people who showered us with laughter and conversation. The girls would grab my hand, and we'd escape to our room, shut the door, and chatter like reunited sorority sisters. Then we'd launch into our study of John. Without fail my pupils had studied the lesson with scholarly meticulousness, with their answers written in German and their insightful comments and questions spoken in careful English. After our study we'd chat about upcoming events in our lives, even about boys we thought were cute. Spontaneously someone would hug me or slip her arm into mine and say, "Thank you for coming to see us." At first their affection surprised me, but before long I took great joy in their unguarded tenderness.

Before we left each Wednesday evening, the women filled Don's car trunk with pastries, canned peaches, huckleberry jam, pumpkin bread, and homemade sausage. He delighted in the goodies, but I knew he cherished the friendship of his new Hutterite family even more. When they appeared with the delicacies, he would throw his head back and laugh out loud, his dark teeth in plain view and his ample belly quivering beneath his messy T-shirt. Unlike folks on campus, the Hutterites never seemed to notice Don's ragged appearance but instead looked beneath it to his heart.

Our small Bible study group invited us to spend a Saturday with them touring their farming operations — the only area where the Hutterites embraced modernization. In the sterile industrial chicken slaughtering house, cauldrons of boiling water bubbled next to swirling vats that removed the birds' feathers before clippers snipped off their dead feet. The concrete floors of the pig and horse barns were fastidiously clean, smelling not of dung but of Lysol and fresh paint, as neat and orderly as a hospital operating room. Shiny stainless steel automated milking machines lined the dairy barn, pumping milk into the processors that pasteurized and bottled it.

Quiet and earnest, they ushered us through their stark white church with its barren walls, hardwood backless pews, and altar devoid of the traditional platform, podium, and musical instruments of modern Western Christianity. In that place all playfulness drained from Rachael's face. They led us into an immaculate communal kitchen, where a group of women prepared lunch in steel ovens and stoves, solemnly kneading bread and chopping vegetables. Before long the men arrived from the field, hung their stiff black hats on the wall in silence, and seated themselves in order of age and rank. Only after the men finished did the women sit down at the opposite side of the dining area and eat. Everything the Hutterites did followed an age-old metronome, set in motion centuries ago to maintain precise order and tempo. Though their stringent code of piety and isolation kept them unattached to the outside world, I was delighted that in private the girls ignored its relentless, homogenizing cadence, their eager smiles like prim windows opening to welcome in a fresh spring breeze.

When the official tour was over, the girls grabbed my fingers and we fled the crowd. In their rooms each one took turns showing me the quilts she'd stitched and the treasures she'd collected over the years, as the others looked on in silent respect, their hands politely clasped behind their backs. Out of memento boxes from under their beds tumbled the highlights of their lives: a church bulletin from a trip to the Spring Creek colony in Alberta, a wheat stalk that a young man had given her during harvest season, a lavender sachet from the Fortymile community in Wyoming. Then they each presented me with a gift from their riches: a special drawing of the colony, a dried flower, a crocheted doily made in honor of my visit.

As we drove home a feeling haunted me, one that had been mounting for months now: what kind of real choices would my new friends ever be free to make? There was so much they would never experience, so much that would remain forever off limits to them: attending college, traveling anywhere except under the supervision of a man, wearing blue jeans. They would never be allowed to speak up in church or attend a community meeting. I agonized over the thought, because I knew the capacity they had to embrace life — the intelligence, curiosity, and mischievousness that occupied their tiny frames. I consoled myself with the idea that at least they had each other. I could see them in their old age, clinging together as they had throughout life, sharing gossip and hand-quilted blankets, bonnets they had knitted for one another's great-grandchildren, and, I hoped, covert books. But somehow I knew they deserved more than their closed world would ever offer them. It was then that I first questioned the odd whims of religion. Religion was the reason Rachael, Sarah, Miriam, Mary Ellen, and all their bright young cousins would never cast a ballot for president, see Paris, or attend Harvard. Religion would keep them from voting even in their own colony. But I didn't let myself dwell on the notion for too long, because I knew it had implications for my own circumscribed life. I closed my eyes, pushing the thought into a back closet of my mind and quickly locking the door.

The preacher and elders endured our presence until late the following spring, when Rachael decided to leave the colony. I knew that something was wrong the night we arrived and all the girls but she looked grave, their faces again wearing the same somber expression as on that evening we first met. Once we were alone I found out what the crisis was all about.

"I've decided to move into town with Edna," said Rachael, beaming.

The room was silent.

"Do you need any help?" I asked.

"I don't have any jeans," she replied in an apprehensive voice.

"I have just the pair for you."

Distress lined the other girls' faces. They understood, as I did not yet, that the inevitable had arrived like an overdue bill from an extravagant shopping spree. The next Wednesday, Rachael's grandfather showed up with a long double-barreled shotgun. He was drunk, and waving the gun in the air he shouted, "Leave us alone! You'll never understand our ways."

Before we left that night, the girls hugged me and shyly touched my hair as they had the evening they'd fashioned it Hutterite style and covered it with Sarah's scarf. It did not occur to me that except for Rachael, I would never see any of them again nor that I might be the only outsider they would ever have a chance to befriend. They asked me not to forget them and slipped me forbidden photographs they'd taken of one another, smiling directly into the camera as though, unlike their patriarchal church elders, they realized the beauty and godliness of their own images.

On the way home Don told us, with a catch in his throat, that we couldn't go back. The colony preacher had forbidden us to return; he was afraid for our safety. Within a month Rachael called me from a pay phone in Lewistown. She had moved in with Edna and gotten a job at the hospital. I raced into town to spend the day with her. By the end of the afternoon she looked stunning in a pair of my jeans, which fit snugly down her long, slender legs, with her hair shining and curled and falling softly around her shoulders — and with black mascara on her lashes.

In Church History class that quarter, I learned how our doctrines were connected historically with the Hutterites through the Protestant Reformation. The Reformation had been built on John Calvin's teachings, and the Hutterite and Baptist faiths shared them as well. Calvin's doctrines had been encapsulated by his followers into the acronym T.U.L.I.P. The T stood for "Total depravity": humanity had inherited Adam's sin and was incapable of goodness and worthy of damnation. "Unconditional election": even before creation, God chose to save some from hellfire, others not. "Limited atonement": since God had already chosen the saved, Christ's death atoned for only those he'd picked. "Irresistible grace": if God chose you, you couldn't resist Him. "Perseverance of the saints": once you got in, you stayed in. If you landed on the lucky side of this divine coin toss, praise God. If you didn't he had simply left you behind, like choosing one child to save from the Holocaust and sacrificing the other, similar to Meryl Streep in *Sophie's Choice* — only God designed the whole scenario and executed it without guilt.

Although I accepted Calvin's assessment of man's sinfulness, the idea that we had no free will and that God arbitrarily rescued some and sent others to the slaughter made me wince. If Calvin was correct, humans were simply pawns in a universal chess game where the moves had been preordained and carried out before the foundations of time. Our duty was merely to endure the match. So what was the point of trying to win people to the faith?

Like doing our assignments in Personal Evangelism class. Part of our course work was to hide Christian tracts all over Lewistown. Each quarter fifty Bible college students slipped pamphlets in department store bathrooms, hotel lobbies, and onto grocery store shelves — under, say, a can of beans. Merchants asked Mr. Foreman not to require students to inundate the small town with religious materials, but he didn't budge; the Lord's work had to be done.

Although I was troubled by this apparent contradiction of thought, after much prayer I finally realized that it wasn't my job to decide whether the unchurched were chosen or not, but to obey my duty and tell them about Jesus. After this internal acquiescence, I didn't even flinch when Mr. Foreman escalated the class requirements to include the Pamphlet Crusade. The project required us to dispense what he called "the gospel bomb." The bomb consisted of tightly wrapped religious literature in the form of a cylinder tied together with a thread. As you'd drive through town and throw these torpedoes out onto someone's lawn, the string would break and religious tracts would burst all over the grass. For an A, students had to do all of the above, plus personally talk to people about Christianity. This involved approaching a stranger on the street, handing him or her a religious tract, and asking, "Excuse me, but do you embarrass easily?" The tract also had DO YOU EMBARRASS EASILY? printed on the cover. Inside it read, "You certainly will be embarrassed if you die and face judgment without accepting Jesus as your Savior."

Anxious to get the assignment over, my classmate Sarah drove into Lewistown and approached the first person she saw, who happened to be a dusty old cowboy sauntering bowlegged down the sidewalk.

"Excuse me, sir, do you embarrass easily?" Sarah called out.

The old cowpoke hesitated, looked down, and drawled, "What — 'smy fly open?"

I told myself that even if these assignments were awkward, they would teach me humility, as the apostle Paul requires in the Letter to the Corinthians, where he says that we must be "fools for the gospel's sake." And I also had to remember that before long Jesus was going to break through the clouds and make his appearance in the Second Coming. Then I would be very glad that I'd been such a good witness.

Besides, as we all knew at Big Sky Bible College, the Rapture was upon us. By that spring of 1976, the world situation looked grim. Earthquakes rocked the globe, first in Italy, then China, then Guatemala. Famines in Bangladesh, Ethiopia, and India were followed by revolutions and uprisings in Latin America, Soweto, and the Sudan. Floodwaters rolled across Indonesia, Brazil, South Korea, and the United States, precisely like the signs and wonders Jesus speaks about in Matthew 24, signaling the end of days. Even more alarming to Bible scholars was that the European Common Market was now looking exactly like the ten-member Revived Roman Empire that the Bible talked about in Daniel 7 and Revelation 13, which would usher in a world government, making way for the Antichrist. On top of that, the Soviet Union, which was certainly the King of the North predicted in Ezekiel 38, was right on track for its attempt at world domination, thereby plunging the earth into the final Great War by oppressing its people and even refusing to allow Scripture within its borders. All these events were coming together so fast that Hal Lindsey and other Bible teachers were confident that Jesus would return around the year of 1981. Lindsey shouted from pulpits across America that we were on "the countdown to Armageddon."

Many of us at Big Sky Bible College could feel the Final Days approaching and wanted to make the most of our time left on this earth, and so we volunteered for summer missions. Jean decided to go to Belgium to participate in revival meetings and march in the street, holding up a placard that read REPENT FOR THE KINGDOM OF GOD IS AT HAND. Dan and David signed up with a mission headquartered in West Germany that smuggled Bibles into Eastern Europe. I stood back and watched them as if they were volunteering for the army. When a representative from the Slavic Gospel Association, another organization that sneaked Bibles into Eastern Europe, visited campus, I decided to join up too; getting Bibles behind the Iron Curtain was the least I could do in God's final crusade. I kept it secret that I was glad to be based in the most beautiful place that any of us were going: the northern tip of France. It took some talking, but I finally convinced Dad that I would be safe and that it was a good opportunity for me to prove my commitment to the Lord. As always Mom was supportive of my spiritual adventure, and I wished I could take her along with me to see Europe for the first time.

I boarded a plane to Chicago, where I spent three days at Wheaton College, taking classes on cultural sensitivity along with fifty other Bible college and seminary students, from places like Boston, Philadelphia, Chicago, San Francisco, and Houston, who would form our team. On the fourth day we flew to Amsterdam, loaded our baggage into a fleet of white vans, and headed out across Holland for France. As we sped west past lush vineyards and tiny cottages, waves of excitement shot through my body as if my nerves had been shattered into a thousand tiny slivers of ecstasy. The entire landscape held an elegance and grace that made me feel that life was permeated with exciting unknown possibilities. Such beauty revived a deep inner longing to experience all the sensual pleasures this world had to offer.

I stepped out of the van and onto the street of the French village of Billy-Montigne, which would be my summer home. Our Bible smuggling hideout was a splendid three-story former hotel, resembling a brothel out of the Wild West. The rectangular multipaned windows lining its facade all opened onto small wooden balconies. Inside the hotel it was quiet and bright and smelled richly of historical presence: aged woodwork, smoke in the fireplace, weathered Turkish rugs in the once grand sitting room. Behind a great winding stairway on the first floor a door opened into a lovely French kitchen, where tired parquet squares of the antique floor warped under pot racks hung with skillets, colanders, saucepans, and great copper-bottomed stew pots. Rows of Old World cabinetry still held the remnant smells of coq au vin simmering in deep, velvety red wine, and apple tarts baking in the big brick oven.

I let myself fantasize that I had been in this grand old hotel at different times in history, to see the place at its turn-of-the-century glory or later, in 1945, after Billy-Montigne had been liberated from the Germans and people danced in the streets. I imagined myself as a beautiful French girl with coal black hair and Audrey Hepburn eyes, standing in the doorway and keeping watch on the cobbled streets in expectation of my handsome British lover in his crisp blue officer's uniform. In my fantasy we met often, rendezvousing in this romantic hotel with the smell of fine French wine and beef burgundy soup seeping up to our top-floor room overlooking the village. I'd see him in the distance, and my heart would race as he ran to the door, and we'd rush up the spiral staircase and into each other's arms. Kissing my bare shoulders, he would unzip my blue silk dress and let it slip over my hips and drop in a rolling swell on the warm-scented wooden floor.

Such thoughts left me feeling a mixture of elation and despair. They felt lovely but feverishly immoral, and I was afraid such passion would send me to hell in a wink if I weren't careful. Now that I was in Europe, a place where it would be easier to fall deep into sin, I had to keep my mind pure. The last thing I wanted was for God to be angry with me and let the Communists capture and torture me just as payback for my wickedness. More praying—I would do more praying. I began to rise at five and tiptoe down the hall to the hotel broom closet.

It was a good thing that I got myself under control, because it was clear that the Great Dragon controlled the Soviet Union. Our Bible smuggling operation would put us in a face-to-face conflict with him. The SGA staff taught us tactics in espionage and staged mock interrogations to prepare us for the road ahead, filled with forks and hairpin turns that could drop us into enemy hands at any moment. In years past several of their students had been caught behind the Iron Curtain and interrogated. In the midseventies Communist authorities strongly embraced Marx's belief that religion was the "opiate of the masses" and were dead serious about keeping Bibles out of their countries. They strictly forbade the possession of religious literature, imprisoning and, in some instances, torturing those who possessed it. The idea of young American religious zealots driving vanloads of Bibles across their borders threw them into a fury, which in turn filled us with a great zeal.

To get us ready for the spiritual warfare we were about to enter, SGA divided us into teams of three and gave us the details of our assignment: the route and location of our border crossing, the address where we would deliver the literature, the story we would stick to if caught by the secret police. Our route took us via Argonne and the Vosges Mountains to Stuttgart, through to Vienna and then over the Carpathians, dropping down and crossing the Hungarian border at Mosonmagyaróvár. Once in Hungary, we would separate, and our leader, Pete, a student from Gordon-Conwell Theological

Seminary, would deliver the Bibles while we kept watch in a coffee shop across the street.

SGA was serious about training us in a realistic fashion. Once I learned the bogus story, I was blindfolded, and someone with rough hands grabbed me and pushed me forward, down some stairs into a dank basement filled with a series of narrow passageways — they were below the old hotel; I didn't even known they existed — while an unfamiliar voice kept shouting in a heavy Eastern European accent, "Keep moving!" Disoriented, I hoped that God would help me avoid confessing details of the mission. Finally my captor pushed me into a stale-smelling room, threw me onto a chair, and tore off the blindfold. I looked up at crumbling cement walls and a drippy ceiling, then into the face of a stout, brutish-looking man I had never seen before. A single bare bulb swayed overhead, and the small table in front of me didn't separate me far enough from another stranger, a skinny, rodentlike fellow with a scarred face and a lumpy potato nose. The swinging light cast shadows from side to side, further distorting my interrogator's vile, smirking expression. (Later I learned that the men were actually Hungarian Christians who called themselves George and Jake and who, before their escape to the West, had been interrogated and tortured by the KGB for smuggling Bibles into Russia.) But at this moment it was easy to forget that this was all playacting and that these were really the good guys, not here to disfigure me but to prepare me to be a successful Bible smuggler.

"Your friends have told us all about your mission," Jake whispered in a sinister voice.

I said nothing.

"What did you think you were doing, transporting illegal literature into our country?"

I stared back at him.

His accent began to rise. "You are no longer in America, silly girl. We have your passport!" He leaned into my face with ferocious eyes. "Don't you realize the seriousness of your situation? If you do not cooperate with us, you will never see your family again. America can't help you now!"

I suddenly felt tied to the noble fraternity of Christian martyrs, tortured for the gospel's sake, whose stories Jean had horrified me with back in our college dorm room. I would handle myself with the stoicism of Faustines and Jovita, who silently endured their agony with such dignity that their tormentor, Calocerius, finally cried out, "Great is the God of the Christians!"

I stared at the fearsome figure across the narrow table and confessed nothing. In the end George and Jake gave me high marks for my ability to resist. The intrigue of the interrogation simply reinforced my determination to enter the Trojan horse and be wheeled into enemy territory, to present my body as a living sacrifice to God. I knew that this kind of commitment would, of course, hurl me into spiritual warfare with Satan. But as long as I kept up my morning prayers and stopped my mind from loitering with thoughts of sinewy British soldiers, I was sure that God would find favor with me and reward my self-sacrifice and zeal.

Once our preparation ended, each team was assigned a white van from a fleet camouflaged in a nearby warehouse. We pulled up the floorboards, placed Bibles in the empty spaces, and nailed the planks back down. The next morning several teams fanned out over Eastern Europe, heading from various checkpoints to the borders of Hungary, Bulgaria, Yugoslavia, and Romania. Within a few weeks, Hungarian border guards apprehended one of our teams. The terror-stricken expressions on the young American faces must have aroused suspicion at the crossing. Police pulled the van over and found the Bibles — contraband as serious as arms or illegal drugs.

They confiscated the vehicle, separated the students, and threw them into dank prison cells, where a crooked-nosed official, with the same intensity as Jake, shrieked in their faces that they would never see their families again. He demanded they tell him the location of our base in France and the destination of the Bibles. Since the students would not confess, they spent a week isolated from one another, with little food and water, not knowing if they would ever see American soil again. Then suddenly one morning the police took them to the border and set them free. It took them several days to make their way back to our headquarters in France.

When the lots were drawn, I was happy to be assigned to go into Poland; the Poles needed Christian support from the West now more than ever. That summer workers' strikes against the Communist party racked the country. Six years before, such protests had prompted the government to send tanks into Gdansk and fire on demonstrators — the dead had numbered into the hundreds. Now in June of 1976, the same kind of labor trouble had broken out all over the country again. A man named Lech Walesa, chairman of the strike movement, had just been fired from his shipyard job as a result of his trade union activities — an action that was prompting rioting in Poznan, Gdansk, Ursus, and Radom. The local French paper reported that the secret police had gone into action and hundreds of workers were being arrested and sentenced to prison. I decided not to write to Mom and Dad and tell them where I was headed.

My assignment was to take Christian textbooks into a religious camp north of Poznan and remain there to sing at tent meetings. The SGA leaders had heard that I sang alto in my high school and college choirs and decided to recruit me for the vocal/transport mission. My partner, Dee, a pretty girl with straw colored hair and such long limbs she seemed to have given up on controlling them, was a music major from Wheaton College and sang in a lovely soprano. Together we threw our open suitcases onto our beds and tucked Christian booklets into them as we discussed the summer's political unrest and wondered what we might be walking into. And even if Poland turned out safe, we had to get the contraband through East Germany, the Doberman guard dog of Eastern Europe. We boarded a train from Lens, France, with tickets that would take us through Berlin to Poznan.

All night the train tossed back and forth like a boat in heavy swells. I couldn't sleep, thinking about my suitcase heavy with Christian literature, and so I slipped away past the snoring bodies slumped together, slid our compartment door apart, and made my way toward the open window to watch the train hurtling past Belgian cow pastures and West German villages. I let the rhythmic knocking and clacking mesmerize me as I stared, sleepy eyed, into the dark landscape.

"Are you an American?" I heard a smooth, guttural masculine voice say.

I looked over my shoulder and into the eyes of a slender, narrow faced young man with thick golden curls.

"Yes," I said. "And are you German?"

"West German," he said, and introduced himself as Tomas Schuster, a philosophy professor at Humboldt University of Berlin. His vocation showed, I thought, on his intelligent face: premature creases around ice blue eyes framed by round wire-rimmed glasses. He wore a silk Armani shirt, jeans, and Nikes, like a hip academic with a taste for Italian fashion; he spoke quietly, as if he were in church or about to cross behind the Iron Curtain.

"I hate the Reds," he murmured. "They rape Berlin daily. Yesterday a beautiful young woman stepped out of her car in the dead zone between checkpoints, and the bastards shot her like a dog."

I looked back out the window, feeling every click-clack of the rails in the pit of my stomach. I was a kilometer from Checkpoint Charlie in East Berlin, with a suitcase stuffed with contraband. Letting the breeze from the open window blow my hair into my eyes, I listened for the train engine five cars ahead of us, hoping it would drown out my panic, but its noise was only a distant rumor.

The train screeched to a halt at Checkpoint Charlie, and passengers returned to their cabins as steam rose up the sides of the railcar. I fumbled with my passport, and Dee darted a firm "hold tight" look at me, herself becoming as serene and poised as Princess Grace. The cabin door flew open, and a tall, steely eyed East German policeman entered as though he'd stepped out of a sepia-toned World War Two movie, smirking with a cocky, affected assurance. He circled around the cabin and grabbed our passports one by one. His face looked flinty and papery white. As he reached for my passport, his lip twitched but revealed no real emotion; I tried to look tranquil while the bile percolated up my throat. Then, for some odd reason, he grinned and repeated the address listed on my passport.

"Camas Prairie, Montana." He threw his head back in a belly laugh, his brittle face cracking as if there were a secret joke about the place called Camas Prairie, Montana.

Still laughing, the policeman handed me back the passport, turned on his heels with a click, and left the cabin without checking a single bag. Dee looked at me wide-eyed, then shook her head in disbelief. It was a sign, I told myself, that God had found favor with us and was rewarding our service for the cause of Christ. The train pushed on, and we traveled through the night, crossing the border into Poland without event. By 8:00 a.m. we were in Poznan.

We stepped from the train and out into the dirt road, where a wizened old man drove us away on a wood-wheeled wagon brimming with newly cut hay. We rocked down the dirt road, past fields that looked like a Constable oil painting, eventually reaching an open meadow filled with tents. The camp had no electricity or running water. Even though the Poles understood little English, and we spoke only a few words of Polish, they laughed and yelled out, "Hullo, hullo, hullo, wulcome, wulcome," as the wagon rocked into camp. The fact that our presence might easily have meant danger to them never seemed to cross their minds. On the contrary, they acted as though hosting us was akin to having the royal family over for dinner.

Tucked into the center of the camp was an ancient farmhouse, where giggling Polish grandmas prepared borscht on a fiery stove, while a strapping teenage boy, grinning shyly, pumped water from the well for us to wash up after our long journey. We slipped down from the wagon and into the old stone hut, quietly delivering our religious literature to the camp preacher, who immediately led us back outside to a long table. Steaming dishes lined the twenty-foot rectangular table: dumpling soup and cabbage rolls, potato pancakes, kielbasa with sauerkraut, rye bread, poppy seed cake, and raisin pudding.

For two weeks we camped there and were stuffed with food by our hosts. They also provided us with our own interpreter, an effusive, portly fellow named Toleck, who shadowed us and translated every word of Polish we heard. During the sweltering, lazy afternoons we swam in Goplo Lake; then at night Dee, in her flawless soprano, and I, in my faltering alto, sang hymns in front of the gregarious crowd of a hundred Eastern European Protestants. Although the Poles were fearless of official suppression and told us not to worry, our voices skipped a beat as a shadowy figure materialized from the woods each evening when we rose to sing to the crowd. Our hosts recognized the dark intruder as a government agent there to take tally. The secret police left Dee and me alone but periodically reappeared during the day to take a Christian camper in for questioning. After two weeks of duets and pierogi, Dee and I left Poland with wonderful memories and several extra pounds. We traveled back to Billy-Montigne, satisfied that we had served God with honor, spiced by the hint of danger, behind the Iron Curtain.

By August our Bible smuggling missions were over, and SGA gave our team two weeks to explore the French countryside before we flew home. We took our white vans and hit the road to Rheims, Amiens, and Lyon, exploring fragrant boutiques, ordering brioche in tiny bistros, and visiting World War Two museums. We slept on the beaches of Dunkerque, then headed south to Paris, the City of Light. As we approached, I looked into the enchanted cityscape and felt the energy of a thousand years in one moment. The stunning lines of the Eiffel Tower and Notre-Dame against the sky lured me into a renewed love of the world and its history and left my body bristling with a strange vitality. In the Louvre, I marveled at the enigmatic face of Mona Lisa and the marble white perfection of Venus de Milo, caught a glimpse of the French Revolution of Antoine-Jean Gros, and the Italian Renaissance of Raphael. We drove out of Paris to the royal court at Versailles, where, walking the granite halls, I could almost hear Louis XIV shouting, and Marie Antoinette's bewildered cries as she was seized by the mob. Back in the boutique district, I bought crystal at Aurelia Paradis, and lace panties from Etam. At Montmartre, in the midst of a village of lively painters, I had my portrait sketched and drank espresso at the Closerie des Lilas, where, fifty years before, the virile Ernest Hemingway watered more than a thirst for wine.

Thoughts of Hemingway's Paris caused the carnal yearnings trapped inside my young flesh to burst forth like ale from a tapped barrel. On the Left Bank, I watched a young girl lean over to kiss her companion on the cheek, twice, once here and then once there. The slow beauty of it was so insouciant: the way that they did things in Paris. You could feel it, the passion of Sartre and Picasso, Joyce and de Beauvoir, haunting the narrow streets. I thought of Hemingway, living there in the 1920s in a stone apartment, with flowers cascading from windows that overlooked the Seine, standing, gazing above the rooftops of Paris as he agonized to create his "one true sentence." All at once I was his lover, observing him bare chested and warm, pulling him away from his literary angst to make damp love to me while sheer silk curtains billowed in the summer breeze.

Paris enticed me into a warm lust for life. For a brief glimpse, the city illuminated the dark lens of religious pessimism that I had faithfully worn as prescribed. Its beauty revived a deep longing inside me to experience all the sensual pleasures that the world had to offer, its sumptuousness washing over me, releasing the oppression that had dogged me since the drive over the empty prairie highway to Big Sky Bible College. I felt an urge to flee from the group, to slip away to attend the Sorbonne and live *la vie de bohème.* As I looked around at the city, I wondered how I could ever return to Bible college, and at that moment the doubts that would come back to trouble me years later first surfaced in my soul. Suddenly Christianity seemed a shortsighted, silly assessment of the human condition — just then our driver yelled, "Load up!"

At that moment, I decided to ignore such questioning and plunge forward into the future.

Four

A Leap of Faith

I FELT AS THOUGH I were a hologram, one that changed as it was tilted under the light: one tilt, I was a dedicated Bible smuggler; the other, a lustful sinner — diametric opposites, never appearing at the same moment, but always present. The hologram shifted a degree, and I stepped into the van. As we pulled out of Paris, I sat in silence feeling as though a clammy burial shroud were being wound about my limbs. In desperation I remembered the apostle Paul's battle with the flesh and his cry for help in the Letter to the Romans: "O, wretched man that I am! who shall deliver me from the body of this death?" God answered by instructing him to deny his flesh and serve "the Law of God."

I told myself it was my weakness and lack of dedication that brought about such lust and wrestling with the spirit. I asked God to forgive my wicked, wandering heart and tried to ignore the world's enticements, keeping my head down as we traveled back to Billy-Montigne, so that I might avoid all the voluptuous temptations of the magnificent countryside.

The next week I flew home from France just in time to start the fall quarter. When I arrived at the Great Falls airport, my parents, my brother, and David Brant met me. Dan and David had traveled throughout Eastern Europe, performing far more dangerous assignments than anyone on our SGA team. Instead of literature, they had smuggled currency to Christians behind the Iron Curtain. Transporting American money was a greater offense than sneaking in Bibles and carried a mandatory prison sentence in Romania, Bulgaria, Albania, and Hungary. David had sewn hundred-dollar bills inside the lining of his jacket and, without knowing the language, sneaked them to Christians in each of those countries, miraculously avoiding detection, just like Roger Moore in *The Spy Who Loved Me*. As I listened to him tell hair-raising stories of near apprehension and imprisonment, I thought about how brave and handsome he was. It was obvious that he didn't wage the same battle with sinful thoughts that I did.

Once I got back to campus, Jean threw her arms around me and told me about her steady walk with the Lord, which had brought on a very fruitful summer. Her mission group had led twenty Belgian souls to Christ, many of them Catholic converts to the faith, finally come to know true Christianity as we Baptists did.

Back in the quiet of my room, a fall rainstorm beat the window with a fiery sounding crackle as my faith shivered. Why was resisting the flesh — just following the Bible and rejecting the world and everything it offered — so hard for me? I started having nightmares about my wayward mind, dreaming that I was making a distressing journey though a succession of hostile landscapes. I was a dazed wartime nurse, lost among the rubble of London in 1945, running through a labyrinth of bombed-out multistory buildings; then a bewildered Puritan, shaking in a dank prison and waiting to be examined by the magistrate for the devil's mark. In the final dream I was fleeing from the German inquisitor (a man who had the same mailbox mouth as Mr. Foreman), hiding in a barn loft and peering out into the quiet snow that whispered softly down to the earth.

I woke with a start and, from my top bunk, looked out the dorm room window into an early snowfall.

I crawled down from the bunk, put on my bathrobe, and headed for the shower. As hot pinpricks of water hit my face, I thought about the philosophy of the nineteenth-century Danish theologian Søren Kierkegaard, who said that a life devoted to art and pleasure would fill a person with despair. He reasoned that once they experienced this hopelessness, they would often try to alleviate it by leading a more ethical, rational life, which would also lead them to despair. The only way to find true meaning, he argued, was to embrace a nonrational act: the leap of faith. Kierkegaard taught that true belief begins when people understand the limitations of art and intellectual thought, and take a leap over reason into paradox — to know by not knowing, to see by not seeing, to believe beyond thinking. Since Christian asceticism and dogma embody ironies that are offensive to reason, faith must be adopted by virtue of the absurd and not the rational, he said.

Ah-hah, I thought. Just the approach I needed. Instead of dwelling on the difficult aspects of Christianity, I would throw myself into the arms of God and thank my lucky stars that I had been saved and set apart from a lost and corrupt world. A great gust of relief began to sweep over me as I imagined my "hallowed standing in Christ," as our professors called it. I was a chosen child of God. It seemed that the Lord rewarded my obedience a few weeks later when David Brant stepped up to me in the checkout line at the bookstore, where I was buying a copy of *The Collected Works of Søren Kierkegaard,* and said, "Carlene, I would be honored if you would accompany me to the winter banquet."

The eyes of the freshman in front of me widened, and she looked back and grinned as if to say, "It's your lucky day, girl." My mind started to race, and I felt too jangled to breathe, with barely enough breath to blurt out, "That would be great!" Inwardly I grimaced, knowing I had sounded far too eager and desperate as I clutched the cover of my not yet purchased book, searing sweaty fingerprints into the image of poor Kierkegaard's dour head. David smiled shyly. "How about if I pick you up in front of your dorm at six thirty?"

"Sounds great," I squawked, now completely out of oxygen.

I ran back to the dorm and burst into Jean's room. "David Brant just asked me to the winter banquet!"

"Well I'll be a son of a gun," she said, which was the closest thing to strong language I had ever heard from Jean. She jumped up and grabbed me. "You see? Look how God has rewarded you for working so hard at your studies and doing a dangerous summer mission." I knew she felt a little like Rex Harrison in *My Fair Lady;* I was her Pygmalion. "You've made a marvelous transformation since I first met you. David Brant isn't going to mess around with anyone who isn't completely dedicated to the Lord."

Within days the campus was buzzing about our date, because although many of the girls had crushes on David, he hadn't asked anyone out in the three years he'd attended Big Sky Bible College. When people brought the subject up around Jean, she said it didn't surprise her one little bit, because I was just as dedicated to the Lord as David was, being such a serious student and Bible smuggling missionary and all.

The evening of the banquet, Jean and I chatted happily as we slipped on our long gowns. She wore a Kelly green velvet formal that brought out the highlights in her auburn hair and took her from quite handsome to strikingly beautiful. I put on my floor-length white dress with capped sleeves and an empire bodice, which had small pink roses circling the scooped neckline. "Let me do your hair," Jean said, grabbing the brush and pulling it back into a loose bun, letting long wisps fall down my face and back. "There, that'll get him," she said, beaming.

David stood on the front lawn, tall, dark, and Clark Gable handsome, grinning his take-no-prisoners smile as I stepped onto the grass, which immediately swelled beneath my wobbly feet. The tingling warmth rose through the soles of my white high heels, up my legs, and radiated through my body — a thrumming wave. "You look lovely," he said, and my knees collided, causing me to grab the car door and duck into his yellow '69 Galaxy before sheer anxiety caused them to give out completely. I was glad we were sharing the ride into Lewistown with another couple; we could chat about classes, and my body would have a chance to regain its composure. We arrived at the Argosy Banquet Hall, where David and I walked to the front of the room and took our chairs on the raised platform. President Longston had asked David to serve as master of ceremonies for the evening, and he and his wife sat next to us, smiling broadly in presidential fashion.

The banquet waitress delivered our food as the crowd mingled below, starched and uncomfortable, inhibited by their formal attire, new dates, or perhaps both. David smiled sideways at me and placed his hand ever so lightly on the fork, an inch from my hand. He leaned toward me, grinning a mischievous, conspiratorial, we're-in-this-together grin.

"Someone needs to liven this crowd up," he said.

I could feel his body close to mine, and his presence made a jolt of heat course up through my spine as he held my gaze for a moment before turning and rising to the podium. I'd never seen anyone move so comfortably; such poise and control in a man was, for me, a disarming sight. Time slowed down. Inside my head the room grew quiet, still and warm. David greeted the crowd, telling jokes and introducing the speakers with his signature wit and lighthearted humor. The crowd relaxed immediately, laughing and teasing him back. People whispered and smiled at us sitting on the platform. I could see them commenting to one another, and I imagined them saying, "What a marvelous preacher that David Brant is going to make — Carlene Cross had better hold on tight to that guy."

We laughed our way back home that evening, David still in master of ceremonies form. Sitting in the passenger's seat I had a chance to study him, intimately, as I had never seen him before from the auditorium of the chapel or the sidelines of a basketball game. I noticed a dimple in the side of his mouth that appeared only when he frowned, a dimple to break your heart. Close up, I could see that his eyes had tiny flecks of green and that he had a wild patch of white hair in the back of his head, contrasting with the jet-black waves. Once we got back to campus, the other couple thanked David for the ride and jumped out. He pulled his rumbling yellow Galaxy up to my dorm, shut the motor off, and walked me to the front door.

"Would you like to get together to memorize Scripture?" he asked.

"Sure, that sound's great," I said, acting casual but catching the signal he was sending me, which extended into the future and made my insides melt. I smiled as I backed into the dorm, tripping over the mat. "Thanks, David, I had a wonderful time."

As the door closed between us, he stood motionless with his hands clasped together and called back, "Me too."

I was in heaven. In our circles, asking a member of the opposite sex to memorize Scripture with you was a portentous sign. Bowling at Snowy Lanes or having pizza at Big Cheese Pizza was one thing, but memorizing the Bible represented completely different motives — something significant and eternal.

We met in the lobby of the administration building the next day, a Saturday, and although it was bone-chilling, it was one of those bright Montana winter days that make you feel as though spring might get impatient and burst forth any minute. David was waiting inside, standing tall and erect as always, with his Bible tucked under his arm, authority radiating from every pore, along with a boyish sexuality.

"Great day, huh?" I said.

"Just wonderful," he replied. "So, what book do you think we should start with?"

"*Start* with" — I liked the sound of that.

While our mouths did a dialogue dance about which passages might be appropriate — something very formal and serious — our bodies were busy having another conversation. The tingling which started in my chest was now moving down into my hands and toes. David must have been affected by the same feeling, because suddenly he leaned toward me.

"Let's talk about something other than the Scripture," he said softly, in a murmur that carried a kind of miraculous intimacy and fidelity. It sounded as if he were whispering to me in bed, or at least that's what I imagined since I did not know that kind of love yet. It was odd: at that proximity he felt like the sun to me, warm and delicious. *Dear God, I want to put my hands on him — not anything carnal, mind you, but just as a test.* Just to touch his face or his arms and feel whether the heat coming off them was as hot and exciting as I imagined it to be. I knew that if I did touch him, if I felt his skin and then the muscle beneath it, I could get to the soul underneath that hard muscle. But then I realized that I shouldn't be talking to God like that, He being completely holy and without sexual cravings and so on. So I said to David, "Do you have a cat back home in Washington?" which was the only question I could think of in my addled state.

"I have a dog named Pandy," he said, smiling. "He's a cute little thing with white hair and black spots, but with a bad itch that we can't seem to cure."

David told me that his family had taken Pandy to every vet in their hometown, but none of them could figure out what was wrong. He went on and on about the dog, and even though I was not particularly fond of dogs, I listened politely, which is the thing to do when you want to get a better look at someone. The skylight illuminated the waves in his raven hair, and his eyes were soft and warm as he spoke — which made it obvious that he loved Pandy the dog a lot. Then he asked me the dreaded question about what it was like to grow up on a cattle ranch (which he knew about because he was friends with my brother, Dan). I told him more than I wanted to about the boring ordeal, but he listened to me as if everything I said, even commonplace occurrences like chasing cows, was the most noteworthy event he'd heard recounted in a long time — he was a real gentleman.

David and I began to meet daily to memorize Scripture, and I quickly realized that the rumors about his intellectual prowess and spiritual commitment were all true — he had at least ten whole books of the Bible memorized and could quote them, word perfect, from beginning to end. And although the attraction between us was sometimes almost unbearable, he never once tried to touch me. David was an avid follower of the Fundamentalist leader Bill Gothard, who taught that Christian couples should refrain from all contact during courtship. "I believe that if we follow Bill Gothard's suggestions, God will bless our relationship," he would tell me.

"All right" I said, being less of an expert on both Bill Gothard and God.

"That way we won't have lust obscuring our senses," he added.

Such a commitment, along with the fact that we were seques-
tered in the mountains at this remote Bible college, did give us plenty
of time to memorize Scripture and talk about important doctrines
like dispensationalism, transubstantiation, and premillennialism.
Even so, some of our talking evolved into a rather interesting non-
verbal kind of communication. Like the day when we were having
lunch, going over chapter 4 of Philippians, and David grabbed a
large red apple out of his brown paper bag and slowly started taking
bites, watching me hungrily as I quoted verses 1 through 4. Suddenly
with a soft smile on his face, he handed the apple to me. I held it in
my hand and gazed down at the marks his teeth had made, raising
it to my mouth and putting my lips and then my tongue on the spot
where his teeth had been. The apple's juicy sweetness warmed me
as it made its way down my throat. Somehow the whole procedure
made me look in the opposite direction from David, in an effort to
keep him from knowing what I was thinking.

"All right," he said, "we'd better start on verse 5, 'Let your mod-
eration be known unto all men. The Lord is at hand.'"

That very day my brother Dan called on the intercom after I returned to the dorm. "Hey, sis," he said, "do you have a minute to talk?"

We met in the student union building, where we took a chair
amid the buzzing crowd, everyone stomping the winter snow
off their feet and milling around the tables, holding paper cups of
coffee by the rim to keep from burning their fingers, laughing and
commiserating about the upcoming Christian Epistemology test.

"It's wonderful that you and David have been spending so much
time together," Dan said. "You know he's one of the most incredible
Christian men I've ever met. He is such a strong spiritual leader and
mentor to all of the guys in the dorm." Dan hesitated for a minute
and then said, "He would be such a great catch, Carlene."

I told Dan I would think about his advice. He was a smart guy, and it was good counsel. David would be graduating in the spring, and there was a long list of girls behind me who would jump at the chance to swoop him up. I also knew that besides Dan, David was the most respectful boy on campus when it came to a woman's rights.

Within a week David and I had finished memorizing Philippians and were discussing which book to tackle next, when he said, right out of the blue, "Carlene, my father was a very violent alcoholic," a fact I already knew from campus legend. Then his eyes sort of glazed over, and he began to talk in a tone and mood I hadn't heard before, describing his childhood in a way that would have sent Dracula into a cold sweat.

"Dad enjoyed being mean to us — it was his hobby, like some men watch football or tie flies, Dad's passion was cruelty. He was a squat, flat faced man with a permanent expression of contempt. He looked like one of those ratty, cigarette reeking carnies with Brylcreem hair swept back in hoodlum waves, the kind of guy who would love to see a kid stumble off the Ferris wheel and puke all over the grass — that would give him a real hoot. He logged trees for a living, but his real calling was alcoholism. He'd come home smelling like turpentine, his red suspenders stretched tight over his filthy T-shirt and liquor belly, with the darkest, deadliest expression a man could wear — like he'd kill you for a nickel. And we were never quite sure that he wasn't about to. He'd crash through the front door, collapse into a dining room chair, and demand that Mom get him something — anything: water, coffee, a Lucky Lager. He'd shout that she was such a slut the least she could do was have coffee ready when he got home after a long day. He'd say she'd probably been sleeping with the milkman all afternoon. That was the only provocation Mom needed."

David continued, his eyes still trancelike, "She would tear the percolator plug from the wall and throw the whole thing across the room at him. Then Dad would burst off the chair like a crazed bull and leap on her, slugging her with his closed fists. Jimmy, my younger brother, and I would jump on his back and try to pull him off, which made him leave her lying in a heap and start punching us until we couldn't see straight. When Dad wasn't beating us, he was telling us how completely worthless we were. 'If you don't break it, you'll shit all over it,' he would say." David then laughed the way people do when they don't really think something is funny at all. "When I played third base on the high school baseball team, he refused to go to any of the games, because he said he knew we'd never win."

"Oh, my God, David," I said, "that's terrible."

"Well, it's a good thing he got saved a few years ago, or he probably would have killed someone. Dad and I got along great for a few years after his conversion, but lately he's been getting pretty mean again — not drinking or anything, just dry-drunk stuff. You know, verbally abusive to Mom." With that David abruptly ended his story and said, "I'm not feeling so great, let's call it quits for the day."

Hours later, as I sat on my bed in the dorm, I was still feeling a bit shaken by what David had told me when Jean popped her head into the room. "Hey," she said, "what's new with you and Mr. Good-looking?"

"Well we've finished memorizing Philippians, and we're starting in on Colossians."

"No, goofball, I mean on the relationship front — what's up?"

"Well he *is* very sweet and incredibly smart."

"I think you'd better put your hooks in this guy before he graduates," Jean said in her no-nonsense way. "Know what I mean? You aren't going to find a man like that walking the streets of Anytown, U.S.A. He's a rare breed. And, come on, he's nuts about you."

That night I thought about what Jean and Dan had said to me, and I told myself that I had never been one to shirk the responsibility of a decision — some might even say I was too impetuous — but I was nineteen years old, and the way I saw it, once the Lord spoke to you through things like powerful attraction and sympathy for someone, together with direct counsel from two spirit filled Christians who happened to be your best friends, you'd better jump on the God inspired counsel before He got weary of trying to get your attention.

The next day, when David and I met to start memorizing Colossians, I said without flinching, "I think God wants us to get married."

"Wow . . ." David looked up from his Bible, smiling shyly. He hesitated for only a moment before saying, "Well, I'm not about to argue with the Lord."

So just like that, David and I started to chart our life together. Our plan was this: After he graduated in a few months, David would move back to Washington State and get a job. I would stay in Montana and finish my degree, and a week after I graduated from Big Sky Bible College, we would get married, move to Seattle, and start seminary together.

That spring, the day he left, it rained lightly as I stood in my dorm room and watched the rich ferns and evergreens drip on the sidewalk two stories below. Down on the street I could see David loading cardboard boxes into a white panel truck. Half the boxes were lined up on the curb; the other half, in the aluminum lined interior of the truck, stacked neatly, carefully bound with brown shipping tape. It was a long step down from inside the truck, and as I watched him hop heavily onto the asphalt, I felt a rush of love flutter deep within my rib cage, a sensation that was exhilarating but almost frightening too, as though all the light of spring were filling my lungs, making them visible through the cotton material of my shirt. In a year I would be married to this handsome man. I watched him, olive-skinned, his arms rippling with muscles, his dark curls wet with rain. He was breathing hard too, though from loading boxes and not, like me, from longing. David swung himself up into the truck and lifted another heavy package.

"I love you," I said to him even though I knew he couldn't hear me. And I did love him: his great outward calm, his unflappability, his even temper, his brilliant mind, his sad past, his obvious respect for the opinions of women. That last trait comforted me the most. It was something that had been dancing in the back of my mind for some time now: how lucky I was to have found a Christian man who didn't talk about the importance of women's submission. In the past I had worried about how once a woman got married, her husband took over as head of the household and insisted that her main role was to serve as his godly helper. I knew that David would never demand such blind obedience. I could tell by the way he treated me now; Jean thought so too. What a great life we were going to have together — equals in the Lord's service.

I looked down at my watch and realized that I was almost due to meet David in the academic center to say good-bye. I put my Gore-Tex raincoat on and ran across the street. As I opened the huge black-glassed door of the foyer, David reached out from the entryway and grabbed my hand, which was unusual since we tried to keep our physical contact to a strict minimum. I followed him silently up the corridor while a yielding feeling settled over me like a spell. There was something magical about him, I thought. He pulled me into the empty auditorium with its high domed ceiling and orderly rows of black seats with a spiny projector jutting up front.

"I'm going to miss you," David said, the enormous, carpetless room returning his voice with an echo.

"I'll miss you too."

I felt like something important was about to happen. I found myself sucking in my upper lip and biting a row along its underside and then taking the bottom in and doing the same, as though I were finishing an ear of corn. He pulled me against him for the first time ever, and I could smell the wet musk of his hair. I looked up at his dark, shapely ears, which lay snug to his head in a way that made me want to feel them, so I reached up and touched them lightly; they were softer than I had expected. He shivered and grabbed my face and kissed my lips — our first kiss. My knees went limp; he held me against him. My breasts were young; they wanted to be touched, and I think he knew it, but being so dedicated to the Lord, he dropped his hands to his side. Hearing laughter down the hall, we broke away from each other, afraid that someone would burst into the auditorium and find us there, doing things that people committed to Bill Gothard's teachings would never do. We both stumbled backward, and he smiled and said, "I think I should go now." I could still taste him, smell him. What loveliness it was. What utter loveliness.

We ran outside into the rain, which had darkened the concrete sidewalks and was pushing heavily against the tree branches, moving them gently back and forth above our heads. Suddenly I was crying, gulping back the air — holding it in, letting it out. I felt as though a giant hand were squeezing my chest, rhythmically expelling the blood in my heart, *swish . . . swish . . . swish . . .* David pulled me to him again, clutching me to his body, his jacket bunching around his shoulders, and whispered in my ear, "I have to go now, my love. I'll call you tonight, when I get to Missoula." I watched the white panel truck pull out as my tears melted into the rain dripping down my face and neck.

David did call that night, and he wrote letters almost every day during the next year. I was so heartsick and lonely for him that I trudged through classes almost oblivious to the months ticking by. He moved back into his parents' house because he didn't manage to land a job and thus didn't have any money, and I could tell when his voice came scratching across the line that his spirits were low. Then one night the phone rang, and David's voice sounded desperate, almost as if he had been drinking. "Did I ever tell you about the time that I was in high school and I came home from class to find Dad demolishing the furniture with a sledgehammer? When he started to blow holes in the ceiling with a shotgun, I went to the phone and began to dial the police. He aimed the shotgun at me and said, 'Put the phone down now if you know what's good for you.' I know I should love him, Carlene, now that he's a Christian, but he is still so angry and cruel. And Mom doesn't help. She craves the battles they fight and even encourages them. Even though they don't physically abuse each other any more, it's still the same mental torture."

"Isn't there any place else you can go? Take a job anywhere and move out?"

"It looks like maybe this position at Boeing, as a machinist's helper, will work out, and as soon as it does, I'm gone," David said. "Maintaining my spiritual life was so much easier at Bible college. This last few weeks I've really been fighting the flesh."

"Fighting the flesh." The words stuck in my mind, but I didn't ask David what he meant because it could have been so many things, various temptations we considered a direct assault to spirituality, ranging from lusting over the opposite sex to neglecting to spend an hour on our knees in prayer each morning. He was such a fine example of a "prayer warrior," he must be having difficulties with his prayer life, I thought. I was more concerned that the sound of his voice, which I had come to recognize as strong and confident, now sounded weak and afraid.

"I think you should get out; this is taking too much of a toll on you."

"Well, Bill Gothard says children should resolve their conflicts with their parents, and until I'm married I am still under the authority of my father, which makes me think I should stay here and deal with my feelings of anger toward him."

"Okay, I understand," I said, but I was not sure that Bill Gothard, never having any children himself, was necessarily the authority on father-son relationships.

I was glad that David could at least feel complete acceptance from my parents, who adored him. For years my brother had reported to everyone at home what an amazing Christian David was, winning preaching awards and being such a perfect example to the other students on campus. Dad and Mom had met him at the airport the summer he and Dan returned from smuggling Bibles into Eastern Europe, and had immediately taken to the handsome, self-assured young man. Once we decided to marry, they knew he would make a great addition to the family. They were also proud that David and I had decided to attend seminary together in the fall, after our marriage.

I hardly saw David that year; our primary contact was over the phone and through letters. Our wedding was planned a week after my graduation, and the closer it approached, the more jitters I was getting. I was a twenty-year-old virgin and had never known any real intimacy with anyone. I hadn't seen David in so long the physical passion that had developed between us as we memorized Scripture and during our brief encounter in the academic center seemed like a distant dream. But a week after I graduated from Bible college, I stood in the foyer of the small white church in Lolo, Montana.

David stood up front, twenty-six years old, tall and slim, his solemn face revealing an uncharacteristic lack of self-confidence, something I had never seen in him before. He seemed as apprehensive as I was as he faced me, looking down the aisle in the presence of God, friends, and family. The sun streaming through the stained-glass window merged him with the wedding party up front — Jean, Dan, and the others — in a slow rainbow of color, white softening to pink, purple merging from scarlet and royal blue.

In the foyer, waiting for the wedding march to begin, I gripped the wad of pastel dyed daisies and baby's breath, the words *What am I doing?* battering around in my skull like swallows trapped in an attic. Was I really sure about this? It was too late now for such questions, I told myself. In the pews all eyes shifted to the doorway, waiting for Dad and me to start down the aisle. As the wedding march began — their signal to rise — we stepped through a path of strewn petals.

That night as I stalled in the bathroom, I felt dread and anxiety instead of eager anticipation. I lingered, hesitating to put on my white lace nightgown, brushing my teeth another time, reapplying mascara. I thought, *So this is what Rebecca felt like when she became Isaac's bride — a man that she didn't know.* David seemed as uncertain and inexperienced as I. Gone was the Bible smuggling bravado and student body president self-assurance I once knew. After months of equating physical contact with sin, we fumbled at each other, thick fingered and red faced. *We're just used to thinking of sex as a vastly illegal drug,* I told myself. *We'll learn to relax and this will start to be fun.* But even so I could still feel my teenage expectations crash and lie in splinters on the frigid floor. I would have to gather them and embrace my new life.

Five 〰

A New Life

W E DROVE TO WASHINGTON and found a dilapidated farmhouse that we could rent cheaply. Built in the 1920s, it had chipped paint and lots of bare wood — one unwatched candle and the whole thing would have gone up in flames. The house was not far from David's parents, in the little logging town where he grew up.

In our spare time, which was plentiful because we didn't have enough money even to go to the movies, we kept practicing at making love, and the situation did get better. We just needed to slow down and quit thinking that it was evil and remember that we were married and that God had said sex was okay once you were legally bound in matrimony forever. "Sex should be *fun,*" some preachers even said from the pulpit. One night after making love, the air abruptly filled, every cubic inch of it, with the damp ozone smell of a summer storm. I got up and walked over to the window, where I idly traced the cracks in the caulk. Even though the rain was coming down in torrential sheets, I thought about how peaceful it was. "What a beautiful thunderstorm," I said to David, thinking we would have many more years of seeing such things together, that we would stand in front of the windows season after season, watching the different kinds of Washington rain — there's so much of it, and it changes all the time. It would be just the two of us, watching the rain knock the fall leaves from the broadleaf maples or melt the winter snow into the rusting storm drains. From now onward into forever, this would happen. We would laugh at our children playing in the cloudbursts, splashing in the puddles, jumping up and down in their yellow galoshes. After we died, we would observe it together from heaven, David and I. *Into eternity,* I thought. After the Rapture and the thousand-year reign of Jesus and the Final Judgment, we would still be watching the rain shower down onto the earth.

The rain seemed to affect David differently, though. He didn't like it the way I did, probably because he had grown up with it, and it wasn't so new to him. He started to lumber up out of bed late most mornings, calling in sick to his job at Boeing and falling into deep, unexplained depressions. He said it must be the town, because it reminded him of his violent childhood. We tried to discuss the awful things that had happened to him as a boy, but that didn't seem to relieve the sadness either. I couldn't help but notice, as we talked about the anger he felt toward his folks, that his eyes would become as cold as a barren landscape. Sometimes he seemed to be living far down inside himself, in a secret hidden passageway. His only solace came when he'd have a chance to get away and read the Bible, mostly off at the church library in town, or late at night in his study.

I had to admit that David seemed much different than he had in college. But I knew this was simply a time of adjustment for him. At Big Sky he had clear direction from God. Working for Boeing didn't challenge him or put his talents to use. Once he was serving the Lord again I was sure things would change. It's why I was so relieved when David started — and I went along to audit — classes at Northwest Baptist Seminary in Tacoma. We arrived on the first day after driving down the winding road through the huge old brick estate overlooking Puget Sound. The grounds, built in 1923 by the Weyerhaeuser family, had an Ivy League charm and made my heart race with hope and expectation. Rose gardens, a stained-glass chapel, and a greenhouse surrounded the lofty academic structures. The place was enchanting. But when we stepped into class, I knew something wasn't right when several of the seminarians turned and stared at me. By lunchtime I found out that I was the only woman attending NBS, because it refused to grant theology degrees to women, following the First Letter of Paul to Timothy 2, which forbids women to hold roles of leadership in the church. The fact that I entered the school dressed in blue jeans also added to the offense (any type of denim was completely unacceptable attire for a future pastor's wife). I decided to keep my ears and eyes open to make sure that I didn't commit any more terrible blunders.

It was then that I remembered a seminar Jean and I stumbled into by mistake during a pastors' conference at the Bible college years before. We were headed for the lecture on Christian Apologetics but were so absorbed in our conversation that by the time we burst into room 223 instead of 234, it was too late. Jean looked at me sideways, shrugged her shoulders, and we sat down. Up front was a long rectangular table with seven women perched in a row. On the blackboard the lecture title read BEING A GODLY ADDITION TO YOUR HUSBAND'S MINISTRY.

The first voice to speak came out of a lifeless face that looked like a waxwork in candlelight. "As a minister's wife you must always display a meek and quiet spirit. It's best to keep your voice soft and nonthreatening. No matter how upset you feel, resist the temptation to raise your voice in front of anyone in the congregation."

"Remember that at all times every eye will be focused on you," a portly young lady, looking barely twenty-five, added. "People will look to you to set an example for every Christian woman in the congregation."

"The most important advice I can give is, do *not* make any girlfriends within the congregation," said a dark-haired woman wearing large-rimmed spectacles.

With that, the entire panel nodded their heads severely. "The other women will become jealous, and there will be no end to your grief," added the portly one. "And God forbid that you might slip and tell them something that could tarnish your husband's reputation."

Afterward Jean said, "I would never forfeit my freedom that far. It's why I'd rather be a missionary out in the bushes of Africa than a preacher's wife."

It was the funniest thing, because that first day in seminary when I thought about Jean my throat constricted and tears welled up in my eyes. I excused myself to go to the bathroom, and thank goodness David was so enthralled in conversation with another student that he didn't see me back up and slip out, wiping my eyes. I stayed there, where I knew it would be safe, considering that there were never any women in the building. I missed Jean terribly at that moment.

But I did have to be thankful that seminary had caused David to become more like his old self again. Driving to class each morning, we discussed theology and quizzed each other over our Greek syntax and Hebrew vocabulary. Even the fact that we lived so close to his parents didn't seem to bother him as much, because we spent every spare minute reading volumes of systematic theology and preparing for our church history and apologetics tests.

Then one morning I woke up in a black sea of nausea. The flu, I thought. However, after two weeks of projectile vomiting, I knew I had something more than a common illness. By that time it was also obvious that I wasn't going to handle pregnancy as David's mother had, who loved to say, "Oh, heavens, I never felt better in my life than when I was carrying my first baby!" I, on the other hand, had never felt worse. Each morning I would wake up feeling like Lazarus on his fourth day dead. I'd force down crackers and Mountain Dew and finally, by two in the afternoon, feel that soup for dinner might be a possibility. Since attending Greek class with a bucket at my feet was not a real option, I dropped out of school to concentrate on caulking the windows and finding garage-sale baby furniture.

It was hard being left behind just when David and I seemed to be back in sync. His time spent at school and studying in the church library increased, and so I filled my days with long walks along a dogleg dirt road bordered by rustling willows and poplars. In the evenings I did my counted cross-stitching and thought about all the interesting discussions Jean and I used to have and what I would tell her if she were here now. Then one evening David's mother showed up at the front door and said she wanted to talk to me about something. She sat down as I banged nervously around the kitchen, making coffee and trying to find a spare biscuit. "I'm worried about you, honey," she said. "David leaves you alone far too much in this creaky old house."

"Oh, I don't mind. I know he's got tons of research to do, and Joe, that guy he carpools with, always wants to stay late at school." In truth I missed David terribly, but then I thought about how love can be intensified by absence. Long ago men went to sea, and women waited for them, standing at the edge of the water, scanning the horizon for a black dot to turn into a tiny ship and sail into the harbor. It was my time to wait for David. Besides it was my duty as a Christian wife to put aside my own desires, now that my husband had chosen to follow God's call into the ministry. David would face great challenges ahead; I needed to be supportive and not put a drain on his time.

And then a miracle happened. Jean and her new husband,

Doug, moved into a house down the street. They were headed for the mission field in Mexico but were going to live in our small town for a while to raise their monthly support from churches in the area. Doug had attended Big Sky Bible College with us, but Jean had never dated him there. Where Jean had been an outstanding student, Doug was, well, less than an outstanding student. He had goofed off most of the time, barely getting passing grades in his classes. A missionary's kid himself, he spent his childhood in the jungles of South America bouncing back and forth between Brazilian boarding schools and the Amazon rain forest. It wasn't until after we had all graduated that Doug called Jean and asked her out. After only a few dates, they both decided to accept God's call to the mission field, which made Jean confident that God would bless their union. I was happy for Jean, who had finally found a partner as committed as she to leading natives to Christ.

My loneliness was over. Jean and I did our grocery shopping together and even started team-teaching a women's Bible study at our church. Her presence revived my spirits, and the pregnancy didn't feel so much like an eternity. Interestingly enough, I stopped worrying so much about whether I'd make a good mother, which had occupied my thoughts when I was spending most of my time alone.

In August 1979 our first child was born: a beautiful dark-haired baby girl. We named her Carise — the Greek word for *grace*. And grace was exactly what Carise brought into my life from the day she arrived. My secret apprehension of motherhood vanished with her first cry, as the doctor whipped the tangled umbilical cord from around her neck and cleaned her flawless face. I knew my life had been transformed the moment I saw the miracle of her miniature fingernails, the lips like a tiny rose, and the toes lined up in perfect little rows, and felt her fierce intent to root nourishment from my swollen breasts. I had no warning that with my daughter's first breath a deep mothering instinct would envelop me or that vigilance for her welfare would become the star that guided my way.

David was smitten by his baby daughter too, and he started to spend more time at home, talking about how we needed to protect her from the evils of this fallen world. This concern naturally led us to pay attention to the upcoming presidential election, in which our pastor had taken a great deal of interest. From the pulpit, he was keeping the congregation updated on the work of a preacher named Jerry Falwell, from Lynchburg, Virginia, who was crisscrossing the country, urging America to repent, arguing that the nation had fallen from greatness because it had turned its back on God and abandoned the beliefs upon which Thomas Jefferson and Benjamin Franklin had founded it.

"The 'I Love America' rallies are turning out to be a superb success!" Pastor Bill hollered from the pulpit. "At each stop Falwell is registering thousands of supporters and convincing Christians to become involved in the political process. God bless Jerry Falwell!" he shouted, banging the pulpit with his fist. "He's showing us that political involvement is a duty, not an option!"

How strange, I thought. In the past, our Fundamentalist leaders had viewed politics as a pursuit not so different from drinking, dancing, and card playing. But the change Jerry Falwell was suggesting was a welcome one to me. It made sense that if Christians were going to lead the unsaved to Christ, a great place to start was the political arena. Falwell, like John the Baptist, was a hero of sorts, a voice crying in the wilderness. For far too long Christians had neglected their duty to be a testimony to the secular world.

"All across America," the pastor shouted, "the Moral Majority movement is catching fire."

Pastor Bill went on to tell us that many big-name Christian teachers were joining Falwell on his crusade: Pat Robertson, Tim LaHaye, and Jim Bakker. Even Hal Lindsey had come aboard, still insisting that the Rapture was just around the corner, although in the meantime, he conceded, Christians were still expected to work toward righteousness in government.

"Tune in to KGNW tomorrow at 10:00 a.m.," Pastor Bill urged us. "The station will be broadcasting one of Pastor Falwell's stirring messages."

I'd never heard of Jerry Falwell before, but he sounded like a pretty inspiring guy, so the next morning, after David left for school, I turned the radio on, already set to AM820 KGNW. "In reclaiming America for God, we must have three priorities," a startlingly loud voice proclaimed in an accent like no preacher I knew from the Northwest. *Ah, this must be Falwell,* I thought. "Number one: get people converted to Christ. Number two: get them baptized. Number three: get them *registered to vote!*" he shouted.

Falwell went on to say that the purpose of reclaiming the political process for God was for Christians to use secular law to reestablish the biblical family structure that America had so completely abandoned, as evidenced by the nation's divorce rate, support for the Equal Rights Amendment, disrespectful children, homosexual rights, and the teaching of evolution in the schools. The other indisputable proof of society's downfall was that its men were suffering from a feeling of impotence, a lack of self-esteem, and a failure of leadership, all of which could be traced directly to the new self-assertiveness of women.

"Quoting my friends Tim and Beverly LaHaye," he shouted, "men in America are being 'feminized' — 'castrated.' The integrity and survival of society can only be restored if women are returned to the traditional role of submissive helper." The fiery preacher continued, voice strained, "The only way to redirect this catastrophe is with radical change: America must start with replacing its current president!" Falwell went on to say that even though Jimmy Carter claimed to be a born-again Christian, his political liberalism said differently. Carter supported the Equal Rights Amendment and abortion. He refused to champion the teaching of creationism in the public schools, condemn homosexuality, or clamp down on pornography; he had even done an interview with *Playboy,* for heaven's sake. The air in the living room was electric with Falwell's anger, his voice bouncing off the walls. Carise, who was nestled in a fluffy cotton baby blanket on the couch, let out a distressed sob. I ran over to the radio and turned it down.

"That guy is pretty loud, isn't he, sweetheart?" I said as I rocked her to sleep.

Months later, on the evening of November 5, 1980, I was restless with pent-up anticipation. David was studying at the library, and Carise and I were cuddled up on the couch with the radio tuned to KGNW. The fire in the woodstove crackled as the voice on the radio announced, "The presidential election is too close to call."

"Let's keep our fingers crossed that we can get this nation on the right track again," I said as I kissed Carise's fat little cheek. In my mind, the presidential election manifested a shoot-out between good and evil, with Reagan wearing the white hat. When the results finally came in, I was elated. Not only had Reagan triumphed, but the election had also resulted in further gains for the Right — conservative candidates had dethroned Democrats across the nation. Now that Ronald Reagan was at the helm and we had a conservative House of Representatives as well, Fundamentalists were assured of a godly America. I was relieved beyond words because I was beginning to suspect that Carise might soon be sharing her tiny bedroom with a new little soul.

I came home from the Walgreen's pharmacy that week and scurried into the bathroom, where I yanked open the pregnancy test kit and peed on the long stick, then used it to stir the chemicals in the little plastic test tube. Setting it on the living room bookshelf, I grabbed the latest issue of *Christianity Today* and sat back on the couch to wait out the five minutes. If the liquid remained clear, I was not pregnant. If it turned blue, I was. I had conflicted feelings about being pregnant again. David had one more year to go before completing his master of theology degree, and I knew that another child would put greater pressure on us financially and emotionally. But after being at home so much during Carise's first weeks, he had once again begun spending more time away, studying late in the seminary library, buried behind theology books. Having another child would be great company for Carise and me. Out on the edge of my peripheral vision was a flash of teal. I focused quickly on the test tube, a tiny, ominous column of turquoise flushing slowly to royal blue. Another baby.

Micael's birth completely contrasted with that of her sister. Whereas Carise seemed reluctant to leave the safety and quiet comfort of water and womb during the twenty-six-hour labor, Micael tumbled out in mere hours, slapping her tiny arms and legs against my thighs as she swam from my body. Wide-eyed and determined, she came out like a woman on a mission. And unlike Carise, who politely refused to drink from a bottle, Micael quickly recognized the freedom it afforded and enjoyed switching between bottle and breast. Fierce independence was Micael's style from birth. I marveled at the difference between my two happy daughters and at my own powerful love for them both.

After graduating from Northwest Baptist Seminary a year later, David decided to earn a second master's degree and enrolled at Trinity Evangelical Divinity Seminary in Chicago. I was four months pregnant with our third child when we packed a trailer Dad had welded together for us from parts of an old pickup bed, hitched it to a green '68 Ford Mom and Dad bought for us at a Forest Service car auction, and headed out to Deerfield, Illinois. Across the Midwest we drove, with Carise and Micael peeking their tiny heads up through our piles of belongings looking like baby robins in a nest. Although I had been a bit apprehensive about taking off across country with two small children and one on the way, I did not object. I knew that God would bless our family as I supported David's ministry.

I did worry a little about our sex life, though. Although we seemed to be doing a pretty good job of it, considering our reproductive rate, David often seemed to be thinking about something else. Our lovemaking had become mechanical and detached, like driving a car on autopilot. And when we weren't in bed, David often seemed to have mislocated himself, holding his book and staring off into the back of beyond. And then, when his theological journal got too heavy, with a start he'd jolt back to reality. I assumed that this small problem with absentmindedness would improve once he was through with seminary and the pressures of school were gone. I hoped also I'd see a lessening of his desire for control.

"The fridge looks pretty dirty these days," he'd say on his way out the front door, heading for the library. "And I also noticed last night that you bought Jif peanut butter instead of Western Family. You should know that we can't afford that name-brand stuff," he'd call back over his shoulder without waiting to hear if I had any defense.

I was sure his increasing domination was also just a passing phase: the pressures of school, two small babies with another on the way. He probably felt trapped by this third pregnancy, I decided, trapped by the necessity of making a home — not just for a young couple but for an entire family: Dad, Mom, and now *three* kids. Within four years David had gone from footloose college student to father of an entire clan, shackled by the needs of his dependents and by his grave Christian responsibility to assume spiritual leadership of the family and be a stellar example, especially since he was going to enter the ministry. It was comforting when several of the other seminary wives confided in me that their husbands were also going through a similar unwelcome transformation.

I got to know two other wives at Trinity Divinity School. The first, Dianna, was a strong-spirited Midwestern girl, a gorgeous redhaired athlete who had run cross-country while in college at Kansas State University. She was strong and slim, with an athlete's self-confidence. There was no hemming or hawing with Dianna, a ruddy, take-no-prisoners beauty. From the very first time I met her in the atrium of the student union building, I noticed her blue jeans hugging her long sleek frame and wondered how she would ever survive the ministry. I hoped her husband, whoever he was, would end up in a liberal denomination, where the pressures were easier on pastors' wives.

"Hi, I'm Dianna," she said, holding out her hand. "I saw you moving your stuff in upstairs. How far along are you — pregnant, I mean?" She smiled.

"Five months," I said, "but it feels like eight."

"Aw, you look great, but I know what you mean. It's so tiring when you've already got other babies to care for."

"Yeah, like a gravel truck has just run you over," I said.

"Mommy roadkill." Her eyes, blue as glacial ice, sparkled as she threw her head back and laughed at her own joke. "You have the sweetest little girls — maybe we could get them together with my two little hellions, Tommy and George."

"I would love that."

"How about tea, then? Tomorrow at ten? I'll invite another one of the girls I saw moving into A320. I don't know what her name is, but she looks nice," Dianna added.

Amber was just as nice as Dianna but in a different way. She was a pretty, peach-skinned blond with a delicate oval face, and although she was smart, she seemed a little like a permanent traveler in outer space. She wore pressed slacks even on Saturday mornings and had a calm, almost sedate voice, which I thought would serve her well in the ministry. She and her husband would probably be just fine in a conservative Baptist church.

Dianna, Amber, and I started meeting to do our counted cross-stitch together, calling ourselves the Seminary Widows' Club (secretly, of course). As soon as our husbands left for class, we would settle our gang of toddlers, George and Tommy (who were actually very nice little gentlemen), Carise, Micael, and Amber's twins, Kami and Kerry, brew strong coffee, and chatter the mornings away.

"Tim is gone so much, I'm beginning to forget what he looks like," Dianna said one day. "But I'll tell you, this new form of nit-picking is even worse. He keeps telling me that if we're going to be successful in the ministry, I'm going to have to keep the kitchen surfaces shinier. Can you believe it?" She grabbed a dishcloth and swirled it in the air. "Wash and polish, wash and polish. God, it's like I'm a private in the U.S. Navy."

"Fred says the same thing," Amber added, setting her cross-stitch down and twisting her long blond curls around her finger.

"He says I'd better start being meticulous now because when we're living in a parsonage, my housekeeping skills will be out in the open for everyone to see. It scares the wits out of me."

"Can you believe that Dr. Spencer actually quoted First Timothy to his class the other day?" Dianna said, laughing. She stood up and thrust her hands on her hips, then lowered her voice into a deep baritone. "A minister must be one that *rules* his own house. For if a man cannot rule his own household, how shall he take care of the church of God?"

With that we all burst out laughing, but deep inside I think we all wondered whether the implications of Timothy might someday come back to haunt us all. At the time, though, I refused to let such future possibilities frighten me. Instead I was going to enjoy every minute of fun and freedom I still had left with my two new friends and my lively little girls.

David approved of my friendship with the other wives because he knew it kept me cheerful and occupied. The other husbands felt the same way. They were all glad we had something to fill the hours as they darted late to class or gulped down dinner so they could get to the library — rarely stopping to chat with anyone, not each other or their spouses. We seminary wives understood that it was a necessary sacrifice we were called to make — God was preparing us for the ministry. We would have to get used to our husbands spending large amounts of time away.

At the time I didn't think much about the ministry. Carise, Micael, and I were having too much fun. After morning coffee with the Widows' Club, we would go back home and begin our daily routine: chicken salad for lunch, a Jane Fonda workout tape at two, then snuggling together in our chilly student apartment for an afternoon nap. After dinner we would watch the *CBS Evening News with Dan*

Rather and *Sale of the Century,* which got us in the perfect mood to turn on the tape player full blast and rock out to Rod Stewart — me the lumbering Disney elephant encircled by two tiny wildly dancing mice. To this day I'm sure it's why Jason came out so fidgety. Somehow, on the deepest, most visceral level, Rod Stewart and "Do Ya Think I'm Sexy?" bouncing through my belly must have shaken him into a frenzy.

Jason was born in February, during a cold Chicago storm that froze every puddle into a solid ice brick. The wind howled and whipped at the car as David rushed me over snow packed roads to Lake Forest Hospital after my water broke. When we got there, he realized he had forgotten his textbook and returned for it once I was checked in. On the labor monitor I watched the red peaks of the contractions getting higher and higher. I breathed my Lamaze pants and hoped David would get there soon. A few minutes before Jason arrived, he came running into the room. "Sorry, I'm late. Wow, the roads are ghastly out there." When we took our new son home, Dianna and Amber were waiting, cheering with WELCOME HOME signs and two weeks' worth of frozen casseroles. Carise and Micael practically suffocated the tiny, dark, and handsome little boy with kisses, and Carise said, "He looks like a Kewpie."

With three small children to take care of, I didn't spend much time thinking about esoteric questions of God and the meaning of the universe. I didn't even care that we were poor as beggars in a fairy tale. After David left for school, the girls and I would bathe, then lotion and powder our new little family member, dress him in his infant overalls and flannel shirt, and sit him in his baby chair on the couch. Mom had sent Carise and Micael tiny pink tutus, which elevated their dance routine to a more sophisticated level. They would tug on their ballet garb, flee into the living room, and turn on Vivaldi. Carise, a graceful, sparrow-boned four-year-old, floated over the carpet, making sure that her movements were precise and dignified. Micael, a chubby twenty-four-month-old ball of energy, looked more like a baroque cherub spinning, twisting, and pirouetting around the room, stopping only long enough to rush over and put a wet kiss on her brother's giggling cheek.

In June 1983, David graduated with his second master's in theology. In late May he had learned of a Baptist church in the Seattle suburbs that was interviewing for a minister, so as soon as the graduation ceremony was over, we loaded our sparse belongings into our rattletrap trailer and headed west. Dianna and Amber stood next to the car, looking glum as we squeezed the last frying pan into the backseat. "Well, it makes sense that you would be the first to take the plunge," Dianna said, "being the oldest and all." (Dianna, at twenty-six, was actually the oldest member of the Seminary Widows' Club.) She laughed as she threw her arms around me, then burst into tears. Amber followed, crying as though I were headed for the Final Judgment.

"I'll be okay, ladies," I said, hugging them both and whispering in their ears, "I'll just remember: wash and polish, wash and polish."

Tears were still running down our faces as the car lurched out of the driveway. I turned and waved back at them, huddled together, holding hands. But even in our sadness, we ultimately knew that our destiny was to move forward to serve God, our husbands, and the congregations we were eventually going to enter.

Six ⤳

Calvary Baptist Church

CALVARY BAPTIST CHURCH, standing on a hill with its white clapboard walls, its steepled roof reaching toward heaven, looked as though it had been lifted out of a Norman Rockwell painting. For over three decades the same families had attended the church, taking personal and serious responsibility for the appearance of the building and grounds. Cultivating its gardens each Saturday, they added new daffodils or Dutch irises beside the rainbow hued rows of azalea, hydrangea, and rhododendron bushes. Work parties planted bulbs of tulips, white lilies, and pink cyclamen, to pop up just in time for Easter, and trimmed the jasmine that scented the entire grounds as it climbed the garden arbor, reaching higher and higher, like voices in the ladies' choir. Bright perennials bordered the concrete steps that led up to the tall white sanctuary doors.

Inside, at the end of a long row of pews, a wooden podium perched high on a platform above the flock, and behind it a velvet curtain concealed the oblong baptismal. Although it was hidden, all good Baptists knew the baptismal was there. In our faith, baptism by immersion was protocol as unquestioned as washing one's hands before dinner. In fact, it was the issue of baptism that gave birth to the denomination back in 1609. John Smyth and his flock in Amsterdam separated from the Church of England over the doctrine

of infant baptism, which placed a baby under the covenant and immediately into the church family. Smyth insisted that the rite should
be performed only once an adult became a believer. Thus baptism,
following a profession of faith, symbolized a mature union between
the Christian and the church. Since immersion uniquely character-
ized the belief of Smyth and his followers, the baptismal took on
great significance, giving its name to the movement. Today in Baptist churches around the world baptism continues to loom large in
doctrinal statements and building plans.

The beauty of Calvary Baptist delighted me. It was clear that
the members of the congregation took religion — and church main-
tenance — seriously. And the salary they offered of $1,200 a month,
with a parsonage to live in, would get us out of our nomadic, graduate school poverty. We had scrimped and scraped for five years, with
no income other than from preaching jobs that David picked up
here and there. Each jam jar was rinsed out, dried, and shelved to be
used for canning, and all wrapping paper was carefully folded and
hidden away on Micael's birthday in May, to reuse on Carise's in August. Every piece of garage sale baby furniture was kept in trust for
the next kid, every pair of socks mended, every plastic bag reused.
My parents had been a godsend in those lean years, paying for much
of David's seminary tuition and constantly sending us bits of money
for the extras — "mad money," as Mom called it. Now the idea of a
full-time income made me breathe a long sigh of relief. I knew it
would take enormous pressure off David and lighten his mood. But
we didn't have the job yet, so we needed to be in top form during the
interview, because other eager seminary couples had also applied to
shepherd the picturesque church. "We've been working toward this
for five years now," David said. "Let's do all we can to make the right
impression."

"What dress do you think I should wear?" I asked.

"That floral one," he said. "Conservative but not dowdy."

We arrived early on Sunday morning, and I took Carise, Micael, and Jason down to children's church, praying they would behave as perfect cherubs. I had outfitted them in their best: the girls in matching red silk dresses and white laced pinafores I'd sewn, Jason in a handsome black suit and crisp white shirt that Mom and Dad had sent especially for the occasion. We were as ready as we'd ever be for the test ahead.

David preached his most stirring — and well practiced — sermon, and the congregation erupted in applause at the end. The outburst made my heart leap because I'd never seen congregants show such emotion in church. After the service gray-haired parishioners lined the back of the sanctuary, bathed in dappled light beaming down through the stained-glass windows, calling out to David and me as we filed past during the last hymn: "Praise the Lord, what a sermon!" . . . "Uplifting message, Pastor" . . . "Glory be to God!" Out on the manicured lawn the elders grinned with delight as members whispered in their ears what looked to me to be further positive assessments. Then Don, the assistant pastor, a short, bald, heavy through the chest fellow with a wide, flat, pie-shaped face, stepped over to us and slapped David on the back. "You passed with flying colors, young man," he said. "Now the board wants to take you to lunch, to see if you are as charismatic in social circumstances as you are in the pulpit." He laughed genially as if to say, "Not to worry — you'll be fine."

On our way to Ming Court for lunch, Janet, Don's wife, and I chatted in the backseat of their car. "Now, this is the time the elders will size you up," she said. "Don't be nervous. They'll just ask a lot of questions, but remember that everyone loves the Lord and is quite harmless."

I was grateful for Janet's warning, because as we walked into the dimly lit restaurant and took our seats opposite a long row of elders and their wives, the group stared with ravenous expressions as though it were me they planned to devour for lunch instead of the pork dumplings. It felt like I was in one of those awful dreams where you suddenly realize you have to take a test that you haven't studied for, and you aren't wearing any clothes, and you can't get out of the room, because your legs won't move. As the waitress set out flower rolls, crab Rangoon, barbecue pork, and pot stickers, the elders began tossing live hand grenade questions at me:

"Do you enjoy teaching children's church?"

"Do you have much experience teaching women's Bible study?"

"Do you like to entertain?"

Thank the Lord I suddenly remembered the sallow-skinned pastor's wife from Bible college saying, "As a minister's wife you must always display a meek and quiet spirit. It's best to keep your tone soft and nonthreatening." I lowered my voice an octave and tried to defuse each question while nonchalantly taking bites of appetizer.

"Oh, yes, I have lots of experience teaching women's Bible study" — which was mostly true.

"Yes, I love to entertain" — which was entirely true.

"Yes, I love teaching children's church" — which was a bald-faced lie.

Just that moment I bit down on a piece of pork I'd covered in an innocuous looking white sauce as, too late, I heard one of the elders say, "This horseradish dip is absolutely deadly. I've never tasted anything so strong."

A bomb exploded in my sinuses, and my eyes watered as I scoured the table for water. None to be found. Thank goodness I had a napkin in which to hide my face. I sat perfectly still for several seconds, trying desperately not to choke or spew horseradish all over the elders and their wives. After my eyes stopped watering, I silently apologized to the Lord for lying about children's church and chastised myself for being so unsophisticated and reckless — I had never eaten horseradish before. Now that I was about to become a minister's wife, I would have to be more careful and look both ways before moving in any direction.

After several more meetings and mercifully uneventful luncheons, David was hired, and we moved into the roomy four-bedroom parsonage only a few steps from the church. Light poured through huge windows that spanned the entire front of the house, filling the open rooms with warmth and making me eager to take my counted cross-stitch projects into a gallery to have them matted and framed and then mount them on the lovely walls. After David said he thought we could afford the purchases, I bought yards of fabric and began sewing curtains and throw pillows, tablecloths and chair cushions, even opening a Bon Marché charge account to buy our first new couch in six years of marriage. "Isn't all this sunlight wonderful?" I said to David. "And the parsonage is so big it feels like Buckingham Palace."

"Yes," he said softly. "It's nice to settle into a place where we can make a new beginning."

I hugged David and imagined our new life together, now that he was free from the pressures of school and we had a steady income and a little extra money for nonessentials. We'd start to do things together, like occasionally getting a babysitter and renting a cottage by the sea, even though it would cost more than a month's grocery budget during our seminary days. Holding hands, we'd walk along the soft, wild dunes and watch the terns and gulls flying overhead and the waves rolling in and out. We'd make reservations and eat in a fancy restaurant that overlooked the crashing, rolling Pacific, its cool mists dampening the salt breeze. We'd stroll back to our cozy cabin with old knotty pine paneling that gave off a warm, golden glow. David would make a fire in the hearth as the light faded to gray and night slid into the room, and I would peel off my clothes and jump shivering into bed. Then I would watch him undress against the flickering flames and slip in next to me. Once fire's heat filled the tiny place, we'd kick back the sheets and frolic like newlyweds, free to make all the noise we wanted. In the morning we would wake up in each other's arms, smelling of musk and lovemaking. We'd brew strong coffee and sit around, grungy and full of opinions, reading the *Seattle Times* out loud to each other, our bare feet touching, longing for nothing, not to be older or younger or in another place or time — simply together.

I imagined that in our new life all the pleasures would be homey ones: the smell of our children's skin, their hair damp as we pulled them slippery and giggling from the tub; an overstuffed armchair to match the new couch; a postcard from Jean and Doug in Mexico City, telling us that the Lord was blessing their ministry; the luxury of grocery bags jammed full of unnecessary things like Brie, hot chocolate, ginger ale, and salmon, sitting on the kitchen counter waiting to be unpacked. That's what I imagined as, there in the parsonage, David and I stayed in each other's arms for a moment, hugging, on the lookout for the future that we expected. I think that was the happiest day of our life together, though we never knew it.

Suddenly David froze as two noses pressed against the window. In the glare of sunlight, the interlopers could not see us standing in the kitchen. The man spotted the new living room couch and said, "That material doesn't look practical to me."

"It's far too light for a house with three small children," added his wife, her hair pulled back neatly in a bun. "It's pretty now, but give it a week and it'll be a mess."

"Forget the color — how can they *afford* a new couch? *We* certainly can't buy furniture like that ... Maybe we're paying them too much."

David whispered, "Don't worry; just stand perfectly still, and they'll go away."

Once they left we laughed, and David said, "Kind of like living in an ecclesiastical aquarium."

After several weeks of curtain sewing and picture hanging, David and I felt that the house looked so warm and inviting that we could ask the elders and their wives over for dinner. I had been careful not to put too many nails in the parsonage walls, the house being church property and all. But I couldn't help making one minor adjustment: the carpet. A matted green dreadlock shag straight from the 1960s, it had a thick plastic runner over it, starting at the front door and extending down the hallway and making the entire entryway feel like an ice hockey rink. Even though the carpet was already knotted and worn, the elders apparently felt that if everyone walked lightly, it had another decade or two left in it. I carefully rolled up the fourteen-foot vinyl monstrosity and hid it in the closet, replacing it with a friendly doormat.

That night, after the house had filled with the starched elders and their stern wives, Phoebe, a no-nonsense cricket of a woman, inquired about the hard plastic. "Where is the runner?" she chirped. "With all the people who will be in and out of the parsonage, I'm sure you understand the necessity of protecting the church's carpet."

"Of course," I said in my practiced minister's wife voice, soft and submissive, and lugged it out of the closet and rolled it back over the deadly green shag.

After Phoebe and the other guests left, I looked at the cold, cheerless plastic, rolled it back up, and returned it to the closet. *I'll simply take it out right before Phoebe visits again,* I told myself, thinking that I was getting this minister's wife thing down pat — surely she would never peer in the windows, like a neurotic landlord, and see it missing. But the next week Janet pulled me aside and whispered, "Phoebe peeked in the parsonage windows and saw that the runner was missing again. She isn't very happy about it. She asked me to tell you that she is very concerned the church carpet is going to be a mess before you know it."

Phoebe was right about one thing: an army of people paraded in and out of the parsonage. Young people burst in to use the bathroom or grab something from the fridge, the way they'd rummage through a stand-up cooler at the convenience store. One day while David was taking a shower, two teenage girls exploded through the back door. They were halfway into the bathroom before I hollered out for them to stop. After that, David mentioned our lack of privacy to Pastor Don. The next day Janet left a package at the front door. Inside was a pink bathrobe with a note attached: "Now if anyone barges in on you, at least you'll be wearing a pretty housecoat." I examined the clump of material that looked as though it had been whipped up from a 1950s chenille bedspread, and realized that having a beautiful parsonage to live in would be a double-edged sword: nice kitchen and plenty of room for parties, but such amenities would come with very little solitude or privacy.

But after receiving a letter from Jean, who had recently arrived on the mission field in Mexico, I realized I needed to stop feeling sorry for myself. God had called her and Doug to a small village near Guanajuato, where they lived in a tiny hut with no electricity or running water. Jean's letter sounded sad, and I was suddenly thankful for all of the luxuries that accompanied being a minister's wife in a nice church in America, even if people did peer in the windows and walk unannounced through the kitchen.

The traffic that streamed through our house increased as the congregation grew that fall. When I discussed our lack of privacy with David, he always answered with what he called "the voice of reason," a tone both sympathetic and evasive. "Of course we deserve to have some space to ourselves," he said, "but for now we're going to have to let these little inconveniences run off us like water off a duck's back. Honey, this won't last long. God has something great planned for this church and for us. We'll be out of this parsonage and into a bigger place before you know it." He hugged me to him, pressing me close against his chest. "Give me your hand," he said, "the right one." He spread it out, passing his palm over mine as though he wanted to clean it, to disencumber it of everything but the important things, dusting off the selfish things — the things of no concern to our future and a growing church. Then he smiled at me the way we smile at things that belong to us.

David's speculation was prophetic. It didn't take long for word to get out that Calvary Baptist had a dynamic new minister. Every Sunday morning more fresh faces appeared and the church parking lot began to fill early, forcing a long procession of cars to snake farther and farther up and down the streets. The grounds swirled with energy as children raced across the balding lawn to meet their friends, darting around parents who introduced themselves to visitors. The elders didn't even seem to care about the worn-out lawn, proclaiming with exuberance that in its long history, Calvary Baptist had never overflowed its capacity. It was exciting, even thrilling, to see the beautiful church packed tighter each Sunday with people who called out "Welcome, Brother," and shouted "Amen" during the sermon. It was gratifying to watch the collection plate fill to the brim and know that it was because David was such a good preacher that all these people flooded into Calvary Baptist. It was a great life if you liked free stuff too: cars that people said they no longer needed, and wanted their minister to have; unexpected envelopes of money slipped into your hand before your upcoming vacation; tons of free vegetables and fruit from everyone's garden.

Within a year the church had added so many new members that it purchased the house next door for us to live in, turning the parsonage into an education center for children's church and Sunday school classes. Church members remodeled the parsonage basement into a study for David that could also accommodate counseling sessions and board meetings. David began conducting four Sunday services, and the board discussed new building proposals now that the congregation was growing.

Even in this whirlwind, David often seemed preoccupied. He'd drop out of mental sight, say, in a nice restaurant, going into a transfixed state, staring at the breadsticks in the wicker basket, or at the coffee cups or the appetizers in the middle of the table. I knew he was thinking about somewhere else, carrying on a serious conversation with persons unknown. I could almost see his lips moving. I ignored his emotional absences as much as possible and busied myself learning the nuances of being a good minister's wife: entertaining and teaching children's church (which I still didn't like to do, though no one would have guessed); singing in the choir; baking casseroles for the infirm, the elderly, new mothers, shut-ins, church members in the hospital; organizing the Calvary Baptist prayer chain; and learning how to memorize hundreds of names as I greeted people filing in and out of services each Sunday. I began homeschooling the girls and enrolled them in ballet and tap lessons, keeping busy enough to hardly notice that David and I still hadn't gotten away to the coast.

Then, the second year, I added teaching women's Bible study to the weekly agenda. David announced my new class from the pulpit, and the next Tuesday morning they arrived, their Bibles tucked quietly under their arms. First came Lydia, a tall, straight-lined woman with curly brown hair arranged on her head like a football helmet. She had an open, eager smile, lacking in any distinct cleverness but friendly. Behind her came Irene, wearing a baggy brown cardigan with an olive green skirt and tan ribbed stockings — appropriate for the retired Christian schoolteacher that she was. Next was Paula, a young mother of two — a bone-thin girl with a thoughtful, almost desperate quiet about her. I welcomed them in and offered them a cup of tea. Janet entered, darting a glance from side to side, sitting next to Paula — having come, I feared, to take mental notes and report back to the other elders' wives.

Then Susan walked through the door, and it was as if the Red Sea had parted. Her hair was dyed coal black and spiked short on top. She wore tight jeans and bright red lipstick; her cheekbones were high and glamorous, her eyes smoldering — even on a Tuesday morning, sensuality drenched her. I'd seen her for the first time on Sunday, just a glimpse of her as she strode out the back of the church in her formfitting blue tailored suit. I immediately liked her. She exuded the take-no-prisoners confidence of someone who would never think twice about making a move before she made it — first thought, best thought. She moved past me and flashed a knowing smile, as though we already shared a secret even though we'd never met. I was glad she was there. She must be new to religion, I thought.

After everyone introduced themselves and gave a brief personal history, I found out that I was dead wrong. "My dad was the pastor of a very conservative Baptist church in South Dakota," Susan said when it came her turn. "A tight lot. You know the story — no drinking, no cards, no dancing, no makeup. I graduated from Oral Roberts University and married my college sweetheart." I could tell she took great pleasure in the look of shock that crossed everyone's face. She was a wild child, held back only by the reigns of religion — Seabiscuit ready to break out of the chute.

After Bible study Susan whispered to me on the way out, "You're gonna need a friend who understands this gig. Let's have coffee. I'll call."

That first class was small, but before we knew it the house was packed and buzzing with the kind of well-scrubbed middle-class Christian ladies you see photographed in a Baptist church directory: 700 Club viewers, Girl Scout leaders, PTA members. Some were quiet, others boisterous and ready to share their opinions. Women's Bible study soon became a place where young mothers could meet with those who had raised their kids and exchange all the instructive anecdotes that women share: when the first teeth arrive, what to do when my two-year-old throws a tantrum, how much weight you gain during pregnancy. Everyone started coming early to chat and stayed late to share impromptu lunches. As they talked, I could see that the class had become a refuge for a group of lonely women who had little contact with the world apart from Sunday services and their respectable Christian homes. We started our study in the Gospel of John, then went through Colossians and Ruth. Then, one packed-to-capacity Tuesday morning, Paula uncharacteristically spoke out: "I have a question: How submissive does the Bible say we really have to be?"

"Not as submissive as our Fundamentalist churches teach," Susan piped up.

"I'm sick of it myself," Paula said. "When Herb and I were dating, the subject of submission never came up. Now he's always pointing out my duty to defer to him as head of the household."

"I think a lot of men use the Bible to keep women beaten down because they're threatened by our intelligence," Irene added. Everyone laughed.

"Amen," Lydia shouted from the corner. "Since Peter attended that silly Basic Life conference, he treats me like I'm a second-class citizen. He claims it's God's will that I dress the way he likes — even wear my hair the way he wants it."

I secretly agreed with Lydia. For years David had attended the Basic Life conferences. Bill Gothard had begun giving the seminars in the early 1970s, and since then millions of Christians had become avid devotees of his Fundamentalist principles. Although he himself had never married, he used both Old and New Testament verses to validate his teachings on marriage and family life, picking his way selectively through scripture like a happy truffle hog, rooting out only the morsels he wanted and leaving the rest — declaring certain Old Testament laws essential to Christian life while curiously ignoring others. He placed much of the blame for the breakdown of modern marriage on women's resistance to male authority, tracing it right on back to Eve: "A wife now desires to control her husband."

After we married David had insisted that I attend a Basic Life conference with him, and so, along with thousands of other Christians, we crowded into the Seattle Coliseum. On the second day of the conference, a woman raised her hand. She said she had a Christian girlfriend who was being physically abused by her husband. "Wouldn't it be appropriate for her to leave him and seek refuge?"

"A policeman may have a terrible disposition," Gothard intoned. "Still, that is no basis to disregard his instructions. God is working in your friend's life to perfect her character of humility. She needs to read First Peter, two and three, and accept her suffering."

No one in the packed coliscum so much as flinched.

I told the women in the class that I thought Gothard's teachings were antiquated and that the church had often gotten carried away on the issue of women's submission. Then, like the coward I was, I changed the subject. That night I stared at the ceiling while the clock ticked away the hours. The next day I called Susan. Since that first Bible study, she and I had become great friends, meeting clandestinely so that the other women in the congregation wouldn't feel that we were spending too much time together. Susan remembered the grief her mother had gotten over the issue of playing favorites. "We're going to have to keep things on the Q.T.," she had said. "The church knitting circle will scream bloody murder if they see that you have a close friend."

Several sentences into our phone conversation, Susan said, "Hey, you sound like you need to talk about something — get on over here."

The August afternoon baked waves of heat up from the blacktop as the kids and I arrived at Susan's beautiful suburban home, surrounded by professional landscaping and a fleet of fancy vehicles. Her husband, Robert, had his own construction business and collected real estate the way a ten-year-old collects trading cards. Robert was a tall, muscular figure with a grave, long face. Deep lines were etched on either side of his mouth, and his eyes drooped in the corners. His voice was thick and harsh, and he didn't look or sound to me as if he belonged with Susan, who had such a sunny, cheerful disposition. Susan made pretty good money herself, selling upscale kitchen cookware.

As I walked into the house, the marble entryway felt exquisite and indulgent on my bare feet once I'd kicked off my sandals at the door. Carise, Micael, and Jason rushed to hug Susan's two children, and the happy mob dashed toward the skyscraper jungle gym out back. My kids loved visiting Susan's house because she kept them stuffed with ice cream bars, Lay's potato chips, and Dad's root beer. My charitable host mixed us two strong martinis (Susan had introduced me to the delights of good gin early in our relationship). Then we peeled down to our skimpy swimsuits, grabbed our sunglasses, and took refuge under the umbrella of her Ethan Allen lawn furniture. As always, grapes and kiwis, blueberries, provolone and Camembert, crackers, and biscuits were neatly arranged on her delicate English bone china. Whenever I marveled at her generosity, she'd say, "After wearing my brother's hand-me-down loafers as a kid, I'm serving my friends only the best — it's Bombay Sapphire for you, lady." She lifted her chilled martini in a toast.

For months Susan and I spent many stolen hours in her sunny backyard, gossiping and discussing world affairs, young motherhood, and the Religious Right's attitude toward women. That afternoon a second martini took our discussion to a deeper level.

"I was such a chickenshit yesterday," I said. "I should have been truthful and said what I really thought — that the church has an appalling record in its treatment of women."

"Come on, like you could ever have gotten away with *that*. Janet would have taken your scalp right then and there — zip — clean off your seditious little head." She laughed, "Anyway, what are good friends for? I answered the question for you — the way you wanted to."

I finished my drink.

"Susan, I've never told you about the real relationship I have with David."

"Well, I've never told you about the real relationship I have with Robert either. So, you go first — there's plenty of gin and lots of sunshine left."

I looked up to make sure that the kids were all out of earshot, safely swinging upside down, squealing and jabbing each other like sugar saturated monkeys.

"David seems to get more controlling all the time. He's even started checking the closets and cupboards to see that everything is lined up in perfect rows. The other day the silverware drawer didn't pass inspection, so he flung the entire contents across the room. Then he said in this weird calm voice, 'Maybe you'll keep the cupboards in better order from now on.' After that, he left the house and didn't come back until late."

"How late?" Susan asked.

"About eleven."

"Whoa. You'd *never* guess he'd be capable of acting like that, watching him up in the pulpit. Amazing!" She shook her head and took another sip.

"And get this. Last week there was a single rose sitting on the front porch with my name attached to a card that read, 'I love to watch you from a distance. A secret admirer.' I was petrified, and when David finally got home that night, I showed it to him. He laughed and said, 'Good for you. You passed the test. I wrote it to see if I could trust you.'"

Susan stared at me from across the table. "My God . . . the guy needs therapy."

"And he's starting to accuse me of being too chatty with other men after Sunday services. What — I'm supposed to stand at the back of the church and ignore anyone in pants? Like I'd have time for an affair anyway. I hardly have enough time to brush my teeth in the morning."

"Carlene, he's gotta get some serious counseling."

"I don't think he'd ever go," I said. "He's so proud of his reputation as a great counselor; he'd be petrified someone from the congregation might find out."

"Wouldn't he go secretly?"

"I don't think so."

"Promise me you'll try and get him to."

"Okay," I said, "I'll try. So enough about *my* ghastly marriage — how about yours?" I said, hoping to erase the horrified look on Susan's face.

She got up, visibly shaken. "Damn, I need to stand up and process this for a minute. Not that I'm in a much better boat, only the chauvinism around here is a little more traditional."

Susan shifted her sunglasses to the top of her head and stepped inside the house. I could hear her grinding beans and scooping them into her shiny stainless steel Krups coffeemaker as I watched the kids kicking a soccer ball across the lawn. She brought out two black coffees and set them on the glass table, then slumped down into her deck chair across from me and pulled her sunglasses back over her eyes. "Robert constantly makes decisions without consulting me — big financial ones. Like he'll just go out and buy a piece of property and then casually mention it weeks later. Whenever I object to being ignored in the process, he tells me that God has appointed him head of the household and I should keep my opinions to myself."

"Unbelievable," I said.

"He even decides where we're going on vacation without consulting me. If I object, he says, 'I'll just go by myself.' And then he *does*. I've started to have this fantasy that when he's on one of those dangerous river rafting excursions he loves so much, his boat will capsize and he'll drown," she said nonchalantly, taking a long sip of her coffee and gazing absently at the running, shrieking children. "The bottom line is, we're trapped, you and I. The Bible says that we're in this for life. And even though I think the church is screwed up in many ways, I believe that Christians are bound by the Word of God."

On the way home I thought about how Susan had so casually wished her husband dead. It chilled me and, knowing what a generous woman she was, made me suspect that the verbal abuse she endured was probably worse than she had revealed. But she was right about the Bible. The Gospel of Matthew did make it clear that unless David or Robert had affairs, our marriage commitments were unbreakable in the eyes of God. Besides, I was determined that my marriage would work. Susan was right — I should insist on counseling. But the thought of suggesting such a thing to David made a cold bolt of fear shoot through my chest. Maybe I'd bring it up after we got back from the pastor's conference we were attending the next week.

Each year, ministerial couples from throughout the Northwest converged on the Christian campground at Black Lake Conference Center near Olympia for the annual getaway. David and I were returning for our third year to the forested grounds set about with tiny log cabins, a mess hall, and a chapel that looked out onto a deep, black lake. But this year after we arrived, I suddenly had a new awareness of the women around me as they stood mute next to their husbands, who were busy one-upping each other with talk of bigger programs and building proposals. In the morning I watched solitary female figures wandering through camp, apparently without the energy or inclination to interact, simply roaming the dirt pathways alone. In the afternoons when the men met to discuss church growth, the women were ushered away to receive pointers on how to become better ministers' wives — much like the talk that I had heard years before at the Bible college.

During the final afternoon, fifty women entered the conference chapel and mingled with poker-faced politeness. After three years in the ministry, I had learned that for gamblers and preachers' wives, bluffing is not only a fine art but also a necessary survival technique. Everyone chatted courteously, keeping their cards close to their chests, until, unexpectedly, someone tipped her hand.

An even-toned, silver-haired woman who had been a minister's wife for thirty years was delivering the last lecture. After her cheerful introduction and a few words on ministerial etiquette, she said, "It's *essential* that you keep a professional distance from the other women of the congregation. I know it sounds tough, but if you have a close friend in the church, other women will get jealous, and your husband's ministry could be affected." Her voice rose in pitch. "And most importantly," she leaned forward for emphasis, "if you have a confidante in the church, you might tell her things about your husband that could *ruin* his ministry."

It was then that I noticed a ruddy-faced young woman in the second row starting to weep. Her quiet sobbing did not interrupt the lecture, but her thin shoulders shook with the conviction of someone who had fallen into a deep crevasse and entertained no hope of being rescued. Finally the speaker paused and looked at her. "Are you all right?" she asked.

"Yes, I'm sorry — I'll be fine," the pretty redhead replied, then started crying all over again. A woman beside her quietly slipped her arm around the girl, and the meeting soon ended.

Afterward a small group gathered around to offer comfort. As I approached, another minister's wife, whose rigid face had softened since the beginning of the lecture, looked at me and said, "She's having a hard time with the pressures of the ministry."

"God will give you the strength to withstand," someone told the girl.

"Satan assaults only those doing the Father's work," added another.

"The Lord will *never* give us more to endure than He knows we can handle..."

Advice came at her from every direction. I stepped back, and suddenly the crowd looked like a herd of sheep, like those my uncle Bud raised on his ranch back in Montana. "Blah, blah, baaaaah," they bleated. "Sheep," I remembered my uncle saying, "are the damnedest critters. Cattle will spook and stampede, squeeze past a broken fence, or push through a pole gate to freedom — but not sheep. They'll stay happily corralled and easily made into mutton without one single protestation." I turned and fled the room, closing the gate behind me.

I walked down to the lake. Pale mist lay over its deep, black stillness. I wondered, what kind of system would demand control over a woman's friendships, isolating her until she went mad with loneliness? What kind of woman would put up with such oppression? I looked into the patchy vapors drifting on the smooth surface, and without warning an answer rose up from the dark depths. *You. You have come to accept your own subjugation.*

For years now I had kept silent about David's increasing demand for control: monitoring my weight and the clothes I wore, scrutinizing every household purchase. Instead of demanding more freedom, I made justifications: the stresses of seminary, children, shepherding a growing congregation. Now my only measure of freedom came during those stolen hours when I sneaked away to Susan's house. And if it hadn't been for her friendship — a confidence that I'd been warned repeatedly against — David's behavior would still be a guarded secret. I knew he expected his actions to remain that way — counted on it, in fact. I told myself that I was about to surprise him. On the long ride back home from this conference, I would inform him that I was no longer going to put up with his tantrums and unreasonable manipulation and suggest that we discuss our problems with a marriage counselor.

But later that day, as we wound down Interstate 5, the conversation did not go the way I had planned. "I guess the elders are unhappy that so many new people are still joining the church," David said. " 'We just don't have any more room,' Don told me the other day. Can you believe that?" he almost shouted.

"Isn't that what we're here for?" I asked.

"Everything was fine as long as the new people just filled the offering plate. But now that they want to fill board positions, the old guard is freaking out. Don told me that the board is afraid the new members will try to seize power."

"Seize power? Sounds like a corporate takeover rather than a church election."

"Don actually said, 'You have to understand, we've been operating this church since the 1950s. We bought the building, landscaped the grounds, and raised our children right here.' He said, 'We feel like we're giving up a house we've paid off the mortgage on.' Can you *believe* that?"

"But they can't just freeze the elections, can they? It's a congregationalist church government; everyone has a vote — and the new members make up well over half the church," I added.

"When I mentioned that small fact, Don said, 'Well, they haven't paid half the bills for thirty years.' Then he suggested that we compromise — make fewer positions available, so that even though there's some new blood, the old board will remain in charge."

"What did you say?"

"I told him it sounded fine. We'd just open up two new positions rather than the five that should be rotating. Anyway, we came to an agreement. But then you'll never guess what else he said."

"What?"

"There are rumblings that I'm not preaching enough out of the Bible. 'More doctrine and less philosophy,' Don said. 'Give us more of that old-time religion.'"

"More hellfire and brimstone, that sort of thing?" I said.

"Yes, yes." David laughed. "So I've decided to preach through Paul's Epistles. That should give them some real condemnation to chew on. Then, once we've foiled the power grab and put an end to my secular preaching, Don tells me I'm going to get a raise."

"Well that's nice," I said.

"Being in the ministry is kind of like having lunch with a patron grandfather who's paying your college tuition but also likes to lean across the table at unpredictable intervals and punch you in the mouth. Is it stimulating? Quite. Pleasant? No."

David's voice was full of irritation, and I knew he was in no mood to discuss the topic of marriage counseling, so I decided to wait for a more opportune moment — which actually presented itself a short time afterward. One Saturday night, David brought home the movie *Out of Africa*. As we sat on the couch watching the three-hour saga unfold, he fidgeted back and forth, squirming worse than a five-year-old. This kind of feverish energy usually signaled an eruption on the horizon: an untidy drawer, a wrong look at another man, too much money spent on Tuna Helper. That evening he paced around the kitchen, shutting drawers with too much force and flipping light switches on and off. Suddenly, listening to him crash through the house, a painful realization hit me: *He's frustrated . . . He wants me to go to bed so he can sneak out.* I froze for a moment, then said as casually as I could, "Well, I'm going to hit the hay."

"I'm staying up to watch *Saturday Night Live,*" he said with a sigh of relief.

I crawled into bed and pretended to fall asleep. Some time later I heard the bedroom door open. David peeked in to see if I was sleeping, closed the door, and left the house. I got up: 1:00 a.m. I took a quilt from the closet and sat on the couch, running my fingers down the soft cotton fabric of the sofa. I thought about what it had once meant to me: a fresh beginning, a new life, with vacation pay and extra money so we could get away to the ocean. None of that had ever materialized; I had a terrible feeling that before the night was out, I was going to find out why.

Two o'clock — the house was silent except for the *tick . . . tick . . . tick* from the living room clock, growing louder with every passing second. A deaf person could hear it, the constant, unrelenting sound ratcheting my nerves tighter. I could feel the noise seeping down into my bones, right into the marrow where fear is lodged — compressing it until it exploded up into my chest, making me want to cry out.

Three o'clock — I threw off the quilt, got up, and walked over to the window. The empty street below was drenched in amber light. In the silent, dark room, patterns from the streetlight played across the ceiling as I stared at the signpost — CONWAY AVENUE — until it went blurry and my body swayed as if from motion sickness.

"Calm yourself down," I said aloud. Maybe David was just in need of some solitude, what with the criticism that the elders had leveled at him and the board elections coming up next month. He could be drinking coffee at a local all-night restaurant or walking around the park practicing his next sermon (as he often claimed when he'd been away for hours). But the image of David trudging through Cowen Park practicing his Sunday sermon or sipping a 3:00 a.m. latte at Denny's seemed as ludicrous as the idea of my making excuses for him.

Four o'clock — I was not going to give in to hysteria even though it was really the logical thing to do: scream and weep until he told me her name. Then car lights appeared in the driveway, and I heard footsteps on the basement stairs, creaking up toward the door. The knob turned. David stuck his head through the partly open door and slipped in like a professional thief. He jumped when he saw me, his face startled into the blank, open-eyed look of a screech owl. Even from across the room his breath smelled like floor cleaner. He straightened up and hesitated for a moment, centering and allowing the charming minister to emerge for the battle ahead.

"Come on, relax, honey. I'm not having an affair," he said almost in a whisper.

"So what the hell are you doing?" I asked.

His eyes narrowed, and he looked flatly at my face, deciding rightly that I wasn't going to put up with any of his bullshit stories.

"Just watching women dance," he said, shutting the basement door quietly behind him.

"Watching women dance?" I said. "What's that supposed to mean? *Naked* women?"

"Yes." He looked down. "I give so much to so many people — I need something that makes me feel good too." He shifted his weight from one foot to the other. "It just calms me down, takes the anxiety away."

In place of the fear that had gripped me for hours, I suddenly felt cold inside. Then from out of the chill erupted a fury that rose in my throat. "You son of a bitch."

My anger rattled him; it threw him to hear such language coming out of my mouth. Obviously his heartfelt confession wasn't going to soften me up, and this too seemed to amaze him: that a circumstance had finally arisen that he couldn't talk his way out of. The Reverend David Brant, the great orator who always got an amen, a hallelujah, a "Right on, Pastor," was stuck. A look of bewilderment crossed his face, and his story, which began slowly, quickly picked up speed, plowing ahead like a runaway locomotive.

"Listen, you have to understand: I've been addicted to strip joints and pornography for years now. When I was in high school, pornography helped me find comfort from the violence of growing up in that abusive home. It gave me a warm feeling that I could never get from my mother. You know what she's like — cold, obsessed with her own martyrdom. When I looked at *Hustler,* it soothed me; I felt nurtured. Then the addiction just gradually grew into strip clubs as well."

"So how long have you been going to those places?" I asked, numb with shock.

"From the beginning of our marriage. The only time I've been free from my compulsion was during Bible college. After our wedding I felt overwhelmed with the responsibility thrust on me, so I started to sneak out again."

"You mean all those times you said were studying in the library or at seminary?" I asked, my heart slamming against my chest like a dog at a fence.

"Yes, honey . . . it's bad. Even when you were in labor with Jason, I left the hospital and went to a club. So don't you see? I simply don't have any control over it."

The memory of frantically sucking Lamaze breaths in and out, desperate for David to return to the hospital from his jaunt to retrieve a forgotten textbook, flashed through my mind. I refused to cry — I wouldn't give him the satisfaction.

"But please know that after acting out I'm always devastated. That's why I've fought with depression for so many years. It's not about you; it's about my dysfunctional childhood. I've struggled with this so long, but I just can't seem to resist. I'm afraid at this point it should probably be called an obsession."

"You sack of shit," I said.

"Oh, come on, Carlene, can't you find any sympathy for me?" David said.

"No, I don't feel an ounce of sympathy for you. You've been lying to me for eight years, demanding my biblical submission, censoring every move I've made, while you're running off to girlie shows, insisting that I pinch pennies while you spent what little money we did have on naked women!"

Realizing that the empathy angle wasn't working, he easily swung over to the meanness approach. "Well, you know, the ten pounds you've gained since our wedding day aren't very flattering," he shot back. "You just don't look the way you used to from the waist down."

"Go to hell," I said and got up and walked out of the room.

For three nights I lay on the couch, staring at the ceiling. The hours seemed endless; they were not a measure of time but also of space, like a vast ocean spreading out between me and the rest of the world. I lay numb, caught between consciousness and sleep, drifting off astride the cold, pale horse that gallops across the Book of Revelation, whose name is Death, then awaking with a start to a high, heavy pain in my chest, and tears streaming down my face. What a fool I had been — like a child, utterly confident and utterly ignorant. For years I had seen only what I wanted to see, believed only what I had been told to believe. If David had suggested I leap from a bridge, I might have considered it my obligation as a Christian wife. Now I felt broken into pieces, hit by a bus I hadn't seen coming, lying paralyzed and trying to understand what had happened.

During the day I fed the kids and then collapsed back onto the couch, listening to the noises outside — garbage trucks in the alley, rain rapping against the living room window, the phone ringing in the distance. The once mysterious puzzle was now revealing its secrets, its pieces snapping into place: our honeymoon on Flathead Lake when David had disappeared unexpectedly; his irritability until he was able to find an excuse to break free; his staring into space as if his mind had flown off to another planet. It all made sense now — the depression, the jealousy. Then through the haze came the memory of the brief time we had in college, without his addiction: the sweetness and calm we felt together, the thrill of watching him run down the basketball court, our first kiss in the academic center. Our young bodies leaning into each other for support, the smell of his skin, the feel of his warmth fluttered through my mind like a bird caught in a room.

The phone rang and rang into the answering machine.

Beep . . . "Hello, Carlene, this is Lucille Jones. I have a prayer request for you and Pastor Dave. It's about my niece, Amy . . . "

Beep . . . "Hi, there, it's Janet. Please give me a call about that children's church curriculum."

Beep . . . "Hey, girl, what's up? It's Susan — haven't heard from you for days. Give me a call."

I couldn't make myself talk to anyone. I turned off the machine and slept on, enduring an endless treadmill of nightmares, my feverish, racing brain blurring the days into one, time stalling into meaninglessness, past hunger, past vanity. David would slide through the room like an eel on a rock and appear at the foot of the couch. He looked smaller now that the flawless invincibility he always projected onto the big screen, like the great and magnificent David of Oz, had unraveled at the seams.

"You're making far too much of this," he would say, irritated, anxious. "Don't you think you should get up and return some of those phone calls?"

"Leave me alone," I said, looking at him as though he were a stranger, not allowing the tears to sting in my eyes until after he walked out.

The third morning, I saw my face in the bathroom mirror: papery skin, dark under the eyes, matted hair. "Mama, what's wrong?" Carise came into the bathroom and grabbed my hand.

"I'm not feeling well, honey," I said. "I think I have the flu."

I looked down at my daughter's silky skin, maturing into that of a young woman — a young woman who needed her mother. It was then that I decided to get help. I remembered hearing that James Dobson's talk show, *Focus on the Family,* provided an hour of free counseling for pastors and their wives. The next morning, after David took the kids out to the backyard to put up a new swing set, I dialed the show's number. While Carise, Micael, and Jason bounced around their father with anticipation, I prayed that David wouldn't make an unexpected trip inside. He would be furious if he found out that I was on the phone with one of Dobson's counselors. After an eternity, the operator connected me with a Dr. Jones. I said that my husband was a successful evangelical minister in Washington State, and then I told him about David's addiction and obsessive jealousy and my growing desperation.

"Believe it or not, this is not that unusual," he said. "And it is treatable. But David must get into extensive therapy, *now*."

"I think it'll be hard to get him to see a counselor," I said. "I'm afraid he'll be frightened that people in the church might find out."

"If David has been a victim of this addiction for years, his only hope is in counseling. I've seen it happen before: when ministers aren't held accountable to anyone, they can start to believe they're above the rules," he said.

"I'll try my best," I promised.

Out in the backyard David was chasing the kids across the lawn. He was a good dad, spending hours reading to them and staging home video productions, writing elaborate screenplays with witty dialogue, which the kids and their friends loved to act out for the camera. He took the kids camping and hiking and talked to each of them with respect and affection. The kids adored — and needed — him as they were growing toward adolescence.

Carise's infant seriousness had evolved into the amenable nature of a caretaker. She was graceful, patient, and serene, even when her brother teased her mercilessly. She was the family peacemaker, breaking up scuffles between Micael and Jason as they wrestled around the living room, or throwing her arms around them in a large crowd, shielding them like a little umbrella. Micael's free spirit was turning her into an impish explorer, attacking everything she did with ardent passion. By age six she'd decided that Claude Monet was the greatest painter who ever lived and that the musical of Victor Hugo's *Les*

Miserables was a masterpiece. She talked casually, yet with keen insight, about subjects far beyond her years, and I knew that someday she would be a world adventurer. Jason had a jack-o'-lantern smile and a thatch of black hair tamed only by Brylcreem. He was the family clown, employing whatever means possible to get his sisters' attention, tumbling over himself to get a laugh from them, hiding in their closets to jump out and tickle them into a frenzy.

With the swing set project finished, the kids ran into the living room to play a video game. David slipped casually through the patio door. We were alone.

"I'm making an appointment to see a counselor," I said, knowing that he would rather hang himself from a rafter than tell a psychologist about his addiction.

"Are you out of your mind?" he said, shocked backward. "What for? Okay, okay — I swear I will never visit any of those places again," he added, as if it hadn't occurred to him to promise such a thing before. "Besides, what are you thinking? We can't afford it!" His face was red, his voice irritated.

"I talked to a counselor from *Focus on the Family,* and he said that unless you get therapy, you won't recover."

"Good God, what the hell did you do that for? Are you crazy? Don't you get what will happen if word leaks out that *I* am in counseling? It'll ruin my ministry. Do you want that? Yeah, you must — great way to punish me, honey."

"I'm making an appointment, and I'm going to go even if you don't," I said.

The next week David accompanied me to the session but sat mutely, staring at the therapist as if he were looking at the appalling monster in the movie *Alien* ripping its way out of John Hurt's guts. After an hour of stilted, one-sided conversation, we left the counselor's office and got back into the car. "This entire procedure was a waste of money," David said. "Now that I've promised to give up my addiction, our marriage is fine, and *you* need to get over your anger. Don't you have any ability to forgive?"

"Yes, I do, but I think we need to talk to this guy some more," I said.

"Who is the head of this household?" David yelled as he swerved toward home. "Who makes all the money in this family?"

"I don't care who makes all the money."

"You'd better *start* to care! You don't have any other options!" he shouted, wheeling the car into the driveway.

"I'm making another appointment," I said as he walked through the door in front of me.

"Apparently you didn't hear me," he said, turning in the hallway. "I'm not wasting any more of my money on that moron. Do you understand?" Then, just to add emphasis, David reached up and pulled a family portrait off the wall, and it smashed to the floor, sending splintered glass across the room.

Seven

The Inferno

I DIDN'T TELL ANYONE about David's addiction for months, I suppose out of shock or humiliation, as if the shame of it had numbed my tongue. In some ways, an out-and-out affair would have been easier for me to reconcile — that David had fallen in love with someone, had been coaxed away by another woman's charms — but the thought of him staring owl eyed at naked dancers while I lay at home in a silk nightie was not by any means self-affirming. The story finally tumbled out one wintry December afternoon at Susan's house, once my emotional paralysis was loosened by a few gin and tonics.

"He *what*?" she shouted across the top of her glass.

"Yes, strip joints since the first week of our marriage. And he refuses to go to counseling," I added, telling her about my conversation with Dr. Jones and his assertion that without therapy David would have little hope of recovery.

"Damn," Susan whispered, shaking her head.

"So let's say that Dr. Jones is right and David can't just will this thing away. What are my options? I can't imagine staying married to him."

"Carlene, we are voyagers on this mad ship together. We *can't* leave these guys; we don't have the money or the biblical grounds. I hate to say it, but technically girlie shows don't qualify as adultery. Matthew eighteen says that the only way either one of us can legitimately get out is if the bastard has an affair. Besides, who in their right mind wants to be a single mother in this society anyway? Raising kids alone — broke, in poverty — it sounds unspeakably bleak to me."

"I'm beginning to think that's just why we should leave — for our kids. The other day I stepped into youth group, and Don was giving the class a full-fledged lesson on condemnation. Do we really want our children to become social malcontents huddling inside our Christian ghetto, heaving stones at every humanist, evolutionist, or homosexual who passes by?"

"So how are we going to teach them morals?" Susan said, pouring us both another drink.

"I don't know; I just want to raise them with some compassion. So many Christian teenagers seem pretty weird to me. But who can blame them? From infancy they've been taught that they're superior to non-Christians. While Jesus is going to let cheerleaders and football players slip into hell, God will save their pious butts because they don't dance. Who wouldn't be a little weird?"

Susan looked up into the low, gray overcast, as if for an answer. "But how are we going to keep them on the straight and narrow unless we have the church? Secular society teaches kids that anything goes — try it all; nothing is off limits."

"Maybe that would be better," I said, realizing that I was not being entirely facetious. "At least they wouldn't be afraid of living. Most Christians seem intimidated by the world, clustering together like a flock of quail. And do we want our sons learning to treat women with such disrespect?"

"You may have a point there." A laugh escaped Susan's lips; it was a bitter sound. "But I still think kids are better off being raised in a nuclear family, with a dad and a mom and a solid financial base."

Susan was right about one thing: I didn't have the means to raise the kids alone. If I left David, he would immediately be forced out of the ministry. Fundamentalism didn't allow divorced preachers in the pulpit, so there would be no money for child support, and I had no professional job skills. If I got work, which would probably be at minimum wage, I would have to put Micael and Jason into day care, eating up what little money I did make. And what reason would I give for divorcing David? No one would ever believe that their spiritual-giant minister could be addicted to pornography and strip joints. Not the man who preached the Word of God to them every Sunday, a genius at human nature who could communicate with a small child or a physicist with equal ease. Even if people did believe me, did I really want my children to hear the story from someone whispering it in the back foyer some Sunday? With three small children who adored their father and with no meaningful degree or work experience to support them, I told myself I had no choice but to stay.

I swallowed my panic as I drove home. I felt like the caged wolf that I'd seen as a child in a rundown zoo called the Trap. It was a place that stank of filth and anguish, a falling down roadside attraction where animals were kept in small pens so that tourists on their way to Glacier Park could see authentic "wildlife." In one of the cages a female wolf ran back and forth along a barren wire coop, panting from exhaustion but never stopping, looking past the gawking people into the distant prairie. Even as a child I realized how silly it was to mistake this creature for the real wolf, who had died long ago; what remained of her, there in the cage, was simply the flesh and bones, pacing to keep itself alive.

David must have played the same "no way out" scenario through in his mind too, because after he smashed the family picture to the floor, he behaved as though nothing had happened. I followed suit. We were acting like two patrons of a Vegas nightclub who had been coaxed onto stage, hypnotized, made to cluck like hens and howl like basset hounds, and then, after a snap of the fingers, sent back to their seats without a glimmer of remembrance. But even though we never spoke of it, in the months after David's confession I felt a change come over me. I started to question the church and its culture, a culture that made it so acceptable for men to dominate their wives and at the same time made women so willing to endure the assault. The quandary stayed with me during the day, when I was washing dishes, taking prayer requests from tearful church members, or preparing the evening meal. It came and went, at times as a barely perceptible tinge, and at others it roared in a rush of rage. If love gives us a heightened consciousness through which to apprehend the world, anger gives us a precise, detached perception of its own. I couldn't quit asking myself how the church had evolved into such an unhealthy organization. The dilemma made me decide to study the roots of Christianity, this time letting historical evidence, rather than religious fervor, lead the way. I covertly collected church history and anthropology books, philosophy, comparative religion, and sociology. I canceled women's Bible study, telling my class I needed more time to homeschool the girls, when in truth I needed the stolen moments to read.

Each morning the girls would sit down at the kitchen table with their A Beka Christian schoolbooks opened and their colored pencils, erasers, and rulers strewn out, and start their lessons as their brother danced around the table, jabbing at their ribs and stealing their pencils. I would sneak my stack of heresy out from the back closet and, between the girls' arithmetic and phonics flash cards, read about the history of Christianity.

"Mama, what do your schoolbooks teach?" Carise asked one day.

"Oh, they're just Bible study books," I told her, not really lying.

"Why do you hide them in the closet?" Micael probed.

"Because there isn't enough room on the shelf, honey," I said, lying.

As I studied, I felt as if I were following a light shining far in the distance, breaking its way through the fog. The more I read, the more I discovered that most of what I was taught in Bible college was refuted by the historical record. For instance, history showed that the New Testament was not an errorless document that had been dictated by God to the apostles shortly after Jesus' death. Instead it was a group of letters that hadn't even been compiled until the fourth century AD. The authentic New Testament writings had never existed as one cohesive book. The ones that finally composed the New Testament had been duplicated profusely, were filled with errors, and were countless copies — and hundreds of years — away from the originals.

The history of the Bible's conglomeration took my breath away. In 312, Emperor Constantine had a vision of the cross with the words *in hoc signo victor eris* ("In this sign you will be victor") inscribed on it. The next day he defeated and killed his rival, Maxentius, and became the new Roman emperor. Grateful for his celestial dream, in which Jesus played a starring role, he demanded that all his subjects embrace the Christian religion.

Then came the tricky part for Constantine: which Christian religion to establish as an official arm of the state? A plethora of sects and interpretations of Jesus' life flourished with countless rival teachers claiming to preach Christ's doctrines. There were hundreds of books purporting to be the exclusive testimonies of Jesus. Various groups across Asia Minor, from Rome in the West to Jerusalem in the East, professed to embody authentic Christianity and fought for dominance, so Constantine set out to establish what he believed to be the right interpretation. In AD 325, he convened the Council of Nicaea, which declared that the Orthodox view of Jesus' life would represent official Christianity. Before long, Orthodox priests met to choose the various letters that would reflect their teachings and embody their vision of Jesus' life. Three hundred years after Christ's death, following heated debate, Constantine's priests chose sixty-six books and proclaimed them Holy Scripture — the New Testament.

Unbelievable, I thought. Fundamentalism must have an explanation for this. So I thumbed through conservative Christian apologist Josh McDowell's book on the subject, and even he couldn't help, saying only, "We don't know exactly what criteria the early church used to choose the canonical books." I stumbled over the sentence and read it again. My mind was a tornado. At that moment I felt as though I had been flying blind for years. (Many historians do have an interpretation of this event: that Constantine and his clergy selected only those writings that bolstered Orthodox doctrine.)

I found out that by the end of the century, the Synods of Hippo and Carthage had codified Christianity and entrenched the Catholic priesthood, declaring divergent views heresy, punishable by torture and death. The church began to obliterate all manuscripts and teachings contrary to Catholicism, burning the texts of the gnostics (a divergent sect) and the contents of early libraries. In AD 391, under Emperor Theodosius I, Christians set the great library in Alexandria aflame, destroying its seven hundred thousand manuscripts, which comprised the bulk of the Western world's ancient literary treasures. And in the sixth century, at the command of Pope Gregory the Great, the church torched the Palatine Apollo library in Rome, filled with ancient lore.

I remember the day, sitting at the kitchen table while the girls wrote their lessons, when I closed my history book and stared out into the blank openness of the universe. If, instead of God's direct revelation from heaven, the Bible was simply a compilation of religious writings that supported an emerging third-century religious sect, Fundamentalist Christianity was a house of cards. Its cornerstone belief that the Bible was without error and thus could be used as a textbook for modern ethics was patently absurd.

It was at about that time that David and I attended a lecture at Western Baptist Seminary in Portland, Oregon, and the remaining withered petals of my Fundamentalist faith fell to the ground. We arrived late, rushing under a sky of puffy white clouds crossing the campus lawn, which smelled of newly cut grass. Entering the brick building, we hurried down the antiseptic hallway to 344, a long, high-windowed lecture hall. Twenty stern faced men looked up: pastors from churches throughout the Northwest. I sat in a soft pool of sunlight near the windows and settled into the warmth. The speaker was a small, mild-looking man with a beaklike nose and a high forehead already shining with sweat. On the blackboard behind him were the words "God's Instructions for 20th Century Head Covering."

Once David and I sat down, he began his talk: "As Christians, we say that God's Word is authoritative and relevant for today, and yet many of our churches refuse to follow one very important teaching." He paced in front of the room, his paisley tie swinging back and forth across his paunchy abdomen while he leveled an accusing stare at the audience. "In First Corinthians eleven, the apostle Paul tells us that the practice of veiling is a fixed — changeless — tradition."

Veiling, humm, I thought, *sounds like a good Fundamentalist institution.*

"When Paul speaks of the tradition of head covering, he uses the Greek word *paradosis,* which must be interpreted as a moral and religious obligation! The veiling of Christian women in the sanctuary is not an option . . . "

As he went on, the ministers pursed their lips, narrowed their brows. The lecturer was talking about them. They were the guilty ones, who believed that the Word of God was applicable for today but didn't require the women in their congregations to wear hats. In defense of the majority, one of the ministers called out, "I believe that this passage is cultural and cannot be applied to the modern church."

"You can't throw it out that easy," the lecturer called back. "Alongside it being a 'lasting tradition,' as Paul calls it, this passage argues that women were *created* to serve men from the beginning — this is an *eternal* position of subordination. Women are to wear hats in church to show respect for the position God appointed them from the beginning. That makes this a permanent dictate, not a cultural one."

This guy was definitely a misogynist but, I had to admit, a consistent misogynist. I felt he had hit on the Achilles' heel of Christianity. When Fundamentalists came to a passage they liked, such as declaring the husband unquestioned ruler of his household, they deemed it authoritative, but when they came to a passage that they didn't like — hats in church — they dismissed it as cultural, that is, only applicable to the first-century society in which it was written.

"We pick and choose our way through Scripture, taking Paul's teaching on salvation, then rejecting the veiling of women," he continued. "But we must be consistent! If any of Paul's teachings are relevant, then we must take them all. So, as a consequence, every woman entering a sanctuary should have a hat on — and, by the way, refrain from speaking as well."

David and I drove home in silence as I watched the sun drenched sky turn black. Before long the wipers were chattering rain off the windshield. I fantasized that I was back in the lecture hall, and instead of sitting stone still, this time I stood up, tall and outraged, and said, "The real scandal is not a woman's bare head in church, but using a two-thousand-year-old religious text to dictate antiquated social mores to modern society." I rested my temple on the window and felt the comforting chill press against me as I watched the dark clouds and felt the rain laden wind drive heavily against the car. And then a terribly heretical thought crossed my mind: *I suspect that the Bible is not the Word of God but a wax nose — to be turned in any direction at will.*

I thought about my recent clandestine studies as I peered out the foggy window: Scripture had been used to justify acts of imperial conquest, torture, and coercion throughout history. During the Holy Inquisition, Christians used Matthew, Thessalonians, John, and Acts to hold the Jewish nation responsible for the crucifixion of Christ. They persecuted and killed Jews, accusing them of kidnapping children for blood rituals, poisoning water, and stealing consecrated communion bread to desecrate the body of Christ. They also excluded Jews from public office, denied them citizenship, and forbade them to own property. During the fifteenth, sixteenth, and seventeenth centuries, the church used Isaiah, Leviticus, Deuteronomy, and Exodus to justify the imprisonment, torture, and murder of an estimated forty thousand women as witches. Taking verses from the Bible, Catholic priests created *The Witches' Hammer,* an official document that came into wide use in the late 1500s, giving specifications for identifying a witch and torturing her to extract a confession, and procedures for her sentencing and execution.

During the Reformation, when Anabaptists cited the Book of Acts to justify their separation over the issue of adult baptism, Protestant reformers Martin Luther and Ulrich Zwingli countered with Old Testament law and demanded that the Anabaptists be drowned or beheaded for their heresy. The books of Isaiah and Matthew were used to justify the Thirty Years' War, along with other aggressive Christian onslaughts. Religious leaders used the Bible to teach slaves not to challenge their masters and to willingly accept punishment.

The Bible had also been used to defend either side of countless moral battles. Matthew was cited to condemn capital punishment, while passages from Genesis, Exodus, and Leviticus were said to support it. (In reality, I found that an unbiased reading of the Bible requires capital punishment for those who work on the Sabbath, commit adultery, disrespect their parents, eat or drink to excess, or masturbate.) To some Christians Proverbs and Isaiah forbid the drinking of wine; for others, Isaiah, Matthew, and John justify it. To forbid work on Sundays, they've used Exodus (ignoring the fact that the Sabbath is actually Saturday); to condone work on Sundays, Matthew and Mark. To oppose war they have used Luke and Isaiah; to justify war, Matthew. Many claim that Exodus, Ecclesiastes, and Leviticus condemn homosexual relations, while others say the Book of Samuel suggests that David's love for Jonathan could well have been sexual. The Catholic Church has used Corinthians and Matthew to enforce the celibacy of priests; those opposed to an unmarried clergy have cited Corinthians, Timothy, and Titus.

And if the Bible is authoritative concerning the attributes of its own God, He himself is a being of rather dubious character. In the Old Testament, He was jealous, played favorites, and punished children for their fathers' sins. He changed his mind, created evil, and had a temper. He violated his own laws against killing and tempting people, sanctioned slavery, deceived people, and told them to lie. He ordered men to become drunk, steal, beat slaves to death, and take prostitutes. He demanded virgins as a part of war plunder, required a woman to marry her rapist, and ordered the killing of innocent women and children. He ordered the slaughter of entire cities and fifty thousand people merely for looking into the Ark of the Covenant.

Biblical criticism also reveals that errors are scattered throughout the manuscript. Using the Bible to force hats on women, or to enforce any other moral dictate, seemed as ludicrous as using it to predict the Second Coming of Christ. I laughed inwardly at the thought of Hal Lindsey's end-time scenario and the apocalyptic vision that had once scared the bejesus out of me. I hadn't heard much about Lindsey lately, the poor man having fallen out of favor with Christians once 1981 came and went with no Jesus in the clouds. And then there were all those other embarrassing missed predictions: the European Common Market had not turned out to be the ten-member Revived Roman Empire spoken of in Daniel (by that year, 1987, the ECU had twelve members); the Jews had not rebuilt their temple in Jerusalem on Mount Moriah; the Soviet Union had not turned out to be the great enemy from the north and was no longer a threat to world peace; and the nations of Africa had not united with Russia to invade Israel. But most shocking of all for Christian prophecy buffs was that the Israelites had occupied the land for over a generation, and Jesus had missed his Rapture rendezvous.

Suddenly I saw myself at seventeen, sitting in our old farmhouse kitchen while that wild rainsquall beat against the windows, sending rivers of water down the glass much as it was now doing on the car windows. At that time long ago, imagining the fabulous Beast of Revelation rising out of the sea, his seven heads bobbing and slavering toward the shore, I was young and naive and full of faith. *When you're a child, everything is simple,* I thought — *you know it all.* You leap into the boat and begin rowing without hesitation, without shame, without reflection. Then one day you lift the oars from the water and let your arms rest, take a moment to look around. Suddenly you begin to hear it, miles away and still out of sight: the faint roar of the current as it swirls and crashes over the sharp rocks downstream. You sit up and taste the mist in your mouth and feel the chill of disaster in the distance, the long falls plunging and crushing everything into the rocks below. Only then do you realize that you must row — this time for your life.

Tears filled my eyes, and I turned my head toward the Cascade Mountains, obscured in fog. I cried, not over my loss of faith, but because I didn't have the guts to pick up the oars and save myself from the catastrophe ahead, to leave the church or my marriage. Although I no longer believed in the prescripts of the Bible demanding that I stay, I felt I couldn't make it on my own. I feared that all of my family and friends would react as Susan had when she said, "I hate to say it, but technically girlie shows don't qualify as adultery." Her additional argument chilled me as well: "Besides, who in their right mind wants to be a single mother in this society anyway? Raising kids alone — broke, in poverty — it sounds unspeakably bleak to me."

Lightning smacked in so close that it sounded as if our own bones were being snapped, yet David stared, unnoticing, glassy-eyed, through the sheets of rain, lost in his own fantasy. He had vanished again, temporarily escaping these fleshly bonds, like a man gazing out from the railing of a cruise ship toward an island that he dreams he is on. *Who knows — or cares — what David's thoughts are?* I told myself. Over the months a great, dark chasm had formed between us. I had given up. I didn't care to bridge it. I wondered when I had fallen out of love with him. Had it been over the years of emotional distance he so expertly maintained between us? Was it because of the control he insisted upon? Was it my own selfishness? Had I ever really known him or loved him, or had we both been too young, too naive, and too blinded by religion? At that moment I had to acknowledge that our marriage had been in trouble long before his girlie show revelation.

We pulled into the driveway at home cold as two sarcophagi. There, next to a bright blue sedan, stood Dr. Martin, the church's district superintendent for the entire northwest region. The sight of Dr. Martin stunned David. He jumped out of the car, hand extended, and walked briskly toward the man.

"Welcome to rainy Seattle," he crooned. "What a delight to see you!"

I stepped into the mist and breathed the cool into my lungs for a brief moment while I listened to the trickle of water run down the drainpipes and watched its wet spill over, leaf by leaf, onto the emerald lawn. I loved the damp of the Northwest and couldn't wait to see the kids. I was glad Dr. Martin was here; he was always full of secret stories about the latest sacred scandal in the district.

Dr. Martin, a large fellow with winter-white hair, always dressed in immaculate three-piece pin-striped suits and expensive woolen overcoats, all custom made and costing a bundle, I was sure. He had an old-fashioned face with meditative, dark brown eyes, widely set apart and vaguely sad. He stood as if planted in the driveway, looking a bit confused. I knew that he had a tough job to do, which was to keep the churches in the Northwest in order, patching up organizational disputes and overseeing discipline. The superintendent was a big fan of David's, claiming he was one of the district's most promising, up-and-coming ministers. It wasn't unusual to have him drop by whenever he was in town. Although he was decades older than my husband, he always came to David to share confidences and get advice. He trusted him completely.

"Come on in, Dr. Martin," I said, "and please stay with us for dinner."

"Heavens, no, I didn't even call and give you warning first."

"Oh, we wouldn't hear of anything different," David said.

"Well, then, all right, that would be very nice," Dr. Martin said, relinquishing.

While Dr. Martin and David sat down across from each other in the living room, I scurried around the kitchen, making coffee and grabbing red peppers, celery, and green onions from the fridge. Throwing them into the sink, I pulled the knife from the drawer as I heard Dr. Martin's weary voice drifting in.

"I'm so discouraged. Many of the district's parishes are in a mess: churches embroiled in petty ecclesiastical power battles, wayward ministers . . . " Then, lowering his tone to a whisper, he said, "I swear, David, some of these pastors make Jimmy Bakker look like Desmond Tutu." I scooped the vegetables from the sink and laid them on the counter, watching them drip onto the Formica like the cold sweat that suddenly streamed down my back. *Oh, my God,* I thought, *maybe he knows about David. But how?* I held my breath and chopped until the peppers, celery, and onions became tiny specks of confetti, then disappeared into pulp. "Fallen ministers are the worst to deal with. You know Tim Dean in Clearview, don't you,

David? Well, we just found out he's run off with a teenage girl from the high school."

"Oh, no." David sounded horrified.

"I'm going to recommend that he take a leave of absence and, of course, seek counseling."

"My goodness, you've had a rough year." David shook his head.

The previous spring, one of the district's pastors, a father of four, had hopped an Amtrak train with a sixteen-year-old from his youth group. A week later he finally returned, broke and apologetic, with the girl at his side. But almost as amazing to me as the event itself was the district's dedication to "restoring these men to Christ" rather than reporting them to the police. In every case I'd witnessed, the church dealt with the scandal internally. Although the guilty preachers were forced to step down, I couldn't understand why they weren't doing time in a state penitentiary.

I took two cups of coffee in to the men and set one next to Dr. Martin and the other next to David, who was leaning back in his chair, hands clasped behind his head, cool as a cucumber. I was sweating from head to toe, while David basked in the sunlight of self-assurance, as though it were unimaginable that anyone might suspect impropriety out of him. And apparently it was. I darted a glance at Dr. Martin, who was gazing back at David, completely taken with his charismatic protégé. Dr. Martin could never believe David capable of misconduct, even if he had a file folder full of indictments in front of him.

As for the dinner itself, it went so smoothly and without incident, it might just as well not have happened. No one made a questionable statement or spoke out of turn; no one drank any liquor or challenged any of the fundamentals of the faith. The pureed seafood chowder was a nice complement to the dull conversation about the necessity of prayer in schools. As Dr. Martin left that evening, he said, "I wish all of our pastoral couples were as happy and *dedicated* as you two."

David had his arm around me, smiling graciously as he closed the door. I turned and went into the kitchen to wash the dishes. David followed me and stood behind me in silence while I squirted Ivory liquid onto a big green sponge and then picked up the five-gallon stew pot and began scrubbing it, running it under water as hot as I could stand, then scrubbing it again. He turned and breezed past me, and I could hear the bedroom door shut. Standing at the sink in a cloud of steam, I felt my eyes go molten as the sweat continued to stream down my back. I placed the sponge and the soapy pot on the side of the sink. Pressing my hands over my face, tears began seeping through my fingers, warm and oily. I tried to turn my thoughts toward planting the new perennials I'd just picked up at Swanson's Nursery, or to the girls' upcoming dance recital, and not to the spiral of destruction overtaking our lives.

Since confessing his pornography addiction to me, David's drinking had increased, as though his dark side, now exposed to the light, could grow unimpeded. During the first years of our marriage, he had refused even a sip of liquor, saying that because he had a serious drinking problem as a teenager, he didn't want to tempt fate. I abstained as well, oblivious to what I was missing, since we had never had alcohol on the farm. Then after we arrived at Calvary Baptist, David gradually started to order wine with meals whenever we'd drive to Seattle for dinner, away from the watchful eye of the congregation. I followed suit and soon grew enthusiastic about the taste of a good merlot — the tangy leather feel of it on the roof of my mouth, the biting edge of it on my tongue, the warmth of it moving down my throat, filling the emptiness, the hot surge that waved along my limbs in a ten minute countdown. By our third year in the ministry, our wine consumption had drastically increased (I had also secretly added Susan's top-shelf gin to the list); David and I were downing a bottle of wine for dinner and then several more glasses afterward while we danced at the club Parker's in Seattle every Saturday night. Then to my surprise David came home one evening and said, "I asked Robert if he and Susan wanted to join us this weekend."

"I didn't think graduates of Bob Jones University danced," I said.

"Hey, if the pastor can dance, so can the flock," David said, laughing.

Several months before, Robert had been elected to the board of elders. David liked Robert from the first day he saw him, just as I knew I would get along so well with Susan. They had started to have coffee together, and David had encouraged Robert to run for a position on the board of elders. "Thank God Robert got on!" David said after the vote. "What a lively addition to that group of old dolts."

Robert and Susan didn't seem to be one bit squeamish about the idea of drinking and dancing. Susan called me the next day to say, "Wow, I had such a wonderful time. Let's go again next weekend!" Once they were adequately incorporated, David added one more couple from the church roster, Hal and Tina, to round off the group. I had the feeling that our companions were being handpicked for some odd reason, but my fears quieted as the months went on, because our partying seemed quite innocuous. Then slowly they became nights of increased revelry, too much drinking and worse.

The six of us piled into Robert and Susan's minivan one night under a moonless sky without clouds and drove up suburban streets, the lawns black and the trees dark sticks of shadow; the headlights of oncoming vehicles looked like the lamps miners wore as they traveled deep into the belly of the earth. We sped onto the freeway and crossed the University Bridge. The water below us, dead now in the quiet, was curiously beautiful, moving beneath us like melted candle wax. Over the bridge's crest, the skyscraper lights of Seattle illuminated the darkness, looking particularly radiant, maybe because Susan and I, having gotten a jump on the evening, had already consumed a strong gin and tonic. We pulled off the freeway into Seattle and up to the fluorescent marquee of the Fenix Underground.

The nightclub was dark and noisy and crowded. Color flooded Susan's high cheekbones, and she looked stunning in her tight black Lycra dress. We girls ordered a martini for ourselves, and the men ordered shots of tequila, while a Glenn Frey look-alike sang "The Heat Is On." One gin . . . two gins . . . three gins later, my mind was jumbled. I caught my reflection in the polished table and stared stonily down at it, dazed, glassy-eyed. I looked confused, frantic, letting go. I turned away. "Let's get out of here and do a little hottubbing," David suddenly said.

We stumbled to the van and drove out of the city to Robert and Susan's backyard and onto their cedar deck, which smelled fresh and warm from the summer sun. The starry night stretched so close over us, it looked like a holey tent roof. Robert pulled the cover off of the sunken hot tub while pinprick clouds of gnats disturbed the air. Giggling, we windmilled our hands in front of our faces to keep them away.

"How about a nightcap?" Susan asked, with a snicker.

Then David raised his hand as though he had something very substantial to say, the same way he did when he came to the climax of a particularly moving sermon. "You know, nakedness is nothing to be ashamed of," he said, unbuttoning his shirt and unzipping his pants. "God made our bodies, and we shouldn't be afraid to take our clothes off in front of one another." With that, everyone smiled blankly and followed their beloved pastor in his spiritual call to nudity. I listened to zippers whizzing down and shoes hitting the deck as I took off my silk dress and panties, thinking, *Amazing . . . In a culture where short skirts are forbidden, David's got us all stripping to the flesh.*

Susan brought us another drink while we sank, loose limbed, into the hot water. Robert turned the conversation political, as he often did. "Can you believe that slimeball Gary Hart? Just like a Democrat to be screwing some young intern."

"Are we sure that they actually had sex?" Hal asked.

"Are you kidding, man? Why else would he take her on a boat named *Monkey Business*?"

"Oh, come on, Robert, maybe they were just out for a little pleasure cruise," Susan added. "Besides, she's a model, not an intern."

"Right, hon," Robert said, rolling his eyes. "Those slick-shoed liberals are always doing something unethical — not a moral man in the entire party."

The distant streetlamp cast what looked like moonlight onto the water, and a silvery glow across everyone's skin. We looked beautiful, we thought, all of us young and taut-skinned and part of God's amazing creative handiwork. We drank more Bombay Sapphire while our laughter mixed with the sound of crickets, and Robert carried on about the corrupt Democrats and the liberal media. Holding our drinks above the water, we listened to the notes of a slow, bluesy jazz song by Ella Fitzgerald as it floated like candle smoke out of the expensive speakers. David smiled contentedly at the head of the hot tub, and then, before I knew it, he was standing above us on the fragrant cedar, looking like a magnificent lion. He paused for a moment to let everyone stare at his powerful naked physique. He was the untamable cat, the fearless leader and sexual conqueror, in complete control of his pride — mind, body, and spirit. Now that he had triumphed, he paced slowly, lazily around the pool, content as all eyes gazed leisurely over his beautiful, glistening skin. David was the great restless beast, at last satisfied. But I had a feeling that before long he would be hungry for flesh again.

I darted a glance at Susan who was staring straight up at David, the tiny spider lines that usually fanned out around her eyes were gone, loosened by alcohol. Her skin looked alabaster and a tranquil expression, one mixed with admiration and awe, glazed her eyes. After months of listening to David's sermons, Susan seemed to have erased his girlie-show past from her memory, and now she often commented to me about what a great teacher of God's Word he was. I could tell by the look on Susan's face that by this point anything he might suggest carried the authority of Moses.

David and I didn't speak of the incident the next day, but I could see a new buoyancy to his step. He loved this life of doubles, opposites: Pastor Dave striding confidently up to the pulpit, orator extraordinaire, effective counselor — the Halloween mask of amiable minister in the tailored suit of Dr. Jekyll, morphing effortlessly the next second into the dark-cloaked Mr. Hyde. The temptations of both — the sacred and the profane — great, seducing dividers embraced in the same flesh.

Although I should have, I didn't feel much remorse about my own hypocrisy. I no longer believed in the Bible or in the church — or even in the possibility of God, for that matter — and I justified my duplicity by telling myself that a similar pretense thrived in Fundamentalism: ministers preaching on iniquity and hiding a closetful of sins from the world; obese pastors condemning every sin of the flesh except gluttony; self-righteous church members using an error filled Bible as a weapon of censure. Solely as an act of self-preservation, however, I did start to worry that someone from the church might discover our hidden life. The humiliation, the loss of income, would be devastating. And since I was sure that now, with the taste of blood on his tongue, David would insist on nude hot-tubbing as a weekly adventure, I decided I'd better protest before it was too late. The next Saturday night as we flew down the freeway with our church drinking pals, David said, "Hey, let's go back to Robert's and relax in the hot tub."

"I'm really tired," I said, "I have to get up so early tomorrow morning."

"Come on, Carlene, you're always the stick-in-the-mud!" Tina called from the backseat.

I had to come up with a better reason than that. Everyone needed to get up early to make it to Sunday school class. "Hey, you guys — I'm having my period," I said, putting an end to the conversation.

I looked across at David in the driver's seat. His brow was crawling while his mouth had become set in concrete — I knew the look. Though he hadn't moved a muscle, though to the entire world he was the most spiritual, patient preacher in the universe, he was puffing himself up inside, full of rancor. He always got his way, whether it was a matter of silverware drawer orderliness, my weight, or what we were having for dinner. He was angry, highly irritated that I wasn't going along with his plan like every other fun loving person in the car.

After we dropped our companions off, David pulled back onto the freeway and hit the gas. "You are such a pain in the ass; I know you're not having your period!" he hollered as he accelerated to eighty. Then suddenly he slammed on the brakes and skidded the car to a dead stop in the middle of the freeway. Vehicles swerved by us in a blare of honking horns. David opened the car door and leaped out, running across the four-lane highway and down into the ditch. I sat paralyzed for a moment and then, with a knee-jerk survival impulse, leaped into the driver's seat and slammed down on the gas, leaving David in the gully. I was still trembling hours later when he burst into the house. "So what the hell did you leave me standing there for?" he screamed. "It's a good thing I was able to catch the bus in Lynnwood. It was the last one running for the night." I sat in silence, huddled on the couch in the dark living room, remaining as lifeless as possible, holding tightly onto my mind. Our life had descended into madness, and I felt a sense of the Dionysian orgy let loose, and us dancing in the flames of what was sure to consume us: abuse of trust, spiritual hypocrisy — the flames of hell itself.

Our descent continued when David asked Hal and Tina, the most malleable of our drinking circle, to join us the next weekend for a getaway to Orcas Island. Hal and Tina worshipped David, and I knew that he sensed he had his tabula rasa before him. They came to every church meeting and hung on his every word; they taught Sunday school and attended Wednesday night Bible study. He could seduce them, possess them, and carve out his pleasure on their soft sandstone wills.

By the time we arrived at our rented cabin at six that evening, we had been drinking since noon and were already seeing double. By late evening, Jack Daniels had completely stolen our minds, and Tina was in full party mode, moving her shapely hips inside her floral sarong. She'd taken off her shoes, holding them in her hand as she danced, pressing her toes against the floor as though she were trampling grapes for a new batch of pinot noir. Standing next to her was Hal, with a narcotized stare and rumpled cotton shirt, three drinks past his limit, blinking myopically. I was just as far gone, my hair covering my face, swaying in place and shaking my arms like a Hindu mystic, to an Aerosmith song blaring from the tape player David had brought along. Only David seemed the least bit in control when he coherently said, "Why don't we have a little fun and swap partners?"

In a drunken stupor I thought, *Why not?* I'd already steered my life into an iceberg — maybe sex with Hal would warm me. Suddenly I felt nausea radiating inside me, going deeper, getting fiercer and more intense. I clenched my teeth and ran to the bathroom, to hang my head over the toilet while, in a freezing, sweating instant, my insides spewed up the night's whiskey. I could hear the vomit splattering onto the sides of the toilet, feel it splashing back up into my face. I stumbled into bed and fell asleep.

Later that night I awoke to hear David giving Tina instructions on how to undress me. She had taken my shirt off and was kissing my neck and chest. David laughed. "Go ahead, take all her clothes off." I pushed them away and crawled deeper under the covers. In the pitch dark of my drunkenness, I thought, *Well, David, you've always been a creative sort — wife-swapping with a little lesbian twist.*

The next morning came hurtling out of the sky like a missile aimed straight for my brain. I opened my eyes and stumbled into the bathroom. There to greet me was the image of a hunched-up old woman who, at twenty-eight, looked finished, already tasting the bitterness at the bottom of her life. Mascara had melted like wax down my colorless cheeks, and lipstick smudged my clown painted face. I hung my head over the toilet and threw up again, trying to expel the cesspit of self-loathing that festered inside me. *You are as hypocritical as the worst of the religious charlatans,* I told myself. *If the wolf in front of you is David, the precipice at your back is your own deceit.* I sat on the toilet and thought about the act of lying. The major problem is that it infects your entire life. No matter how hard you try to contain it, pretty soon it's spurting out through every seam and buttonhole, spewing like a broken sewer, overflowing into every crack and flooding places you never thought it could reach. I threw my head back and slumped against the toilet. I was sick of the taste of lies on my tongue, sick of the sound of them in my head, in my voice. *It's beyond stupidity when you lie about God,* I thought. If He does exist, you're in deep shit; if He doesn't, you may as well get into a new line of work. But here I was, doing just that, faking spirituality like faking an orgasm, too gutless to stop the sick drama.

But breaking free wasn't so easy. I was actually becoming afraid of David. Now that drinking had become a way of life with us, I was petrified at how it transformed him. Once he began his descent into drunkenness, each swallow let loose another jackal, a new legion of demons locked inside him. The impeccable self-control on his face slackened. I could see a brooding rage replace his usual veneer of calm, and he looked at people as though they were pieces of furniture. Once it started, I knew he would soon drag me into his torment, beginning always with a litany of insults. "You are incapable of showing me any real love." "Your parents must have starved you of affection; you can't seem to show any to me. I bet you'd like to screw Robert, though, wouldn't you? Come on, admit it." "I can tell you don't like to kiss me; you are so frigid." Although David's verbal badgering was not as physically threatening as the assaults his dad had perpetrated against his mother, once he was drunk I was never quite sure that it wouldn't escalate into that. Over time I grew so desperate that I actually hoped he would hit me, just to give me tangible evidence that everyone's beloved pastor was not the man they believed him to be. One night in an effort to obtain such proof, I waited until he was stumbling drunk, then stood toe-to-toe with him after his barrage of accusations and screamed, "What the fuck do you want from me? We have sex almost every night, and still you're never satisfied. If I'm so worthless, then just hit me, smack me right here in the mouth!"

Anger flashed across David's face as a vein the width of a child's finger rose in his ivory forehead, as if his heart and brain were exploding at once. Then suddenly he stopped himself, stood back, and calmly said, "I'll never give you the black eye you need to leave me." Leaning down, he kissed me on the cheek and walked out of the room.

But most of the time I wasn't so brave. After long hours of taunting, I would simply acquiesce, confessing to whatever offense he'd leveled: not enough affection toward him, too much conversation with some man after church, ketchup stains on the fridge, five extra pounds. We would have sex, and he would fall fast asleep, contented, triumphant, satisfied again. The whole thing sounds revolting and pathetic, but if a person has never been a codependent, it's hard to understand how it happens. It comes much like the science experiment demonstrating a frog's compliance. When placed in a pot of water, a frog acclimates to its surroundings. If the water is incrementally heated, the frog slowly adapts and will eventually die without leaping to freedom. That's how it happened with me: I gradually accepted the control and growing disrespect until one day I no longer felt the will to save myself. Instead of wondering why I didn't put up more of a fight, I began to believe that the free-spirited farm girl I had once been simply no longer existed, that she belonged to another time. Few vestiges of her remained, her spontaneity and strong will having been replaced with the skills necessary for survival.

I continued my routine for months, entertaining, singing in choir, homeschooling the kids. Each Sunday David would preach a moving sermon, then step down from the pulpit and into the aisle. I always sat on the outside of the second row so that once he reached me I could stand and join him. We'd move past the smiling, often tearful faces — those who had just repented of some great sin — and stand near the back door to shake hands with the congregants as they left, uplifted for the week. Everyone who walked by us, and even those who didn't, thought our marriage was perfect: David was always affectionate and attentive toward me, never missing a chance to compliment me in front of a crowd. "My sweet wife is such a support to my ministry," he would say, or "My wife is as lovely as the day we met — I am such a lucky man!" These accolades would prompt the women in the room to smile wistfully and comment on my great fortune in being married to such a loving, devoted husband and spiritual leader. I would nod and say, "Oh, I'm the lucky one." One lie, fifty lies — who was counting?

Then one day, a stunning young woman named Carrie walked into the back of the church, and I sat up straight up. Maybe she was my salvation, my one remaining loophole. If David had sex with her, I could be free of my marriage and the people who made up my entire support system would not reject me. In their eyes I would have justification for leaving. If I had the emotional support of my family and friends, I knew I could survive even financial poverty.

Over the next few months, I realized that, yes indeed, Carrie might be my ticket to freedom. From day one, Carrie always wore provocative outfits to church, her red silk dress being my favorite — red, the color of life, of blood, of the sexual chase. Its scandalously scooped neckline exposed her generous, swelling breasts. She accentuated her tiny waist by cinching it tight with a wide crimson

belt. As she walked slowly and deliberately up the center aisle looking for the perfect seat, she let her hips sway ever so slightly, like
an actress on the way to the stage to accept her Academy Award.
She would select a spot in the front pew, snuggle down into it by
shifting her weight from hip to luscious hip, then cross her shapely
legs and gaze up at David while he sat on the platform. As he stood
to approach the pulpit, she'd keep eye contact with him, then lean
forward to exchange her hymnal for a Bible just at the moment when
David's eyes were glued to her tanned breasts spilling over the satin
fabric. David pretended that he didn't notice her voluptuousness,
but I observed with delight that his eyes widened significantly.

Carrie soon asked David to counsel her and her husband, Ralph,
through their failing marriage. Each week they would arrive at his
study, Carrie looking radiant while sad-sack Ralph, slumped and
tired, plopped his body down in the chair as if it were a burdensome
bag of sand. The fact that Carrie didn't come in earnest gave me real
hope. She had confided to a mutual friend that she was madly in love
with David and wanted to sleep with him. When she and her husband
separated and Carrie started showing up for individual counseling, I
was elated and made sure not to interrupt her therapy sessions. My
heart gathered real hope during one of their meetings, as the clock
inched past the designated hour — an hour and fifteen . . . twenty . . .
twenty-five minutes — only to have my hopes plummet when David
came waltzing into the kitchen, his face beaming with amusement.

"You'll never guess what just happened. Carrie Jenson just made
a pass at me." He shook his head, laughing. "I told her it would probably be best if I didn't counsel her anymore."

I tried to act shocked, shaking my head back and widening my
eyes to conceal the disappointment. My escape route had vanished.
There's no way out now, I thought.

Eight ⟋

A Way Out

I T WAS IN OCTOBER 1988 on a typical Sunday, when David stepped up to the pulpit with effortless poise. I watched closely, waiting for a flicker of doubt to cross his dignified face — any sign that he might feel a twinge of guilt about the double life we were leading. But since deception is by its nature invisible, it hadn't disqualified either of us from the ministry. In the place of truthfulness, David radiated self-confidence, over the years his face taking on the chiseled beauty of a stone monument, as if determined to live up to its own importance. "Turn your Bibles to First Corinthians 11," he said with a smile.

I had to give David credit. He had played the situation with all the mastery of Itzhak Perlman on a Stradivarius. Everyone was delighted with him: the church board, the congregation, our clandestine drinking buddies. The old guard loved him because he'd limited new members to only a few positions on the board, keeping the balance of control firmly on the side of the founding elite. He was preaching solely out of the Bible, but delivering his sermons with such oratory exuberance that the elders felt they were getting that good old-time religion but wrapped in exciting new cellophane. Even better, he had the mettle to critique Christianity in his fiery sermons, which made everyone feel open-minded and discriminating, but he did it without assaulting the fundamentals of the faith:

biblical inerrancy, women's submission, eternal hellfire, and the sinfulness of the entire universe. He stirred things up just enough to stay out of trouble while still making the congregation feel as though they were embracing a modern, intellectual faith.

He also kept his appearance immaculate, which set him apart from other Fundamentalist ministers in the district, who often looked pudgy and exhausted, with expressions and attire that bagged like Goodwill underwear. Not David, whose Hart Schaffner Marx suits molded to him, reinforcing his aura of authority. His hair had grown parallel with his dignity, with flecks of silver gleaming in its once jet-black sheen. As he stood in the pulpit, I watched his lips and eyes smile in collaboration so convincingly that I almost bought the act myself. The corners of his mouth turned upward as he surveyed the crowd, giving only the faintest hint of the endless secrets we had to keep. To the undiscerning, the grin looked playful and good-humored. David had found the perfect audience, and it wasn't surprising to me that within the ranks of Christian Fundamentalism David's reputation was growing — he was a star.

The congregation flipped their Bibles to First Corinthians, chapter 11 and then focused their attention back on their handsome minister. I looked down the pew with its open church bulletins lining the row, the Sunday morning homily "Biblical Guidelines for Communion" in bold print at the top of each page. Under the outline that followed, ample space appeared for parishioners to take notes. I thought of the stacks of church programs piled in Christian offices and studies throughout the city, the faithful saving the snippets of wisdom they contained — as I had done so many years ago in Bible college when I first heard David preach his sermon on Joseph. Ever clamoring for nuggets from God, we were like open-beaked baby chicks, eager for the good news to drop in.

The crowd sat in family groups squeezed neatly together, wide-eyed kids sandwiched between smiling parents. Even the children loved Pastor Dave's colorful, animated sermons, many of them choosing to stay in the adult service rather than file downstairs to children's church. It was like having a front row seat at the Barnum and Bailey circus. I knew that, as always, this morning's Scripture interpretation would be engaging. Several hours from now the elders would sit around their Sunday dinner tables and marvel at Pastor Dave's astounding insight and biblical exegesis. "For a man of thirty-five, David certainly has more than his share of godly wisdom," the board chairman would say.

David began the Scripture reading, and a sea of voices followed: "For as often as you eat this bread and drink this cup, you remember the Lord's death till he returns." A ray of color spilled through the stained-glass window, as if Jesus might descend at any moment and preside over His own memorial. Instead the rainbow vein of light bathed David's brow, anointing him with divine radiance, signaling to many in the congregation that in Christ's absence, their faithful minister could easily serve as God's devoted understudy. As I watched the congregation that morning, I supposed that few would have been shocked to see their pastor's hands suddenly brandish the stigmata.

And David also had Jesus' gift of storytelling. Each Sunday, before he unveiled a new set of rules for right living, he'd warm the crowd with a lively tale: "Several months ago, I was called to serve on jury duty. After I arrived at the courthouse, the clerk informed me of a procedure called *voir dire* — a French phrase meaning 'to speak truly.' It's a process in which attorneys determine who will reside on the jury, by questioning those summoned." David's expression turned pensive. "A similar method of investigation occurs when we prepare to take the Lord's Supper. Instead of an outside entity conducting the inquiry, however, the apostle Paul tells us we are to conduct our own *voir dire*. In verse 32, he instructs us to examine ourselves and confess our sins before we partake of communion." His voice slowed, and he leaned forward against the pulpit, placing his hand flat on its surface as he had years ago in college. "By such confession, we remain separate from the world and avoid sharing in its sure condemnation."

This image of heathen judgment brought a hearty "Amen" from Robert, who liked it most when David preached condemnation down on errant lifestyles, especially the homosexuals, feminists, and liberals who, in his opinion, were responsible for the breakdown of America's moral fiber. Robert was a great fan of James Dobson's *Focus on the Family* radio talk show, and I had often heard him saying, "Praise God for Dobson's stand against gay marriage and homos in the military. These are the atrocities that have eroded the Christian foundation of this nation." Robert said that if we allowed such transgressions to continue, God was going to judge America — that it was simply despicable how far this country had fallen from the path of righteousness. I glanced at Robert, with Susan tucked in beside him, and marveled at his know-it-all face, hard set and jutting forward.

But even though I felt disgust with Robert as he shouted another "Amen," I had to admit that not all Christians were like him. Many lived by the Golden Rule and were generous, gracious, and humane. Take Herm Jorgensen, sitting at the end of the row, a massive Norwegian fisherman with huge hands and an even bigger heart. He was strong across the chest, with a full beard and black-rimmed half glasses that he wore on the end of his nose, like now, until he'd take them off to look you in the eye and say, "And how are ye today, fine lady?" When he spoke up in Bible study, he always interpreted

Christianity through the lenses of compassion, emphasizing the passages that taught generosity and shunned judgment. Herm was a church elder and always voiced common sense in the board meetings. But unfortunately he didn't hold the same status as the old guard, not having been part of the original core of the church. He was also a bit of a renegade — a divorced man, a freethinker with his own theories about God and little allegiance to doctrine. (It was rumored that the original members let him on the board because he had lots of money and gave plenty to the church.) David told me that Herm often said at board meetings, "I think we need to get our pastor and his wife out of that fishbowl parsonage. Let's put a down payment on a house for them." No one listened to him much, though. Most of the time he sat stoically in board meetings and in church; he wasn't the kind of elder who was ever going to stand up and pray or testify in a loud voice.

I thought about such things that morning in October of 1988: the sanctimonious and the kind, the sincere and the not so sincere — evaluations and musings alongside the plans I plotted for my own escape. Several weeks earlier I had experienced an epiphany of sorts, one of those life-changing moments when you suddenly see yourself clear to make a decision that you know will forever change the course of your life. It happened on my birthday. That morning David announced that he had arranged a surprise excursion to celebrate my big day and that we would be leaving for Vancouver that afternoon. Dread shot up my body as Pam, his secretary, burst into the house, ready to begin the prearrangement to babysitting. "This is kind of short notice," I said, grasping at any excuse, logical or not, to release me from the pleasure trip.

"How can you be so apathetic? I'd be ecstatic if I had such a romantic husband," said Pam, ever loyal, ever trusting.

I wanted to say back, "I'd be happy to let you take my place." But of course I didn't. Instead I listened to David describing to Pam and me how he had planned the trip down to the smallest detail.

"I borrowed Don's new Cadillac so we can drive in style," he said, "and I got us a great-view room at the Four Seasons — it's the nicest hotel in Vancouver."

David and I got into the car, and Pam waved to us from the front door, looking starry-eyed and envious. David flashed his killer grin at her and shouted from the window, "Don't hesitate to call us if you need anything!" However, less than fifteen minutes up the freeway, David's mood began to change. Pulling a fifth of Jim Beam out from under the seat, he announced, "I've heard there are some great gay bars in Vancouver, with terrific amateur strip contests. You know I've always wanted to enter one of those — I think I'll do just that." Then, after a short pause, he added, "As a celebration for your birthday, of course."

I sat stunned for a moment and then said, "You know, David, I don't have any desire whatsoever to see you strip at a gay bar."

He ignored the comment and took another swig of Jim Beam, driving on in silence. We arrived in Vancouver and checked into the Four Seasons. As I unpacked my suitcase, David grabbed the phone book and scribbled addresses onto a yellow legal pad. "Twelfth and Howe," he whispered, then almost shouted, "Let's go!" We pulled up to the flashing marquee of the Odyssey, and David jumped out while I sat in the car. Some time later he yanked open the door and dropped heavily into the seat. "Shit, amateur night is Tuesday instead of Thursday," he said, slamming his palm down on the steering wheel. "I knew I should have called ahead. The guy in there tells me that *none* of the gay bars in Vancouver have an amateur night tonight."

We drove back to the hotel, and David picked up the phone book again. "Since I missed my chance to dance," he said in the tone of a petulant child who'd just been denied his daily chocolate, "I'm going to hire a stripper to come here."

"Listen, David, I'm not interested in strippers. Whose birthday is this anyway? If we've come to Canada to celebrate my birthday, I don't want to watch naked dancers."

By this time David had been drinking for several hours, which meant I was on shaky ground. "You're completely unable to have any fun," he said. "Perpetually uptight about everything. Will you at least go out dancing with me, or is that too much excitement for your boring little self?"

Around nine we arrived at Club 212, a wild place with pulsating strobe lights and ear-breaking music. Twenty-year-olds, and those making an unsuccessful attempt to look like twenty, crashed up against one another, while the sober ones in the crowd surveyed one another like starving coyotes in search of warm flesh. David and I sat down at a table on the edge of the dance floor. Before long he disappeared. It took me some time to realize that he wasn't just in the bathroom. *Shit,* I thought, and kept my head down, hoping I'd go unnoticed from the bar lined with men, hunched over the counter with their wolf's hair slicked down, too anxious, too alert. Soon a young man who looked nothing like the prison-break group at the bar asked me to dance. After we danced, he introduced himself as Nathan and asked if he could sit with me. "Oh, my husband will be returning any minute," I told him.

"What kind of a guy would leave his wife alone in a place like this?"

I smiled at Nathan and decided to ask him to join me. He was an economics graduate student at the University of British Columbia, and we talked about his classes and plans for the future. In a quiet Canadian accent, he told me he'd grown up in the interior on a dairy farm and had come to university on a scholarship. We chatted about graduate school and farm life, the difference between raising dairy and beef cattle, and how we both had run for our lives from the backcountry.

After several hours, Nathan looked at me and said, "Let me take you home. I swear you can trust me."

"My husband is crazy, Nathan."

That was David's cue to appear before us, recklessly drunk and furious. "So . . . I've been on the other side of the bar all night, watching that guy trying to pick you up!" he shouted.

I suspected that instead of sitting across the darkened room watching me converse with a harmless graduate student, that David had actually spent the hours away from Club 212 exploring the seedier side of Vancouver.

"You're sick," I said, jumping up and bolting out of the club before Nathan got smacked. David ran after me, charging out into the street, dodging traffic and shouting accusations as he went. "You couldn't wait to get rid of me, could you? I can't trust you for a minute. Give you a little free time, and you pick up some dweeb."

I crossed Government Street and switched back, heading by memory toward the Four Seasons. By the time I burst into our room, David was still at my heels, screaming accusations that by now had migrated onto a familiar topic. "You never show me any affection. You are simply not capable of love. You couldn't love any man."

People who think death is the worst thing that can happen in this life don't know a thing about brutality, I thought as I looked back into David's red-veined, raging face. It was then that it happened. I decided I was finished with David, finished with religion, finished with my marriage. Some of the events of those years have gone from my memory; I have only a gauzy recall of a collection of people passing through — names, faces, fleeting conversations with church members — but the evening of my thirty-first birthday stands solid and clear in my mind. In that instant I realized I would rather be dead than live another minute with my husband. As David slammed around the room, I felt a deep calm come over me. I knew I would never retreat from my decision and that now, for the first time in ten years, David had no control over me. If he killed me while I was making my escape, I would go happily to the grave without God or the hope of any future existence. But now I must save my energy for one last lie, one final battle: to plan the getaway while still under the watchful eye of the minister and his congregation. I didn't fight back that night but simply said, "You are right; I'm not affectionate enough, because I was raised in a very stoical home. I do need to learn to be more loving."

"Yes, very good . . . And do you promise to work on it more?" David's voice was now calming, even gentle, as he smoothed the top of my hair with the flat of his hand as if he were stroking a cat.

"Yes, I promise."

"Good, I know that you can't be blamed for something you just don't know how to do." He whispered, "I'll be patient, but you have to work on it every day," pressing me against his chest and then unzipping the back of my dress, waves of alcohol fumes surging from his open mouth.

"Yes," I said, feeling my body go limp.

Sex between us was like this now. Like the moment an antelope relinquishes her spirit to the lion's jaws, knowing that any further struggle is futile. It is her last act of control, her only dignity, to choose the instant that she will liberate herself from life and deliver her body into the teeth that are cutting into her flesh. David, the lion, pulled me onto the bed, and when he had had his way, he rolled off, breathing hard, his limbs splayed out across the bed, sweat beading on his forehead, a tiny drop of it fixed like a jewel to the tip of his nose. The hair on his chest was glistening, his legs shaking from the conquest. A low growl rattled in his throat, contented and satisfied, as though he had just fed on a lump of bleeding flesh. "Wow, that was great," he said, and immediately began to snore off his drunk.

I lay awake, staring at the ceiling; while the room turned underneath me, not with drunken abandon but slowly, as if it really were moving through space and time. I knew I had crossed over an emotional divide that evening. I was going to leave David. I didn't care about the reaction of my Christian family or friends. I was going to escape, with or without the biblical excuse of adultery to satisfy those around me.

Suddenly I could see myself in the future, waiting tables, the perfect form of employment for a student — shorter hours, higher wages from tips — then, attending community college and on to the university; the kids getting older and more independent; and, once I earned my degree, my break for freedom. I would be patient; it would take some time, but I would stay the course. My eyelids grew heavy, and I let the sleep wash over me like a dark tide. *Job, education, emancipation,* I told myself — my new mantra. I was getting out.

Nine

Leaving the Faith

IN THE DAYS THAT FOLLOWED, I felt excited, almost giddy, but I knew that I couldn't tell a soul about my plans for escape — not Susan, not anyone. No one was going to get a chance to talk me out of it. Even God, if He did happen to exist, wouldn't be able to sway me. The day I walked out of the house and down the lane toward David's study, to begin the first leg of my strategy, I said, "Sorry, God, my faith in life as a martyr has just ended."

David sat engrossed in his Greek lexicon when I walked in. "I'm going to stop homeschooling the girls," I said. "It's time they went to public school anyway, and I want to start working." David peered up from his book, silent for a split second as he pulled the pen from behind his ear, like an archer nocking an arrow.

"I always knew you didn't want to be a mother," he said. His voice was cold, but his eyes were filled with fury.

"We both know that's ridiculous," I answered, turning and walking out of the room before he could send another arrow from his silver quiver of oratory.

I rushed back to the house, picked up the phone, and called the Space Needle Restaurant. Even though I'd never eaten there before, it was the most expensive restaurant I could think of (higher prices, more tip potential). There was only one problem: I didn't have enough experience to get the job. Although I'd waited tables in the 1970s at a truck stop in Montana, my steak and egg expertise hardly qualified me for fine dining. During summer breaks from college, I'd worked at the 4B's in Missoula — a gigantic plaza open twenty-four hours a day, where brawny, tattooed truckers streamed in for a quick meal before climbing into their rigs and red-eyeing it for Minnesota. I knew plenty about slinging hash, nothing about lobster. I told myself just to keep repeating the positive-thinking phrase Susan had learned in her cookware sales seminars. "Fake it till you make it," she'd always say. I intended to do just that. The only problem was that I needed a reference from a gourmet eating establishment. My mother was the only possible candidate.

Mom once ran a small café in our hometown in Montana. It sat on the corner of Wall Street and Main and for thirty years had been owned and operated by a family named Cortner. When Mom reopened it, she kept its familiar name, Cortner's Corner, and put out the tiny parlor's same homemade soups and ice creams. I worked for her one summer, scooping chocolate decadence and minestrone. I called Mom and told her my plan. "I'll just rename it Cortner's Fine Dining and list you as a reference. Don't worry," I said, "If they ask you anything you don't want to lie about, just tell them the truth and I'll try somewhere else. What can they do, arrest us?"

There was a short silence, then Mom said, "All right, but I think you are courting disaster."

Miraculously, the interview went well. And no one had to lie — at least not technically. When Al, the Space Needle manager, called Mom, he simply asked her if she had employed me. "Yes," she said, "and she's a very hard worker," not stretching the boundaries of her unshakable honesty one little bit.

When Al interviewed me, he asked only one question about Cortner's: "What were their specialties?"

"Oh, wonderful seafood and meats."

He smiled, imagining coquilles St. Jacques and steak tartare, I'm sure. I grinned back, remembering clam chowder and beef barley soup.

The Space Needle called that evening and asked me to show up in two days. Only then did I hesitate. Somehow in my determination to get the job, I'd forgotten about the numbing fear I had of heights; the ride to the top of the six-hundred-foot Needle each day, in a glass elevator, would be a real character builder. It also dawned on me that I didn't know the difference between a cosmopolitan and a manhattan or how to open a wine bottle. Although David and I had been drinking for several years, we never brought liquor into the house. As much as I loved to order merlot during dinners out, or gin and tonics and tequila shooters while we were dancing, I knew nothing beyond that about mixed drinks.

Once I stopped to consider what I'd done, I could feel my heart thumping like a kettledrum. David reacted by stomping his foot on the floor like Rumpelstiltskin in the fairy tale, pounding his way into the center of the earth. "This is total lunacy. How can you work and maintain your responsibilities here? I forbid you."

"I'm doing it anyway," I said.

Later I realized that David's anger actually helped me overcome my terror by reminding me why I was waiting tables in the first place. I purchased a corkscrew and started practicing, busting cork after cork but taking comfort in the fact that I'd also have three days of on-the-job training.

I stepped into the glass elevator at 6:00 a.m. on Saturday morning, chanting to myself, "This elevator has never malfunctioned. In twenty-five years of existence, it has never ever malfunctioned . . . twenty-five years — my God, this thing is a death trap!" My eyes closed, squishing back the tears of terror and loss at the idea of never holding my grandchildren. I didn't see the beautiful orange sun rising up between the downtown skyscrapers, but kept my eyelids tightly together until the elevator doors opened. I slipped out quickly. Al was standing there, ready to introduce me to Cindy, a kind, wide-eyed brunette whose job it was to tutor me in survival.

"My job is to show you the ropes, and your job is to pick up all the weird nuances of waiting tables at the Space Needle." She smiled.

Being the tourist magnet that it was, working at the Needle meant ten hours running with almost no time even for a bathroom break. I watched openmouthed as lithe servers shouldering huge trays filled with lobster and lamb dodged one another like country-and-western line dancers. To add to the chaos, the tiny central kitchen remained stationary while the dining room revolved, so that visitors could get a panoramic view of the Seattle skyline in one hour. You'd step from section A onto a fixed kitchen floor and, ten minutes later, rush back out onto a moving dining area that had changed to section D. And just to keep things interesting, in a strong wind the top-heavy Space Needle swayed slightly — the architects had designed it to withstand two-hundred-mile-per-hour winds and to swing rather than snap off in the event of an earthquake. Keeping your balance was like tap-dancing on the bow of the *Stars & Stripes* during the America's Cup race.

That first day Cindy said, "I'm going to have you deliver all the drinks for my tables," which should have been an easy task. But when I stepped up to the bar, I didn't recognize a single beverage on the tray, which was forested with fruit-speared glassware. I had a gut-wrenching feeling that my mother had been right. I shot a quick look at Dennis, the lanky bartender with a sandpaper voice, who was finishing an animated joke to one of the waiters. I made a snap judgment that I could trust him — I would have to. I introduced myself, then leaned toward the bar and made my confession quick: "I'm here to pick up drinks that I can't identify. I haven't actually served mixed drinks before — the only place I've worked is a truck stop in Montana."

Shock darted across his face, followed by a generous grin. He leaned down with his gangling frame and whispered, "I'd be happy to tell you their names."

Thank God Dennis didn't burst out laughing (though months later, after I knew every drink from the rusty nail to the screaming orgasm, he did every time he retold the story). That first day he simply said, "Hey, when things slow down, I'll tell you about the little old ladies from Montana I waited on once." Throughout the day Dennis patiently whispered the names of every drink I came to collect. When our shift was over, he told me his tale: "One day two quaint little characters sat up at the bar and ordered bourbon shooters. When I asked them where they'd come from, one of them said, 'We're from [baaing like a sheep] Mo-o-onta-a-a-a-ana-a-a, where the men are men and the sheep are nervous.'"

Dennis threw his head back and laughed with abandon. It was then that I knew I'd made the right decision in getting a job at the Space Needle. Even driving home that night, when my shoulders ached and my calves began to cramp from the grueling physical labor of waiting tables, I was happy. Even when I got close to the house and my stomach started to knot with anxiety, knowing that David would be in a foul humor, I was content. As I entered the house, David was lying on the sofa, relaxing after a quiet day of Bible study. "We're starving — when will dinner be ready? If you're going to work, you can't just forget about your other responsibilities!" he yelled.

Whispering my mantra, "Job, education, emancipation," I threw a Mrs. Smith's lasagna in the oven.

It was immediately evident that my fellow servers at the Space Needle were a wild crowd — a group that used the word *fuck* as if it were an article of speech. But I also watched them show each other great courtesy and respect. They seemed to embrace life without guilt and other human beings without judgment, reveling in their own individuality and appreciating the trait in others; what people believed in or whom they slept with was their own business. It wasn't as though they were perfect — there were still internal battles at work, and some held on to six-month-old vendettas — but by and large my rowdy, irreligious coworkers were honest and unwaveringly fair; beneath their rough exteriors dwelt sincere, compassionate human beings.

They also had a great talent for having a good time. At the end of a grueling breakfast-lunch shift they'd congregate at Yukon Jack's, a saloon that sat at the base of the Space Needle, to drink and tip away a sizable chunk of their own hard earned cash, arriving at the bar to a rowdy welcome from the Yukon staff. In this solid fraternity, the lucky servers who got our group knew they'd earn more tips from us than they'd made all day. The Space Needle crew filled up a huge rectangular table and boisterously compared experiences: hollered, swore, and sang, then told stories about the great people, best tips, and worst customers they'd waited on that day. I loved sneaking away and joining them after work; it was like an upended church service, but this one felt good for the soul.

As I made friends with my gay coworkers, I shamefully remembered my ignorance and prejudice against Diane and Evie at Bible college, using Scripture to condemn people of whom I had no understanding. This was going to be a different world without a "God-breathed" holy book to do my thinking for me. I knew how much my worldview had changed when one morning my new friend Thomas came in, his voice shaking with emotion. "Last night I found out that my partner, Boyd, is having an affair."

"God, that's terrible!" I said without any hesitation, genuine sadness welling up in my throat. In years past I would have disapproved of Thomas without even taking time to know the compassionate and tenderhearted soul that he was. That was when I was sure how the world worked, sure of my own judgments, sure of the judgments of a God who would show little compassion for Thomas. Now I wondered if God felt as disgusted with the condemnations that religious people attributed to Him as the people being condemned felt.

I didn't attend church on Sundays anymore, starting work on the weekends at 6:00 a.m. and not getting home until after 5:00. I knew that the congregation was beginning to whisper behind their hands about my working on what they thought of as the Sabbath and no longer singing in the choir, no longer teaching women's Bible study, or throwing church dinner parties. My performance as a minister's wife was being scored like an Olympic ice-skating competition, and I knew I was coming up with scandalously low points. I did go to Wednesday night Bible study, however, but eventually, in a fit of recklessness, ended up sullying my image even further.

One evening during a packed study, I squeezed into the back pew. David had already begun his lesson on Luke 16 and was reading verse 22: "the rich man also died, and was buried; and in hell he lifted up his eyes, being in torments, and seeth Abraham afar off, and Lazarus in his bosom," when someone raised his hand and said, "What do we say to people who claim that hell isn't a literal place?"

"We say that Jesus mentions hell over ten times in the New Testament. Are we going to take Christ at his word, or not?"

I sat in the pew and thought, even if the man named Jesus was talking about a literal hell, how would we know? This was a parable Christ was telling. And even though the idea of everlasting damnation never found its way into Jewish theology, Fundamentalists clung tenaciously to the ghoulish notion. In the Old Testament, the Hebrew word for *hell* represents a burning trash heap outside an ancient city, where the fire is eventually extinguished. In fact, I had learned from my clandestine history readings, the concept of eternal hellfire wasn't even embraced by the Christian church until the fourth century, when Saint Augustine began to teach that those who did not receive Jesus as their Savior were headed for the bottomless pit. So I sat in the crowded pew and thought, *How curious that a loving deity would consign 95 percent of the world's population to everlasting torment for not knowing the proper password* — especially when those who chanted the right incantation seemed so profoundly confused.

Then, like someone blithely boarding a bus without brakes, I raised my hand and said, "It's beginning to strike me as strange that God would cast most of his children into eternal hellfire when, even as mere mortals, we would never throw our own kids into a burning pit for disobedience."

David looked at me in disbelief. He didn't respond, and after a few seconds of stunned silence from the congregation, he moved on to the next question. When the service ended, Phoebe, my old carpet runner nemesis, marched up to me and said, "Your role is not to question the sacred doctrines of the church, but to be a testimony to its teachings!" Apparently an overcrowded heaven was something that Phoebe just couldn't abide.

Once we got home David had a word with me as well. "It's suicide to let the congregation in on your disbelief. You need to remember, you are the minister's wife," he said, bowing down from the heavens of his fullness, readjusting my position on the earthly mission that he and God had appointed as mine.

"You're right," I said. "I'll be more careful."

"I don't believe in hell either," he went on, walking into the kitchen, opening the cabinet above the refrigerator, and pulling out a bottle of tequila that I had no idea was there, "but we just can't expose our doubts to the congregation." As he made his way back into the living room, he poured himself a shot and slugged it, then poured another. Downing it, he sank into the overstuffed chair, tequila bottle in one hand, shot glass in the other. "The fact is, I don't believe in any of this anymore. You know, I came across a cassette tape of a sermon I did in 1983, hollering hellfire and brimstone. Back then I thought I sounded so melodious and eloquent, but five years later it sounded just like it was: high-pitched and silly," he said, throwing back another gulp. "Isn't it ironic, a guy condemning sinful society and completely without a conscience himself? I swear, it's like losing a limb; I just don't have one anymore."

Over the next few months, David's agitation with religion continued. He began to complain more each day about the stress of the ministry and the idiocy of Fundamentalism. Then one evening he suddenly announced, "I'm resigning from Calvary Baptist. This whole religion business is like adding two and two together and coming up with five."

David had dropped hints before that he was frustrated with his job: the elder's censuring of his sermons, the old guard's fear of church growth and loss of control. But his sudden announcement made me also wonder if he wasn't beginning to worry that our secret drinking parties with other couples in the congregation might eventually be revealed. Although, since the night I feigned having my period, David had not suggested we nude hot-tub together again, our drinking escapades were escalating. If we separated from the watchful eye of the church we could party without concern.

That Saturday David invited our drinking buddies over to tell them about his plans to leave the ministry. They drifted into our backyard, chatting and grabbing a Pepsi out of the cooler while David lit the grill. Summer was ripening. The ash tree was making its little green berries, and the goldfinches had returned to take up residence in its branches as they did each year. I put on some Kenny G, an airy CD with notes that floated like fireflies over a summer lawn, a thousand of them, winking here and there. Robert took shelter in a chair under the umbrella and said to David, "Can you believe that liberal Supreme Court, voting to protect a traitor's right to burn the American flag? What in God's name is this country coming to? I think you should preach a sermon on the subject, David."

"My sermon days are just about over, old buddy."

"What's that supposed to mean?"

"I'm going to resign from Calvary Baptist."

Everyone froze. You could hear seagulls from the Pacific crying overhead.

"No way," Tina finally said, her lip already quivering. "You are kidding us, right?"

"No, I'm not kidding," David said. "I need some time away from the ministry, to think. I'm completely exhausted. Everything seems so crazy right now."

"What are you going to do?" Robert almost whispered.

"I'm going to do some carpentry work for John Slate for a while. I'm looking forward to a little hard physical labor."

"But the church is growing so fast, and everyone is delighted with your ministry," Susan said.

"I'm burned out, guys. But Carlene and I aren't going far. We can still have great times together."

"At least you're not going to leave the state — then we'd just have to follow you," Hal said, laughing. Everyone fell back into silence, and the backyard looked like that *Twilight Zone* scene where the whole town is frozen, immovable, unable to speak.

The members of Calvary Baptist were just as shocked, and they grieved David's resignation like the death of a saint. We left the church and moved to a nearby town, where he started working as a carpenter. At first David was glad to be free from his ministerial responsibilities, but before long he realized how much gratification he received from preaching, and he began to sink deeper into despair.

I tried to mask my own happiness at the freedom that I felt, sensing the bonds of iron I'd known for so many years turning into spiderwebs. I enjoyed my job and colorful coworkers at the Space Needle, and since Jason was starting school that September, I decided to implement the second leg of my strategy. One evening I told David I was going to start classes that fall at the nearby community college.

"There is *no* way you can start school," he said. "I let you take that job at the Space Needle, and that's it. Besides, you can't possibly do both; you'll never be able to keep up with the schedule."

"I'm going to try," I said, knowing that David was without the patriarchal structure of religion to defend his dominance, and so he had no justification to stop me. "You spent five years of our marriage in seminary. Now that the kids are all in school, it's my turn."

I registered for classes at Shoreline Community College and, hoping that some of the credits from Bible college would transfer, made an appointment to see an academic counselor. After reviewing my transcript, she told me that since my religious degree was unaccredited, I'd have to start from scratch. At first I felt upset and cheated, but I then realized that every moment I spent angry was just wasted time: *job, education, emancipation,* I repeated.

I rushed onto the campus that September morning in 1989, the air crisp and smelling of fall and promise. I was ready, with blank notebooks and great intentions, looking forward to new teachers and interesting classmates — a feeling of anticipation that I hadn't experienced in years. As I ran past a sea of teenagers in a group, I realized just how long I'd been away from school, that I was a thirty-two-year-old mother of three, not entirely sure I could pass a science course, and on top of that, late for class. I stepped into Mr. Peterson's world history and wobbled down the aisle, my legs rubbery with fear, glad to go unnoticed among the swarm of young faces buzzing with excitement. "Two thousand years before Christ," Mr. Peterson called out in a deep baritone voice, "a brilliant culture, located on the island of Crete, possessed vast centers of wealth and power, a written language, a powerful fleet that ruled over the Aegean, and one of the most artistic civilizations in history. Nine hundred years later, this ancient kingdom inspired Homer's mythic vision."

A hand flew up in the front row, and a fresh-scrubbed student said, "I thought everyone in two thousand BC was barbaric."

"Au contraire," Mr. Peterson said with a laugh, "these civilizations were just the opposite."

"What were they like?" another voice inquired.

"The five storied palaces of Minoa, Knossos, and Gournia possessed countless rooms, statues, and courtyard theaters. Luxurious dwellings surrounded the palace, filled with specialized workshops, altars, and temples. Even simple homes had elaborate frescoes and paintings."

"When did we discover these lost cities?"

"The palace of Minos was unearthed in the spring of 1900. Almost immediately researchers realized they had stumbled upon a structure unequaled by anything previously known in ancient history. Excavation of the other civilizations followed. Homer's epic cities, once considered legend, were now real."

As I listened to the spirited interaction in the class — information about recent finds in archeology that were reinterpreting ancient history, students asking questions and challenging the professor, a professor who was not afraid to be challenged — I realized how different this experience was going to be from Bible college. This would not be the herd life of religion, debarring any real inquiry, but a place to think, discover, and explore. *I'm going to like college,* I thought — a new set of rules and a new language, a new life. I felt as though a secret door had opened, a hidden bookshelf panel had turned, and I was walking through a new passageway, leaving everything behind.

In the next few months, I threw myself into a demanding schedule, attending class in the morning, rushing from campus to work the lunch shift at the Space Needle, then dashing home to make dinner and spend time with the kids, and studying until late into the night. When the first term ended and I practically ran to the mailbox to find the letter from Shoreline Community College with my grades inside, I felt a sense of doom gripping my throat, just as it had in grade school when the teacher handed out our report cards. I hesitated and then ripped open the envelope: one B and four As. I screamed, feeling an enormous upwelling of relief inside my chest. *I can do this,* I thought. I ran across the street and burst into the house.

"I made the honor roll!" I shouted.

David looked up from his typewriter, the one he had been spending countless hours at lately writing angst-filled poetry. Then he looked down without a word and started to type again. The weeks had grown taut with the tension between us, the destruction of our lives together spelling itself out in the silence.

"You are amazing," I said. "I spent five years cooking, cleaning, and taking care of the kids while you were in school — typing your papers, rooting you on like a mindless cheerleader — and now you can't even support me one iota."

"So, big deal, you get a couple of As. It's only your first quarter."

"You're going to fight me every step of the way on this, aren't you?"

"Have you ever thought that you shouldn't be in school? That you should be working on the problems in our marriage instead? You're right, I don't want you in college, and I don't intend to make it easy for you."

Since I had started classes, David had refused even to acknowledge that I was in school. If I had a big test the next day, he'd demand that we spend the evening discussing the lack of communication in our marriage. If I had a paper due, he insisted that fixing dinner was my first priority.

The next morning I walked into the Women's Center at Shoreline. As I stood at the front desk, sunlight slanted through its tall east windows. Great rectangles of brightness warmed the cream colored carpet, a glassy light striking the tables and chairs and making the whole room seem as peaceful as a chapel.

"I was wondering if I could make an appointment to see a counselor," I said.

"Wow, you are in luck," the doe-eyed girl with a dragon tattoo on her shoulder said. "Ms. Collins just had a cancellation. I'll ask her if you can take the slot."

At first glance you could tell that Lydia Collins was a liberated, highly educated woman. I took her to be in her late forties or early fifties. She wore a pin-striped suit showing off her kinky salt-and-pepper hair and black-rimmed glasses dotted with ruby jewels around the edge. I stepped into her office, and forty-five minutes later, after the story of my life with David had poured out in a torrent, she said, "This guy sounds like a charismatic, charming abuser. What makes you so compelled to stay with him?"

"I'm holding out until I get my education. I think it would be better for the kids if I waited until after graduation before I left him."

"I think David will make it impossible for you to finish one year, let alone graduate. And as far as your kids go, children learn acceptable behavior by watching their parents. If you continue to raise them in this environment, abusive behavior could easily become their benchmark for normality. If you wait for four more years, your girls could end up marrying a controlling man like David, and your son might very well learn to emulate his behavior."

What a nightmare, I thought, staying in a bad marriage for the kids while inadvertently consigning them to the same miserable fate. I went home that night and began to imagine how I would ask David to leave his own house. It wasn't long until he gave me a compelling reason.

I left around ten the next Saturday morning to work a double shift at the restaurant, both lunch and dinner. "I won't be home until late," I told David

"How late?"

"Gosh, not until after eight at least."

It was cold in Seattle that winter, with the sky bright and fierce, the ground without snow — a kind of permanent frozen autumn, as if the calendar had stopped when the wind tore the last leaves from the maple trees. The whole city must have felt the chill and stayed home that day, snuggled up playing Yahtzee; after a pitiful lunch showing it was obvious we weren't going to have any business for dinner. Al reduced my ten-hour shift to four. "Take the evening off, go home, and wrap Christmas presents."

As I turned down our street, the air was damp and still; the low, gray sky seemed to bulge with an impending blizzard, like a river about to overflow its banks. *Maybe we'll get snow for Christmas,* I thought. Plastic Santas waved from their sleighs, green elves and miniature reindeer blinked up and down our street. For the first time in years, I hadn't decorated the house with lights — only a small tree inside, and a scattering of boughs. I felt a little guilty about it, but also relieved, as if someone had lifted an unseen burden that I hadn't really felt until it was gone. No one would be watching the house to see what kind of decorations the minister and his wife had up this year.

Pulling into the driveway, I knew immediately that something was wrong. The front door was wide open, and I could hear playful screams coming from the house. I stepped inside and saw neighborhood children running through the stone-cold living room, playing hide and seek, crashing around the Christmas tree. Bowls of partially eaten ice cream dotted the room.

"Where's your father?" I asked Carise.

"He built a fire in the fireplace this morning and then went to Costco, but he hasn't been back," she said.

"It's cold, Mama; could you make another fire?" Jason danced around me.

I stepped out the back door to collect wood for a fire, and the cold hit my face with an intensity that felt like the grip of permanent night. How irresponsible could David get, starting a fire and then leaving the kids alone? My mind rushed through the horrifying scene: a pop from the fireplace and a spark onto the carpet, smoldering and then running along the floorboards while a roomful of kids played happily upstairs. Then, shooting up everywhere, surrounding the staircase and blocking any way out, flames working themselves up until the heat and pressure were powerful enough to explode the windows. I took the ax and chopped an armful of kindling, threw several large chunks on top, and headed inside. Even after I had a new fire going and it had filled the room with a dry, parched heat, making my face burn, I was still pushing the anger back down my throat. That son of a bitch, I thought. I looked at the clock: 4:00 p.m.

"Did you have any lunch?" I asked Carise.

"We had lots of ice cream," Micael said with a giggle.

I grabbed a handful of potatoes from the refrigerator and began scrubbing them under the tap. I filled a large pot and set it down heavily on the burner, the water spilling over the sides. While the water hummed on the heat, I stood at the stove, looking out the window onto our suburban neighborhood, a world of absolute stillness mantled in lights. I imagined what I would say to David when he got home. It seemed obvious where he had spent the day: he only acted this foolish when he had naked women on his mind. I had been reworking this moment for some time now — pulling the plug on the last death rattle of our marriage. But all my plans had been reenacted for four years in the future, a time when I'd have my bachelor's degree firmly in hand. None of them would work tonight, and now that I was about to do it — years ahead of schedule — my stomach felt as if it had been pumped full of lye. I heated a mug of water in the microwave and made myself some chamomile tea. I drank it down, letting it warm me. The house was strangely still. The kids had been warmed, given a sandwich to tide them over until dinner, and were now bundled up outside, playing. Not a sound could be heard inside; it was as if the house itself had stopped breathing.

Suddenly David opened the back door. I felt my insides jump, but my face was stone. David's cheeks were white, his voice wobbly. "Hey, why are you home so early?" he said. I looked at him taking in every detail: his upper lip beading with fear, his voice pitched too high, the words trapping themselves in his throat, the air around him slippery as Vaseline. He had the exact expression of Jimmy Swaggart the year before, the night he made his TV confession about picking up a prostitute.

"So how long did it take you to go back to your strip joints?" I asked.

"I know I haven't been supportive of you being in school. I've been a real shit . . . I promise to change and help you out in any way I can. I'm really very proud of you, you know." As always, his words were a maneuver, a strategy.

"How long did it take you to go back to your girlie shows after you promised me you'd quit?"

David's shoulders slumped. "A few months after you first caught me," he said. "You were right — I know that the only way I'm going to beat this thing is with counseling. I'm ready to go. I've heard about this group called Sexaholics Anonymous. Let's go together."

"You have a week to get out."

"You can't be serious."

"One week. I'll give you one week."

David's lip began to quiver. "You've got to give me another

chance. You said it yourself: all I need is counseling. Come to this meeting with me, and you'll see that I can change. Promise me you'll do it."

"I'll go to a meeting with you as soon as you're moved out of the house," I said, employing the only leverage I had to get him packing.

David finally took me seriously and rented an apartment ten minutes from us. After that, I went with him to a Sexaholics Anonymous meeting held in a Seattle YMCA, with people milling around, keeping their eyes to themselves. A young male facilitator announced, "Partners meet in room 211, and recoverers stay here in the auditorium." I joined a small throng of about twenty-five women as we made our way down the silent hallway, our shoes clicking on the hard floor, my skin flushed hot with shame. As I entered the room, I continued to avoid eye contact with anyone, pretending to study the wavy old windowpanes and then the enameled wall in front of me, grimy and in need of a new coat of paint. I sat in one of the battered chairs ringing the room and immediately looked down, first at the worn loafers of the woman sitting next to me, then at the twisted leather laces in the boots of a woman across the room. I propped my elbows onto my knees and put my head in my hands to try and cool the burning glare of my cheeks.

Our leader, who was the female colleague of the male counselor in the auditorium, lowered herself into one of the seats as if testing the heat of a bath. When it held her satisfactorily, she leaned back and looked at us one by one, smiling, cautious. Her manner was serious and guarded, and she started the meeting by listing the simple rules of a Sexaholics gathering. Number one: each of us would tell our story; we could say anything we wanted to, whatever was burdening our hearts. Number two: no one could judge what anyone else said — not one word of condemnation or critique, only support.

The stories started to erupt and pour around the room like a lava flow of pain. John had been so good for so long, one woman cried, and then, just like that, he slipped. She was trying to forgive again; God give her the strength to forgive again. One by one, the stories poured out: repeated betrayal, repeated heartache, repeated forgiveness. I was glad no one gave the intimate details of their partners' lapses — the collective sadness was already too palpable. It sounded to me like most of the women had been attending this gathering for quite some time. Voices spun the room like a merry-go-round, making me sick to my stomach, until I realized the woman next to me was talking. She began by rummaging through her purse for something, her hands shaking, her voice quivering. "I found this the other day," she said, pulling a stub from the tattered bag, "in Jake's pocket. It's from the OK Bar on Ninety-nine, where he goes to pick up prostitutes. He's been good for *two whole months,* and now this! I confronted him last night, and he said, 'Well, it looks like we'd better go back to my meetings.'" Shrugging her shoulders she sighed "So here we are."

The smile had long left the facilitator's face. She looked at me. "Would you like to share?"

My throat tightened. "I just told my husband to get out and not to come back. I'm not giving him another chance — taking the risk he'll bring home some disease and give it to me. I'm running for my life."

I guessed it was from thousands of broken hearts and an attempt to mend them that various "Anonymous" meetings have become so strong a pillar in our modern social structure. I knew that these meetings have saved lives and kept people clean, sober, and married. In many cases they make people accountable and give them the tools they need to survive, to cope with unbearable situations. But at that point in my life, I simply didn't have any faith left in David to believe that he could change. He had lived so long in a world of make-believe, covering his obsession with religion, that I was afraid the chances were remote that he would ever come clean. I was also afraid that if I continued down the "enabler" path, I would become as addicted to being abused as David was to abusing. And what imprint would that leave on my children, what scratchy record to replay?

That night as we drove back to the house I glanced at David, seeing the lines deep in his face, desperation in his eyes. I turned from him and looked out the window at the brittle, leafless trees, their branches like bones clicking in the wind. I closed my eyes and laid my head against the headrest. It was as though my love for him had been buried over the years in a deep thick fog — a fog that had risen out of disappointment, disillusion. It had appeared first in thin spirals like ghosts in a churchyard and thickened with the force of a genie from a lamp. At times we had tried to find each other in the haze, but now there seemed no hope. We were drowned in the soupy mist. It had encased us both and it was bitterly cold.

He dropped me off at the house, asking quietly that I reconsider, knowing by the look on my face not to push the issue. As he drove away, I stood outside and looked up at the moon, blood red through the clouds. I put my face into my hands, as though I was praying to God. But now, for me, He did not exist. Instead I cried, remembering for the first time in years how I had once loved David so completely. Remembering there had been a time when we shared such tender moments, a mutual belief that our future was infinite, our children secure, encased together in our arms. I thought of the time when we believed that God had called us to help the world. I felt the sobs wrenching me. If I had been more diligent, less gullible, could I have stopped this heartache — if I had loved David more or myself less. For some time remorse flowed through my body, building up and dying down, building up and dying down. I felt as though I was unmoored, being sucked into a black current, only to pull myself onto a solitary continent of sadness.

I cried for some time and then thought of my children, unaware that I had returned home; they'd be sitting upstairs in front of the television or doing their homework. I dried my tears and walked inside the house. The battle ahead would be a difficult one. I needed to think about how I was going to tell my family and friends.

The first people who needed to hear about the separation were going to be the hardest to tell: my parents. They had absolutely no idea of the life that David and I had been living — they had supported us at every turn, taken pride in our service to God, paid for David's seminary education, and loved him like a son. They believed in both of us completely and unquestioningly.

The next day was a slow one waiting tables, so I left work early, taking the elevator down from the Space Needle, crossing the plaza to the Seattle Center, pausing to listen to the folksingers, stopping to browse through the gift shop, stalling for time to try and calm myself. Maybe I didn't have enough quarters — it was going to be a long call from the pay phone in the Food Circus. I couldn't lie, but the truth was going to be very hard to explain. My practiced explanations kept fluttering away like a great chirping flock of starlings, black against a pale blue sky, veering and swerving then spreading apart and disappearing from sight. Maybe I would wait until tomorrow to call Mom and Dad. Then I thought of the freedom I longed for, the dream of it seeded long ago, after David's first confession, and watered over the years by David's jealousy and demands for control. Now liberation had sprouted in my veins. I was a waitress; I had plenty of quarters.

Mom answered the phone, and my story spilled out. After my confession, she didn't hesitate to tell me that she loved me and that she and Dad would do whatever they could to help. I knew it would be easier to tell the next person on my list — Susan — but as I suspected, she wasn't as agreeable to the plan.

"I asked David to leave the house, and he's gone," I told her that night over the phone.

"What, are you crazy? You just started school. How are you going to pay the light bill?"

"He's been sneaking out to strip joints again, and I've had it. I can't stand it anymore."

"Now, calm down and think this through," she said. "How in God's name are you going to survive?"

"I'll keep waiting tables, and things will have to work out."

"Your kids need the security of a nuclear family, even if it's an unhealthy one."

"I saw a counselor at the community college, and she said that wasn't necessarily so. She said if I stayed, my kids would start to think this madness is normal."

"This counselor is not a Christian and can't understand the obligations we have to follow the teachings of Scripture!"

"I'm sorry, Susan, I've made up my mind. I have to go. I'll talk to you next week." I set the phone down before Susan could say another word.

The people of Calvary Baptist were just as stunned by the separation. Some surmised that our marital problems were the result of my newfound independence: a woman who pursued her own selfish interests and stepped out from under God's protective umbrella of family hierarchy was simply asking for trouble. Others whispered that I was probably having an affair. That accusation made me consider revealing David's addiction and jealous outbursts, but I decided against it because of the effect that such mudslinging would have on Carise, Micael, and Jason.

It was the reaction of my brother Dan that would somewhat surprise me. In the years since Bible college, Dan had gone from being a ruddy faced farm boy to Dr. Cross, with a PhD in theological studies. He was the senior pastor of a beautiful stained-glass megachurch seating a growing congregation of four thousand. Over the years, Dan and David had remained close friends, spending many long hours together discussing the problems and triumphs of church growth, which theology books they were reading, and the latest debate in *Christianity Today*. Dan had always considered David a mentor and a guide.

As the story unfolded, his face, one I had known so well since childhood, looked stunned, agonized, and then determined. "Leave him, Carlene. Get out now," he said. In that moment I knew that love could triumph over religion. It was one of many surprises ahead.

Ten

Going Alone

A STRANGE ENERGY SURGED within me over the next few months. I ignored Susan's warning and steeled myself for the melee that I knew was about to begin. Like a child emperor, David was used to getting his way without question, and I suspected he would use whatever means he could to regain his former power. And he did. When the kids went to visit him, he would tell them that he loved us all very much and was unbearably lonely in his cold apartment; maybe we could convince Mommy to let him move back. One evening when he dropped them off, he stood in the doorway and wept. "I want to be able to help my kids with their homework and tuck them into bed at night," he begged. As their father cried, Carise and Micael looked on in horror, breaking down in tears, begging me to let him return. Jason sat on the couch staring at the ceiling and talking to himself, his seven-year-old's brain not able to process the shock of watching his family fall apart before his eyes.

I told David he had to leave, and I shut the door. Carise and Micael ran to the picture window and watched their father drive away, tears running down their cheeks as they pressed their heads against the glass. I worried about the way such trauma would affect the kids, but my decision seemed justified several months later when David showed up at the door again. This time he burst in, saying,

"I'll do whatever it takes to reconcile. And to prove my sincerity, I've decided to confess a grave sin. Several months ago I picked up a prostitute in Seattle."

"A prostitute?" I said, counting backward on a mental calendar to the last time we'd had sex.

"Don't worry; she just gave me a blow job," he said, as though they'd spent the evening discussing the beatitudes. "See? If I'm willing to be honest about that, you *know* that I'll be truthful about everything from now on, and we can start over, from scratch — erase the slate clean."

To this day I can't understand why David thought that such a confession would save our marriage. Maybe he knew that his visit to First Avenue wouldn't technically give me biblical grounds (as Susan argued) to end our marriage: penetration had not occurred.

"I'm filing for divorce," I told him.

It was as if an invisible club had come out of the air and smacked David in the temple. He staggered back, caught himself on the kitchen counter, then steadied himself against it before plunging forward across the table at me in a rage. "You can't divorce me. I'll kill you first!" I grabbed a chair and held it up between us. This simple act of self-defense stopped him, and he stood motionless for a few seconds; then, releasing the air from his insides like a deflated balloon, he began to cry, propping himself up on the table. It seemed like an eternity before he turned and walked out of the house, leaving the door open behind him.

A few days later I filed for divorce. When I assured David that I would not ask him to pay the legally mandated child support, he agreed without contest. Although I eagerly anticipated the exodus from my marriage, long past caring what the Bible or my Christian friends said about it, when I grabbed up the divorce decree, my heart sank. Even though I scrawled my signature across it like a jubilant ex-con signing her parole forms, I wept the entire rest of the day. The distance between the heart and the mind is often an unbridgeable chasm. I was hit by the stark reality that I had failed at my marriage and now faced the prospect of raising my kids in a broken home. A great sense of shame and deep sadness overtook me; I felt buried alive under the weight of a thousand lost dreams.

After that David began directing his anger in even more un-predictable ways. One night, in a drunken stupor, he sneaked into Dan's church through an unlocked window in the nursery and spray-painted the white sanctuary walls with sexually graphic draw-ings, alongside quotes from Christian theologian Tony Campolo and lyrics from Pink Floyd, scrawled out in ancient Hebrew and Greek. The police called in David, their major suspect in the crime, for questioning — there was a small suspect pool, considering how few people were fluent in both ancient Hebrew and Greek. He con-fessed to the vandalism, and the state sentenced him to several days in jail, community service, repayment to the church of six thousand dollars in damages, and required that he undergo a psychological evaluation.

Dan contemplated contacting David to talk with him but de-cided against it. His church had decided to press charges against Da-vid, and it seemed foolish to try to reason with him. Besides, none of us were quite sure what David was capable of at this point. Over the next few months, he rarely communicated with the children and seemed to have lost interest in seeing them. I had no face-to-face interaction with him but had an eerie sense that he was only a heart-beat away, reckless, out of control, bent on hurting someone.

My fear seemed justified when I received a phone call from a distinguished-sounding woman. She introduced herself as Dr. Blaine, the mental health counselor who had just evaluated my ex-husband. "I've been a criminal psychiatrist for twenty-five years," she said, "and in all of that time I have never come across anyone as skilled at manipulation as your ex-husband. He arrived in my office, sat down, and took over."

I said, "Sounds like David."

"He started asking *me* questions, where I went to school, how long I had been a counselor — like he was the therapist and I was the patient. It was a real struggle to regain control of the interview."

"How did you do it?"

"Finally I said, 'Listen, David, *you* are the one being interviewed here. I'm not going to answer any more of your questions about my qualifications. Now it's time for *you* to answer *my* questions.'"

"Good move," I said.

There was a pause on the line, then Dr. Blaine asked, "How were you ever able to keep your bearings with this guy?"

"I'm not sure. But it's certainly nice to know that you figured him out — that he can't manipulate *everyone* he comes in contact with. Thank you so much for calling me."

Even after his psychological evaluation and finishing his jail time, David continued to grow more reckless. One night — it must have been about 2:00 a.m. — I woke suddenly, thinking I had heard someone step onto the deck outside my bedroom. Then the distinct sound of footsteps shot me straight up into a sweaty, dry-mouthed terror. The only thing dividing me from the intruder was a glass patio door. I could see him silhouetted there, hovering like a restless, menacing ghost, as I huddled up against the wall in the darkness, hardly daring to breathe. Then a fist, covered in a black glove, bashed against the window. The window shook, and I screamed, expecting it to shatter into a thousand pieces. Jumping out of bed, I ran upstairs to call the police. The intruder sneaked back to the highway and fled, but not before slitting my tires.

When the police arrived, I was still shaking all over. I told them I couldn't imagine who it might be, except a burglar.

"Do you have an angry boyfriend?"

"No"

"Ex-husband?"

"I can't believe he would be that crazy or mean," I said, and then hesitated. I thought about the recent vandalism of Dan's church. I told the police the story.

"It's him," the male officer said.

"I'm going to get a restraining order."

The detectives glanced at each other, and the male officer adjusted his belt of dangling armaments while the woman officer looked me in the eyes. "A restraining order will only make him mad. If he wants in, he'll bust the door down before we can get here." Her lips tightened, pulling the skin on her cheekbones taut, hardening her already grim face. "This is strictly off the record, okay?"

"Sure."

"I think you should get a gun. It's the only way a woman can have any real protection against a guy like this. Have you ever fired a gun before?"

"Yes," I said, remembering the long summer days when, as teenagers, Dan and I would drive out to the garbage dump to shoot tin cans.

Afraid of further repercussion from David, I told the officers that I was not going to press charges but that I would take their advice and get a gun.

I felt as though I were watching my life on television while someone else was turning the dial. The normal signals were becoming less

distinct, finally vanishing altogether and leaving in their place something from *The Outer Limits*. Before then, I would never have considered bringing a firearm into my house, but the next day, after my
neighbor helped me get new tires, I drove down Highway 99, pulling
off at a place I had driven past countless times. I stepped out onto
the bare, sun-baked clay and looked up at the sign: DUKE'S NEW
AND USED GUN HEADQUARTERS. Walking through the metal
door with steel bars crisscrossing the window, I smelled solvent and
gun oil. Squinting in the dim light, I saw an old man in the back lift
his eyes from his workbench and watch me for a few seconds before
rising and limping to the counter, fixing me with a gaze as steely as
the gunmetal that surrounded him.

"Can I see your handguns?" I asked. Without a word, he led me
to a long glass case. While I studied its contents, he studied me, as
if it were an official part of his background check.

"Ya know, if you can't pull the trigger, you're better off without
one."

I looked up at him, confusion in my eyes.

"The fellah might just use it on ya," he added, the sourpuss de-
meanor melting from his face.

"I can pull the trigger," I said, thinking, *Does this guy want to sell
me a gun, or does he want to go out of business?*

I bought a Beretta 92 and a package of nine-millimeter bullets.
I stored the gun under my mattress and the bullets in the closet. I
started to sleep at night again.

Before long, and out of the blue, David called the kids to tell
them he had stopped drinking and was back in the ministry. He had
landed a job at a Religious Science church in Seattle, where he was
teaching Hebrew and Christian theology. Now that he had an income, I contemplated trying to force him to pay some child support

but did not pursue the idea out of fear that he would become violent again. Instead of putting any energy into trying to get David to help out, I tried to focus my time on my studies. It wasn't difficult. I was devouring my classes at the community college the way an eight-year-old eats ice cream. Just reading the general catalog made me come alive with expectation, not only of the classes but also of the colorful people I knew I would meet there.

One quarter I stepped into an art history class and sat beside a beautiful blond who looked about my age, thirty-three. She wore a loose tan cardigan with an abstract-patterned silk scarf wrapped around her long neck, and a tight leather skirt inching up her slender thighs. Her generous mouth flashed a wide grin when I sat down next to her. If I could read her mind, she was saying, "I bet we're the oldest people in this room." Instead she cocked her head toward me and whispered, "Name's Dani, what's yours?"

The professor started her lecture before I could answer. "I've just received my PhD in art history, and I intend to teach you every-thing I know this quarter," she said with a grin. By the end of the hour I believed her. She flew through the history of ancient hiero-glyphic art while Dani and I feverishly scribbled notes. As soon as class ended and we were headed out of the room, Dani fished a pack of Marlboros and a Zippo lighter out of the bottom pocket of her sweater and had a cigarette in her mouth before we hit the door. By the time we were in the sunlight, she was inhaling long and easy. She closed her Zippo with a metallic smack, switched the cigarette to her left hand, and held out her right for a shake. "Your name?" she asked.

"Carlene. Great class, huh?"

"The best, I lo-o-o-ove art history," she said, exhaling smoke straight up toward the clouds, "but if we're going to pass that baby, I suggest we break a little sweat, you and me — study together is what I'm saying."

"Sure, I'd love to."

The next morning, and every school morning thereafter, we met in the student union building to quiz each other about Italian baroque architecture or eighteenth-century neoclassic romanticism. I found out that Dani was very bright. While I had to rely on memory crutches for the hundreds of details that we needed to remember, Dani's steel-trap mind never hesitated. When asked about Gustave Courbet's realism, she'd deliver an elegant treatise describing the dark underpainting, heavy chiaroscuro, and the pivotal significance of his work in nineteenth-century France. I hated to admit it to myself, but I had sorely underestimated Dani's intelligence when I first met her. Plenty in life was turning out to be the opposite of the way it seemed.

Then one morning Dani said, "So where do you work?"

"I wait tables at the Space Needle."

"Whew, impressive phallic symbol, huh?" She grinned.

"Yes." I smiled back, never having thought of it quite that way.

"I'm in the same business," she said.

"Phallic symbols?" I kidded.

She burst out laughing and said, "As a matter of fact, yes, phallic symbols and waiting tables. I work at Doug's."

Doug's was one of those establishments without windows, a long brick facade lined with flashing hot-pink enticements — "All Nude, All Night, Beautiful Busty Babes" — in twenty-four-hour neon.

"You know," she went on, "seeing as you have kids to support like me, I have a suggestion. Why don't you start working with me? I swear you could make twice as much in half the time. Give you more time to study and be with your little ones."

"So how does exotic dancing work?" I said, a little stunned but not wanting to hurt Dani's feelings.

"It's really not all that bad. You just have to remember a few things. You can dance as close to the clients as you want, but you can't touch them." Then she whispered, "Of course, that's not *always* possible. And a five-hour shift is such a great workout that you don't even have to have a gym membership to keep in shape. Sure, some of the guys are one bubble off level, but most are just regular Joes wanting a good time."

"It sounds great, but I really do love working at the Space Needle," I said, taken a bit off guard by our conversation, though certainly not blaming Dani's vocation for David's sexual addiction problems.

In David's case — and I thought probably Jimmy Swaggart's as well — the question was not one of sexual gratification as much as control. For sometime afterward, I thought about Dani and Fundamentalism and began toying with the idea that maybe conservative Christianity's "biblical" view of women was actually a contributing factor to pornography, strip clubs, and the objectification of females. Could it be that the church's literal interpretation of Genesis encouraged men to treat women with less respect and think of them only as a means of sexual fulfillment? Maybe there was some correlation. It seemed clear that our cherished Judeo-Christian heritage had done much to keep women in subjugation for nearly four thousand years. For some strange reason, my conversation with Dani made me decide to reexamine the Adam and Eve story and see what I might find.

Eleven

The Goddess versus the Word of God

THAT SUMMER, WHEN MY class schedule light-
ened, I hauled archeology and ancient history books
home by the armload, jumping into bed and fan-
ning them out around me, reading late into the night until I couldn't
keep my eyes open. As I read, I found that Mr. Peterson was right.
Technological advances of the twentieth century had enabled archeologists to glean troves of vital information about the ancient world.
Even as far back as 6000 BC, civilizations across the Mesopotamian
Fertile Crescent had created complex social organizations involv-
ing craft specialization, a variety of agricultural crops, advanced
pottery, and copper metallurgy. These ancient peoples constructed
elaborate art centers that showcased paintings, plaster reliefs, and
stone sculptures. They crafted seagoing vessels that expanded trade
and communication throughout the area.

Amid the rubble of these archeological digs, scholars also discovered a proliferation of carved female figurines. Interpreting
the meaning of these feminine carvings had thrown the academic
community into a heated debate. Some felt that because no writing
existed to explain this prehistoric art, its meaning could not be determined. Others believed that these female carvings held great significance to ancient civilizations, proving that early societies possessed
not only a sophisticated social structure but advanced religious rites

as well, which centered on a female deity. *The Chalice and the Blade* by Riane Eisler had been on the *New York Times* best-seller list for almost a year; in it, the author claimed that these figurines and the sites where they were found were tributes to a goddess.

Dr. Eisler and other archeologists like Marija Gimbutas, Sir Arthur Evans, and James Mellaart argued that the prehistoric world was filled with symbols representing her divinity. The pillar monument, or *asherah,* was one, often depicted as a fig tree — a place where worshippers paid tribute to the goddess Astarte. Researchers had found these stone pillars in homes and religious sanctuaries in such far-flung places as Babylon, Egypt, Crete, and Greece. The snake also epitomized the goddess, her divine wisdom and spiritual rejuvenation embodied as the great and wise winding serpent. The caduceus, the twin snakes entwined around the physician's medical staff, are a remnant of this symbol of wisdom.

These scholars pointed to a third symbol unique to these goddess worshippers: their celebration of sexual union. For millennia in Sumer, Babylon, and Canaan, priestesses had lived within temple complexes, residing there to have sexual intercourse with those coming to pay homage to the Great Mother — a sacred religious rite representing union with her life-giving energy. Early Bronze Age cultures deemed these rites a commemoration of love and procreation — sacraments that connected humanity to the fundamental rhythms of life. The notion that such ceremonies held negative ethical implications did not occur to such ancient people, who had not yet developed systems of sexual morality. Procreation represented part of the divine movement of eternal power, and when humans mingled with the energy of the Great Mother, they came away rejuvenated.

I spent a lot of time on the beach of Lake Washington that summer, reading these fascinating academic and social interpretations of ancient history. The kids and I would throw our wide-striped towels in the back of my rusting green Plymouth, jam the cooler with sandwiches and soda, and head for the shore. Micael and Jason always raced to the beach, laughing and nudging each other as they ran, he diving straight into the brisk water, she wading in right behind him. I watched them splashing each other and realized that they were happier and more relaxed lately. They seemed to be stabilizing since the initial shock of the divorce. Carise stayed with me, calm and peaceful as ever as we chatted quietly and made our way down to the beach behind them. I would fix my eyes on the glistening, deep blue water, utterly calm and so unlike the churning Puget Sound only five miles to the west of us. Unfolding our towels at the water's edge, we would sit, Carise finding the dog-eared page in her current *Baby-Sitters Club* book, and I digging my toes into the wet sand and watching the red nails vanish and reappear. Then I would put on my sunglasses, tinting the sky dark, and return to the ancient world of the goddess.

I read that summer about the replacement of the goddess religion, which Eisler claimed had happened around 5000 BC when tribes of nomadic herdsmen swooped down from the north and west, invading the indigenous people who had lived in the Fertile Crescent for thousands of years. One of these conquering tribes was the ancient Hebrews. Along with their bronze weapons of destruction, these marauders also brought a new form of religion, introducing a young warrior or, in the Hebrew case, a supreme father god.

Then a fascinating aspect of the story emerged, making me sit straight up on the beach, pull my sunglasses off, and stare out onto the water. Once victorious, Eisler claimed, the priests of the invaders began to rewrite the creation myths of the conquered peoples in order to solidify their own position as the new ruling authority. For instance, when the Assyrians overthrew Babylon and brought their god Ashur with them, Assyrian priests took old Babylonian tablets and recopied them, substituting the name of their own god for that of Marduk, the Babylonian god. The work wasn't carefully executed, however, and in some places Marduk's name remained.

And if the conquerors didn't out-and-out rename a deity, they forced it to share power with their god. Eisler and Gimbutas argue that the archeological record reveals that instead of replacing the goddess, the triumphant invaders incorporated her into their own stories. Gods and goddesses merged their power: the Greek storm god, Taru, and the sun goddess, Arinna; Zeus and Hera; the Canaanite Baal and Astarte. They wrote that this sort of "remything" was customary whenever a victorious nation wanted to consolidate its control — marry their god to your goddess. There was one notable exception during this historical period: the Hebrew deity Yahweh, who said, "You shall have no other gods before me."

I watched Micael and Jason's horseplay in the water, pondering what I had just read, until the sun sank below the giant cedars and hemlocks behind me. I dropped my book onto the sand and lay back into the waning heat, pressing my fingertips into my forehead as the immense implications raced through my brain, darting and dancing like overheated molecules. I was still thinking about this ancient remything when I stepped up the porch stairs and into the house that evening, taking off my sandals and walking barefoot across the soft carpet and upstairs into the bathroom. I undressed, turned on the shower, and stepped in.

So what if Genesis three is simply a remything event? I thought. In the Old Testament the serpent (a prophetic and oracular symbol of the goddess) cunningly advises Eve to disobey the male god

Yahweh. Eve takes counsel from the snake and is tricked into believing that she will receive divine knowledge — precisely the purpose of the goddess rites in Babylon, Egypt, Crete, Canaan, and Greece. Eve takes the fruit from the tree — another representation of the goddess Astarte's life-giving sustenance. Once the transgression occurs, Adam and Eve cover their nakedness with fig tree leaves, gaining an understanding of sexual pleasure and procreation — possibly a parallel with the celebration of the sexual act performed in the goddess temples. After the snake enlightens the couple, Yahweh curses both the snake and the couple. He goes on to afflict Eve with pain in childbearing and subjects her to the rule of man.

I stepped out of the shower and went back downstairs in my bathrobe, leaving wet footprints on the carpeted steps. I made my way to the living room and sat on the couch, folding one leg under me and letting the other foot brush the floor. I thought maybe that was why Yahweh told the Hebrews to annihilate the people of the land: to eliminate the female threat found in the goddess worshippers. In so doing, Yahweh (or his priests) had been quite successful in establishing a patriarchal system that ruled without rivals.

I knew that there was much academic controversy concerning this prehistoric time from which no written record remained. Who could be sure about the history of the goddess? Yet as I explored the social climate of the ancient world that summer, I began to realize one thing was very clear: in all the years that I had studied the Old Testament, I had never understood the plight of its women. Whereas in the goddess worshipping societies, archeologists claimed that females held equal power with men, in Hebrew society their value was based primarily on their ability to produce offspring. I reconsidered the life of women in ancient Jewish society and discovered a laundry list of exploitation: If she was not a virgin when

she was married, she was stoned. If a man raped her, she was forced
to marry him; her rapist's only obligation was to give the girl's father
a proper wedding gift and not divorce her. If she was unfortunate
enough to be engaged to another man during her rape, she was to
be stoned along with her rapist because the crime was considered an
affront to the man who owned her (her betrothed) and an offense
against the girl's father, robbing him of the money he would have
received upon her marriage. Ancient Hebrew women, it seemed, had
almost no rights.

One summer evening, after hours of reading, I felt angry and
exhausted, my thoughts beginning to bunch up in a corner of my
mind. I needed some air, so I closed my book, threw on my overcoat, and began walking up the street while a fine mist covered my
face. I pulled my jacket tighter around my chest as voices flooded
my memory: poor Lydia, calling out from under her football helmet
hairdo years ago at women's Bible study, "Peter claims it's God will
that I dress the way he likes — even wear my hair the way he wants
it." And the expert preacher's wife admonishing us at the Black Lake
pastors' retreat, "It is essential that you keep a professional distance
from the other women of the congregation." "Every woman who
enters a sanctuary should have a hat on — and refrain from speaking as well," shouted the paunchy professor from Western Baptist
Seminary. They all tumbled through my mind, frame by frame,
memories overlapping one another, propelling the past into the present. By the time I got back to the house, the sky had turned a vivid
electric green, and rain pounded against the windows. I ran inside
and pulled off my soggy overcoat. I needed to discuss what I had
been studying with someone I respected, someone in the Christian
movement who was both intelligent and thoughtful. My brother
immediately came to mind.

That holiday season I finally got my chance. The whole family was scheduled to meet at the ranch in Montana. The kids and I arrived late the evening before Thanksgiving, to a house warm and fragrant with smells imprinted on us long ago. Carise often said as we drove through eastern Washington, "I love it at Grandma's; it smells so warm and safe there." My mother stood curved over her cooking pot, giving a dash of this or that to the beef stew she always made for our arrival, as logs of pine and fir crackled in the stone fireplace. Boots lay piled in the corner as they had for as long as I could remember: cowboy boots with the toes curled up like croissants, rubber boots for winter, leather work boots for summer, black galoshes. I closed my eyes and breathed in the aroma of being home, feeling protected and seeing my children run to throw their arms around their grandparents. I hugged my brother and looked at his face, grown older since his years at Bible college. Gray hair now flecked his temples, thinning in the same pattern as the men on our mom's side, but his expression still showed that farm boy virtue, strong and sincere. I knew he worried that I no longer attended church, but I took comfort in the knowledge that he didn't know how far my faith had fallen.

I waited a couple of days into the holiday, and then one afternoon when we were alone in the living room, I said, "Dan, did you know that the Old Testament demands that a woman be killed as punishment for being raped?"

"What do you mean?"

I found Mom's Bible, opened it to Deuteronomy 22, and handed it to him. "Read this passage."

As he read the chapter, his face blotched and his expression dropped as he came to the last verse. I could see his eyes dart back to the beginning of the chapter and slowly reread the passage. After moment of silence, he shook his head and said, "I'm not sure what's going on here. I'd have to study these verses more."

"There are plenty of passages like this one in the Old Testament, Dan — passages that I've never really noticed before. I've been rereading it, and it's getting harder for me to believe that its teachings can be applied to the modern world. I'm starting to suspect that it's simply a document priests wrote to preserve their power. The New Testament seems just as bad. The apostle Paul was a sexist."

"That's a misinterpretation of Paul," Dan said, his brow creasing.

"How about in the Letter to Timothy, where he says that if a woman comes into a church without a hat, her head should be shaved like a prostitute's? Or that a woman can't teach a man? And she shouldn't even *speak* in church; if she has a question, she should wait until she gets home to ask her husband. Sounds pretty sexist to me."

"Paul is just illuminating God's twofold truth," Dan said, his voice still calm. "While on earth, wives must submit to the guidance of their husbands. But once they die and enter heaven, the chain of command is eliminated. God views women as morally equal with men, but there must be a leader in any organization, so He simply placed man in that position."

"The Bible never gives women the same moral footing as men," I said. "In Corinthians, Paul says that women are to serve men because they weren't even created in the image of God, but in the image of man. You know the rib thing — that doesn't sound like equality to me."

Mom and several of the grandkids looked up from their pinochle game in the next room, so Dan and I lowered our voices. He said, "I'll send you Gilbert Bilezikian's book *Beyond Sex Roles*. It's supposed to be a good new book from an open-minded evangelical on the roles of men and women in the church. Let's both read it, and we'll get together and discuss this some more."

Once I was home the next week, the book arrived in the mail. In it Bilezikian, a teacher at Wheaton College, attempts the same sleight of hand that I had come to expect from Christians on the subject. Bilezikian claims that although women aren't made in the image of God, they possess a special position that mirrors the fullness of human splendor. "In the presence of God and the angels, she possesses the authority to reflect the glory of unmingled human personhood."

"Unmingled human personhood," I thought. *What a crock!* It sounded like the line I gave my kids about raw carrots: "They're just like orange Popsicles." They fell for that story until they were about four. Then, in an even more blatant attempt to sanitize Paul, Bilezikian simply throws 1 Corinthians 14:34 – 35 out of the Bible — the passage where Paul teaches that women must remain silent in the church because of Eve's fall into sin in Genesis. "This appeal to the Old Testament constitutes in itself sufficient proof that Paul is not the author of this statement," he declares.

When we met at the ranch again that Christmas, Dan and I went for a walk, our boots crackling down the road in the bone numbing chill. The whole valley was frozen stiff, granular ice coating the bare black limbs of the poplar trees, the strands of frosted barbed wire glimmering on the fence bordering the road.

"So when are you going to move back here so you can enjoy this weather?" Dan joked.

"Right after you do," I said.

We trudged down the road in silence for a while. "Hey, thanks for the Bilezikian book."

"Sure. What did you think?"

"You know, my biggest objection was when Bilezikian eliminated First Corinthians from the Bible because he thinks it's incon-
sistent with Paul's other teachings. That kind of selective exegesis
represents the inconsistency rampant in conservative religion. Fundamentalists insist that every word of the Bible is breathed by God
and that it must be interpreted literally — until they come to a passage they don't like. Then they concoct an explanation that con-
tradicts the original meaning, ignore the verse, or simply throw it
out."

"I think you are wrong," Dan replied. "Bilezikian is doing what
every believer of God's Word must do: correctly applying the Bible
to the modern age."

"Christians can't have it both ways. You can't insist that every
line of the Bible is God's inerrant Word, then ignore passages that
don't fit your program."

"All Scripture is inspired by God, and we are expected to obey
every word."

"Christians never obey every word, or even try to. Instead they
use the Bible as a baseball bat. They comb through it, pick out the
condemnations that fit their agenda, then clobber people over the
head with them and ignore the rest of the book."

I could tell that Dan was horrified at what I was saying. Pain
registered on his face as his limbs hung heavy in the cold. I knew
what he was thinking: not only had he lost his best friend, David,
in a nihilistic freefall, but now his sister was abandoning the faith as
well — the faith he believed in so strongly that he'd dedicated his life
to it. I felt sad for Dan, but it was as though something strange had
overtaken me — like the sensation you get when you first go skiing.
You expect you'll have some trouble learning to move on skiis, but

immediately you learn that getting moving isn't the problem — it's stopping.

"Christians want to hold society hostage to certain verses," I recklessly went on. "They attack the gay community using Levitical law, but they ignore Deuteronomy 21, which requires that gluttons be stoned. Like Jerry Falwell, for instance — the guy spews out judgments right and left, but he's a hundred pounds overweight."

By that time we were back on the front porch, stamping the frost off our feet. The door opened, and a flood of children burst out, followed by their limping grandfather. Dan and I gave each other a silent look of truce and started talking about the price of beef futures on Wall Street. I thought about how much I loved my brother. He was a good man, full of kindness and integrity, a conservative minister living the same life that he preached others should live. I respected him for his beliefs, but I could no longer live them myself.

After we got inside, Dan and I poured ourselves coffee, blowing on it to force the steaming heat back onto our red noses. "Oh, you'll never guess who called the other day and asked for your new phone number," he said. "Jean. She and Doug are back from the mission field — some sort of unplanned furlough. She asked for your new number, and I'm sure you'll be hearing from her." He smiled.

Jean did call the next week, and we agreed to meet at a Denny's restaurant halfway between us. Although we had corresponded faithfully over the years, I had never been honest about what was happening between David and me; the notion of putting my spiritual collapse on paper, to Jean of all people, always seemed overwhelming. Now I would have to come clean. As I drove toward the restaurant, I wondered what Jean would say about my divorce from David. She never was one to compromise her Christian ideals. And from her letters over the decade, there was no evidence that she had tempered her convictions. Her, and Doug's, service in the remote Mexican village had been tough. They had no running water or electricity, living in such unsanitary conditions that their children were often infested with a nasty tapeworm. In order to kill the tapeworm, she was forced to give her children medicine so toxic, it couldn't be purchased in the United States, because the FDA had banned it as a potential carcinogen. On the other hand, if they withheld it, the tapeworm could kill the child. They wrestled with the dilemma but always ended up administering the dangerous drug, because leaving the mission field was out of the question. As always, Jean had a burning assurance that her calling was to save "native" souls for Christ.

When we met at Denny's for lunch, Jean's appearance startled me. She looked nothing like the pretty young woman who had left for Mexico years before. Her once peach colored skin and auburn hair had been bleached to a pale orange in the tropical heat, her pearl white teeth were gray from lack of dental care, and her figure, once lithe and athletic, was rail thin and exhausted looking. As her story unraveled, I understood why. "It was so weird," she said, keeping her eyes on the cup of tea she stirred in front of her. "One day I found a sore on my genitals. I took the long trip into Mexico City to visit a doctor, and after my examination he told me I had syphilis."

I sat frozen in stunned silence.

"It took Doug a while, but he finally confessed that on his monthly trips to Mexico City to get supplies he had been visiting prostitutes."

Once my mind thawed, I blurted out, "Thank God this isn't any worse than a curable VD, Jean. You have to get out of this marriage!"

"But Doug has repented," she said. "He's promised he'll never do such a foolish thing again."

"*Jesus Christ,* Jean! David told me the same thing about his addiction. You can't take the chance. You can't go back to Mexico."

Jean's eyes widened, showing life for the first time that day. She was more concerned with my taking the Lord's name in vain than with her own potential exposure to the AIDS virus.

"I've decided to follow the Bible and not my own selfish yearnings. Don't you remember what God promises us in Proverbs?" she said, her voice rising till she sounded like some wild-eyed television preacher. " 'Those who put their trust in the Lord shall be safe'— Jesus will protect me."

And that was it, her final stand, no matter how hard I argued. I felt frantic. I had known Jean for a long time, since my first tentative days in Bible college, when she took me under her wing and transfused her own great religious convictions through my blood. Now I wanted to instill some of my own disbelief and mutiny into her soul. But the space around us had changed; we had both endured personal storms, but we had dealt with them in radically different ways. I had taken shelter from religious life; Jean was determined to soldier on, stiffening her face into the coming gale. A few weeks later, she and Doug returned to Mexico, leaving me to wonder if Jesus, as when he defied the laws of nature and raised Jairus's daughter from the dead, would perform the miracle my friend counted on. I thought about the gullible, greedy innocence of Jean and me as we started out in college. It was like believing letters that come in the mail telling you that you have won a free Ford Escort or a vacation for two in glorious Waikiki. Jean and I had fallen for the cruel hoax, a shoddy piece of scam artistry, so obvious now in my flawless hindsight. It had altered our lives forever.

My cynicism continued to spiral upward when I took a political

science class that semester and began to study the teachings of the
Founding Fathers concerning the separation of church and state — a
feeling that was cemented at a party I attended at Robert and Susan's.
The house and yard were full of people. Some of them were old
friends from Calvary Baptist whom I hadn't seen for ages. I walked
into the backyard and looked at the sea of bronzed bodies, surrounded by a circle of torches whose flames stretched out in the
breeze. Suntanned faces came toward me, white teeth flashing in
the dark: "Carlene, we haven't seen you in forever." The hair on the
back of my neck was wet with nervousness, giving me a little chill,
causing a shiver to slip down my limbs. Hal waved at me with a gin
and tonic in his hand, docile as a frog. "We never see David anymore. It's very sad." I moved on, saying hellos here and there. Over at
the drinks table, Susan was talking, one hand holding a martini, the
other moving rapidly. Susan was a gracious hostess, and she loved a
good party. Her satin dress, the same red as her lipstick, clung to her
breasts, making her look like one of those women on the cover of a
magazine dedicated to country living.

Everyone in the crowd seemed quite contented, eating and
drinking and surveying one another's spouses — everyone, that is, except Robert. He had emerged from the house and stood on the deck
looking irritated and a little tipsy, his gaze roving the crowd — hunt-
er's eyes. Once a fan of James Dobson, Robert had now become an
avid Rush Limbaugh devotee, listening to the man's talk show every
day, then whipping himself into a rage over the "femi-Nazis," the
liberal media, or Bill Clinton's complete lack of morals in the White
House. According to Susan, Robert's demand for control at home
had also escalated that year; any show of independence from her was
interpreted as a lack of submission and thus as disobedience to God.
His intimidation had gotten so bad that during one argument in

their bedroom, Robert went to the gun cabinet, pulled out his rifle, and laid it on the bed next to her. Susan told me that my lifestyle had also alarmed Robert — he was concerned that I didn't attend church any longer and hadn't dated anyone since my divorce from David. It all made him wonder if, at the deep-down core of things, I wasn't a lesbian.

Robert spotted me and stumbled across the deck, careening off lawn furniture like a pinball. "So how's our little Clinton lover tonight?" he said. "You know, Rush Limbaugh was saying the other day that our great Mr. Clinton is addicted to prescription painkillers. Clinton admits to it — from some kind of back injury, he claims. What kind of a commander in chief is that for our great nation?"

"Jeez, Robert, I missed that particular broadcast," I said.

"We have to get these amoral morons out of the White House. Rush has called this country back to God. It's time we bring the Lord back into government and honor the faith of our forefathers!"

"The Founding Fathers were Deists, not Christians, Robert, and they were adamantly opposed to mixing religion with government. Haven't you ever heard about the separation of church and state?"

"The words 'separation of church and state' aren't even *in* the Constitution," he barked back gleefully, pulling a line directly from a ditto-head script.

"I didn't say they were, but the Constitutional Congress built this country on the concept of separation, one that has been upheld in every court decision since the Constitution was formed. Maybe you should read the writings of our forefathers instead of listening to Rush Limbaugh so much."

Robert's eyes narrowed, and he smiled with his teeth bared. How dare I question his authority under his own tiki lamps? Seeing Robert headed toward me, Susan had already crossed the lawn with a plate of appetizers and was now holding it between us, as if her stuffed mushroom recipe might protect me from her husband.

"Take a mushroom, Robert," Susan whispered, "and calm down."

In that moment, I realized how much my worldview had changed — from the terrain of unblemished belief to faith's own boneyard. The Fundamentalist movement now seemed preposterous to me. It was the early 1990s, and Limbaugh (and the Religious Right) were frantically trying to save this country from the moral morass of the liberals, using the argument that Thomas Jefferson and his colleagues had intended Christianity to be an arm of the state, and the United States a Christian utopia. This distortion of history was now accepted truth in the expanding ranks of conservative religion. Moral Majority preachers like Pat Robertson were proclaiming from the pulpit, "Christians founded this nation, they built this nation, and for three hundred years they governed this nation. We can govern it again!"

I looked at Robert, wanting to bounce his tipsy head off the deck. I was tempted to ask him if he knew that Thomas Jefferson had once said that there wasn't one redeeming feature in the American superstition of Christianity. Or that the atheist John Adams said that in the best of all possible worlds there would be no religion. I longed to inform the homophobic, chauvinistic duck's butt that James Madison believed that religion had *never* been a guardian of the liberties of the people and that the worst form of government existed when religion and politics merged. But I could see Susan humming nervously the way Edith Bunker used to when Archie was about to do something rash, so I swallowed the words back into my throat.

It seemed to me that Robert — and the entire Moral Majority movement, for that matter — was confusing the Founding Fathers with the Puritans. The Puritans, who arrived a century and a half before the Constitution, had sought religious freedom and fled spiritual persecution in Europe. However, once in America, they were perfectly contented to establish their own brand of theocracy, denying such liberty to anyone else. They levied taxes to support their religion and jailed those who refused to pay. The Puritans made sure that only members of the state sanctioned congregationalist church could vote. They compensated ministers from government coffers. Their civil leaders enforced Fundamentalist doctrines and persecuted Catholics, Quakers, and other minorities, even executing innocent "witches" in Massachusetts.

Protecting Americans against this kind of religious oppression was exactly what the Founding Fathers set out to do over a century later. Jefferson insisted that the Bill of Rights was to protect the "the infidel of any denomination." He and his Constitutional Convention colleagues realized that most wars, conquests, and tyrannies were a result of the alliance of religion and state (as we have seen today in Northern Ireland, across the Islamic world, in the Balkans and the Sudan). The Founding Fathers believed that true religious freedom would result from pluralism, and so they set out to create a framework for the revolutionary concept that we call modern democracy: the secular state.

Instead of saying what I wanted to say that night, I smiled at Susan and took another stuffed mushroom while mosquitoes dive-bombed my shoulders. From around me, the sounds of laughter, conversation, and music all blended in a murmur that was like some sort of undercurrent I didn't care to be pulled into. I nursed my gin and tonic for a while and then sneaked past the crowd, whispering to myself that I would never return — a promise I would forever keep. Out on the freeway the night was dark — no moon, no stars, the sky locked up tight with a humid fog sweeping in from the Pacific. I thought about Robert and Fundamentalism and America and was glad that "amoral" Bill Clinton kept religion out of politics. God forbid that we should get a Fundamentalist in the White House someday.

It was only a few weeks later that I answered the phone and heard Susan on the other end of a hissing line, her voice frail. "I'm outside on my cell," she said, sounding as if she were calling from halfway around the world. "I'm so freaked-out," she whispered. "I was cleaning the back closet last weekend and discovered a huge box of hard-core porn. After hours of denying it, Robert finally admitted that they were his. And they aren't just *Playboy*s," she went on, "but really violent stuff—women submitted to unbelievably degrading acts." As I hung up the phone, I wondered what Robert might have to say about the amoral state of America now that Susan had discovered his secret.

Twelve

The Dark Night of the Soul

I STARTED TO THINK that Karl Marx had been right about religion being the opiate of the masses. No, I thought, it was worse than any deadly drug. It was like floodwaters roaring into the brain, spilling onto the synapses, short-circuiting electrochemical signals everywhere; religion set up a new household; it rearranged the furniture, pushing the cerebrum to the corner, cramping the hypothalamus, reshuffling common sense in the basal ganglia, jumbling all logic into madness. The best thing to do was to run in the opposite direction of the horrible flood of any organized creed — sprint for high ground and never look back.

I knew my cynicism would only add more confusion to my kids' lives, so I never mentioned in their presence how I felt about religion. I knew that coming to grips with the divorce was difficult enough for them, so I found a good counselor for us to see each week.

"I feel like I should help Dad more — he seems so sad, and sometimes I think things are my fault," Carise said during one session.

"Carise, there is *nothing* you could have done to stop this divorce," Dr. Hines replied. "The issue is purely between your dad and mom. Do you kids understand that?"

Perched on the counselor's brown velour couch, they looked like little birds on a fence. Carise and Micael nodded, and Jason fiddled with the round glass paperweight on the coffee table.

"Dad needs to keep a job so he can buy a car and get to work on time. That's not your fault, Carise," Micael told her sister.

Jason fumbled the paperweight, and it rolled across the floor.

"What do you think, Jason?"

"I dunno," Jason said, crawling under the table to retrieve the glass dome.

I did take comfort in the fact that even in the midst of her anxiety, Carise was still getting good grades, playing flute in the school band, singing in the school choir, and constantly surrounded by a gaggle of happy girlfriends. Micael, as well, seemed on solid ground, starring in the school play, staying on the honor roll, and becoming the crown champion of her fifth-grade *Jeopardy* tournament. I worried most about Jason. His emotions seemed bound up in irons, and it was hard to get him to talk about anything. His grades were starting to fail, and his third-grade teacher kept calling to report that he was being disruptive in class. Besides counseling (and grounding), the only way I thought to help him was to encourage him to participate in athletics. So when I wasn't working or in class, I darted from Jason's soccer and Little League games to the girls' school performances. As I stayed active in their lives, I felt our hearts knitting together with an enduring bond — or maybe we were just clinging to each other for survival.

In order to weather the upheaval of a broken home, I knew it would be important for us to remain close, so when it came time for me to transfer to the University of Washington, I knew that something had to change. I couldn't remain involved in the kids' activities, work full-time, and earn a GPA good enough to qualify for graduate school, which I now wanted to try for. David was unemployed, not even teaching at the Religious Science church anymore, so there was no hope of receiving financial help from him. My only other possible means of income was public assistance. I decided to quit work, even though it meant losing touch with my friends at the Space Needle, and apply for welfare. So in the winter of 1992, I would take a journey into what felt like a figment of Dante's imagination.

I stepped from the freezing rain into the large waiting room overcrowded with empty and confused faces. It was as if having lost your way was a requirement for admission. The place reeked of damp, musty clothing long overdue for a wash. Everyone sat bundled up, huffing, coughing, glassy-eyed from the wet chill. A young mother gazed straight ahead, her expression distant, as if her consciousness were receding like a balloon swept up into the sky. Her children, racing around her chair, crashed into her limbs, eliciting no response. A man whose hands were shaking pulled at his greasy blond hair, which stood straight up off his head like jute rope, rough-edged and matted. He stared at me blankly, his face as impossible to read as a headstone faded by decades of storm, while the overpowering smell of whiskey rose off him. No one engaged in conversation but instead stayed huddled inside their threadbare coats, sheepish and apologetic — I guessed that the welfare office was no place for small talk.

As I approached the front desk, the well-nourished receptionist kept her eyes focused on her document, shoved the sign-in sheet toward me, and said, "If you brought all of your children's birth certificates and Social Security cards, then sit down — your name will be called." I looked up and read the sign hanging above her desk: DEPARTMENT OF HEALTH AND HUMAN SERVICES, but from the feeling of the place, I imagined that ABANDON ALL HOPE YE WHO ENTER HERE would have been more fitting.

Every seat was taken, so I leaned against the wall and blew warm breath into my hands, closing my eyes, silent, buried in my own memories. I began to imagine I was a girl again, lying in the meadow behind our farmhouse on a baking August afternoon, watching the breeze transform the Montana sky. Earth and grass encircled me in a womb of warmth and safety, smelling of fresh alfalfa. The vast prairie stretched before me in miles of gentle rise and fall as the wind swirled the sky into dancing circles of white and blue. If I kept perfectly still, I could follow its movement: the huge Montana sky changing like the Pacific Ocean.

"Carlene Brant, your caseworker will see you," a voice boomed over the loudspeaker, startling me back into the dreary present. The thud of my name sounded like a dull ax hitting green wood: blunt, dead. I rushed toward the door to avoid another announcement of it.

She was standing in the office doorway in front of me, but I could tell by her eyes that she was secluded behind a brick wall, detached and anonymous, like a checker with cold hands who dispatches your change in the market. "I'm Doris, your caseworker," she said impatiently, without smiling. I walked into her office: government posters pasted above a stainless steel desk polished to an antiseptic sheen. The glaring green table lamp amplified the set lines in her jaw. She stared at me over the rim of her half glasses, scrutinizing my appearance like a suspicious parole officer. Once she'd taken her fill, she looked down without a word. As she began reviewing my application, the creases in her eyebrows burrowed deeper. I had a gnawing feeling that she didn't like me. *Relax,* I told myself. I was getting paranoid, mistrustful of everyone lately. Then Doris removed the fountain pen from its holder and, on a yellow legal pad, began scratching out notes. Finally she said without looking up, "It bugs me that they haven't changed the laws yet concerning student status. I believe your financial aid package should be counted as income."

In other words, my caseworker didn't think I should qualify for welfare. If my student aid were recognized as income, I would not be eligible for government help. "But most of the money I get is in loans that I'll have to pay back," I objected. Now Doris had a real reason to dislike me. She glanced up at me, rolling her eyes as though I were Pee-Wee Herman lecturing Pelé on the rules of soccer.

"Where do you shop for food?" she asked.

"Safeway."

"You know, you can get canned vegetables much cheaper at Dilly's. It's a warehouse in Everett that sells discount food in dented cans."

"Oh, I'll check it out," I lied.

"Clothes?"

"Nordstrom Rack."

"There's a Goodwill on Fifth and Olive. How about makeup?"

"Uh, makeup. Well, let's see, Bartell Drug."

"You must think this is degrading, but most recipients aren't as careful as they should be with state money," she said.

I breathed an internal sigh of relief. Doris had called me a recipient. I must be eligible for public assistance. I stumbled out of the interview, sweat damp on my forehead, and sat down to catch my breath next to a young mother with a toddler on her lap. I must have looked a mess, because she shattered the silence of the waiting room by saying, "That bad, huh?"

"God, it was like the Inquisition. Is it always this harrowing?"

"Oh yes, completely degrading. And let me give you some advice. During your reviews don't tell your caseworker anything you don't have to. One day I wanted to get *personal*" — the young mother rolled her eyes — "so I slipped and told her about my son's birthday party. She made me go back and fill in all the gifts as income. I had to write down everything and what it cost — all the socks, underwear, even the Lego set. It was totally humiliating."

From what I already knew about welfare, this small addition could easily have disqualified her and her son from receiving benefits. There isn't much leeway for extra revenue while on assistance, considering that if a family of two has a total income of over $350 in any particular month, they became ineligible.

I left the office as darkness was beginning to descend, washed by rain that had been falling gently but relentlessly for days. I drove through the hesitant light, the headlights of oncoming cars glaring into my eyes. I felt sad and thought about calling Susan to ask her if she would meet me for a drink, but decided that I didn't want to hear one more story about Robert's abuse or turn down another invitation to the new church they were now attending. As my car rattled down the freeway, suddenly an eighteen-wheeler shot past me and around the curve, its trailer shimmying wildly and sending a splash of water onto the windshield. My hands tightened around the wheel and the fear inside me felt like pond water hardening into ice. I would have to face alone whatever battles lay ahead.

And the clashes did continue. Even though I technically qualified for welfare, Doris's attitude remained hostile during each of our semiannual reviews. She would be standing at the door of her office when I arrived, the strain of disapproval puckering up around her lips, digging trenches alongside her nose and the corners of her deep set eyes, making her look like one of those frozen mummies they pulled out of the ice in the Andes. As soon as I sat down in the cold plastic chair of her office, she would say, "The laws should be changing soon — get ready to lose your benefits." Then she'd request a mass of information about my financial aid package at the University of Washington, sending me scrambling back and forth between the welfare office and the university administration center, laden with documents, fear crystallizing in my chest that she would find the elusive loophole she looked for.

But I found that the humiliation of welfare wasn't confined to Doris's reviews alone. Although we anticipated and appreciated the $240 in monthly food stamps, the kids often worried that their friends would see us using them. More than once I relinquished my place at the grocery checkout stand when a neighbor pulled in behind us. When I saw the terrified look flash across the children's faces, I would spin the cart around and say, "Oh, hi, Gretchen, you take my place in line. Funny thing, I forgot the one thing I came for — sugar."

It was an uneasy time to be on public assistance — 1993, the era of welfare reform. President Clinton had just announced his mission to "end welfare as we presently know it." The Republicans answered back in their "Contract with America" with even more radical cuts. Although the proposed legislation did target welfare abuse, it also eventually eliminated the single mother trying to get an education. In the political fury to transform public assistance, the nation was obsessed with ferreting out those responsible for its inefficiency. One day while I was listening to a National Public Radio program, I caught the end of Bob Dole's tirade about a divorced mother he'd heard about who was receiving benefits while attending college and not working. He promised America that he would work tirelessly to put an end to such abuse. *But without an education, how was I going to make a better life for myself and the kids?* I thought.

The government didn't see it that way. The issue had become a political wrestling match, with even the socially minded Bill Clinton anxious to score a point. Yet it seemed to me that this budget trimming frenzy was obscuring the country's ability to visualize the long-term benefits of helping single mothers earn a college degree. With it I could double the money I made as a waitress. Over a life-time, my salary increase would create twice as much in tax revenue and certainly reimburse the system for the $624 monthly supplement I'd received for a few years.

Eventually Doris's desire came true. In 1997, Washington passed the WorkFirst and Personal Responsibility Act, forcing single parents to juggle the rigors of work, school, and child rearing, all but destroying their hope of receiving a college degree. In the early 1990s, Clover Park Technical College near Tacoma, Washington, graduated five hundred nursing assistants, licensed practical nurses, and registered nurses each year under the old welfare program. Today it isn't graduating any. The trend is also evident in Washington's state colleges. Since reform, welfare recipients attending college have dropped by 35 percent. Recent studies reveal that the effect on single mothers has indeed been catastrophic, forcing them into low-paying jobs rather than helping them increase their income level through education — consigning them to poverty. Single mothers who took minimum wage jobs a decade ago are today making only sixty-five cents more an hour. The result of cutting this avenue of help has been so disastrous that eight states have changed their welfare laws, freeing students from the twenty-hour-workweek requirement. Washington State, however, has yet to review its welfare reform.

Back in 1993, political rhetoric also implied that most "welfare moms" were delighted with — even aspired to — their fate. I found this claim ridiculous. Every woman on assistance I knew was there because she was not receiving child support and needed help in raising her children or in going back to school so she could get a better job. It seemed amazing to me that politicians protested so loudly about welfare mothers yet refused to direct their energy toward a real solution: child support laws with clout. I knew from Doris's warnings and the news I read in the papers each day that the clock was ticking on my benefits. I took as many course credits at school as I could and went full-time during the summers.

I started classes at the University of Washington knowing I was in a contest against time. Still, it was a lovely place to run the race, to watch twenty-year-olds bustle through Red Square with brilliant autumn leaves scattering across the plaza, to see the Hacky Sack players, skateboarders, and Frisbee aficionados: an eight-ring circus below the towering fourteen-thousand-foot volcano Mount Rainier.

The student culture was as diverse as its attire: scrubbed young faces hurrying past, looking as if they'd just stepped out of an ad for Banana Republic or the Gap, boys from Seattle Prep in oxfords and carefully messy curls, girls wearing Abercrombie sweaters over crisp white cotton blouses. And another crowd who bought their clothes at secondhand stores like Buffalo Exchange or for twice the price at Encore Boutique. They all looked past me as they would have looked past their own mothers, even though I was technically the age of a big sister — well, okay, a youngish aunt. Either way, I was invisible.

Even as I watched the twenty-year-olds, it was hard for me to imagine what their lives must be like. At twenty-one I had been married and already pregnant. Now, at thirty-four, I was worried whether I could squeeze Micael's birthday cake out of the $240 monthly food stamp allotment, justify sneaking Doc Martens boots onto the overused Nordstrom credit card for Carise, or siphon off enough of the monthly welfare check to buy Jason's Little League uniform. Although I loved my classes that first fall at the university, I kept silent and hung around like a suit in a closet. With all the studying I had to do, I no longer kept in touch with my friends at the Space Needle or returned calls from Susan. I told myself there was no time for socializing.

I began to have a recurring dream: I am standing at a train station wearing a silky blue dress that feels soft and lovely against my legs. I walk to the magazine rack and pick out a glossy *Cosmopolitan* magazine, stepping onto the sheltered platform, perfectly calm and self-assured. The train is waiting, steam chugging out from under it like in the old movies — an elegant train, red and gray and gleaming. But just as I am about to board it, I realize I don't have my ticket, so I start digging through my purse, looking for it. I finally find it, only to drop it, losing more valuable time as the engine of the train quickens. Suddenly the train starts to pull away from the station, and I can't move. It leaves the platform and I'm still there, but now my purse is gone and I'm barefoot. I look inside the station — it's empty, deserted — and I look back down at myself. I'm naked and alone.

David's lifestyle reinforced my sense of isolation and fear as he sank deeper into alcoholism, going for weeks without making contact with the kids, telling them that he had become one of Seattle's "night people," who slept all day and then congregated to roam the city all night. One night at about two, I answered the phone, and he said, "There's no reason to live. I'm going to kill myself, and I'm coming over to your house to do it."

"Listen, stay away from us, David," I said. "I have a gun."

"That will be appropriate," he said with a harsh laugh. "*You* can kill me instead."

Oh, my God, I thought, David had finally slipped over the precipice, had gone from being an egocentric narcissist to a madman. Forget the days when he would drink twenty shots of Cuervo at the Space Needle bar — now he was ready to jump over the side. I slammed down the receiver and called David's parents, who sped over to his house and found him stumbling drunk and wheezing with pneumonia. He had stopped eating and had been drinking for days. Later that month he was admitted to a Seattle detox center. I hoped for his recovery, but still I felt as though David was like a hyena, circling around our lives, persistent and unpredictable, always ready for the kill.

My recurring dream turned into a nightmare in which I would see David, in a blur at the top of the stairs to my bedroom, staring down at me in cold rage, his face distorted with drunkenness. Then he would slowly descend the steps toward me. I would fight to lift my legs, trying to get out of bed, get the clip to the gun, and save myself and the kids, but my limbs were frozen stiff and inflexible as a block of ice. One night I awoke in a cold sweat and grabbed the pistol from under my pillow, rushed to the closet and found the clip, shoved it in, cocked the trigger, and released the safety: twenty seconds. *Maybe I should move the clip closer to the gun,* I thought. David was strong and fast, and I wouldn't have much time. Being able to pull the trigger didn't worry me, but I feared that in my panic I wouldn't have time to load the gun, or I might forget to release the safety. I rammed the clip into the gun and put it back under my pillow.

By the second quarter at UW, when I stepped into an intellectual history class on Friedrich Nietzsche, my sense of aloneness was growing. During the first week's reading, though, I found a compatriot to my cynicism and isolation. Nietzsche, the tormented fellow, despised organized religion with the same passion that I now felt. In *Thus Spake Zarathustra,* he declares that the church is "the most malignant counterfeit that exists . . . sickness is the essence of Christianity." The philosopher had no beef with Jesus, but he disdained the apostle Paul who, he said, misrepresented Christ's teachings and created a storehouse of false doctrines "to tyrannize the masses and form herds." I whispered out loud in Suzzallo Library, "Right on, Nietzsche!"

Even in Bible college I had silently wondered about the disparity between Paul's writings and the Gospels about Jesus. Since Paul never knew Christ, and the Gospels had not been written yet, his only real knowledge of Jesus hinged on a celestial voice he had heard on the road to Damascus. After that, he muscled his way into the tiny sect with his own interpretation of Christianity and wrested control of the movement from Christ's original followers. In the Gospels, Jesus taught in simple parables, broke the commandments, and tore down organized religion. In the Epistles, Paul taught complicated theology, created laws, and reestablished the kind of religion Jesus had condemned. To me, simple literary criticism made it clear that placing the Gospels in the same text with Paul's letters was like attaching *The Bhagavad Gita* to *Mein Kampf.*

It was time to take Christianity and send it to the morgue, I thought — to a huge armory-sized room, its floors spotless and sterilized and lined with stainless steel tables, filled with small machines for extracting and drilling, severing and plucking. Along the tables would be enlightened seminary students, eight to each side — celestial surgeons trying to bring a corpse back to life. These theological students would be charged with resurrecting the religion of Christianity from its entombment by the apostle Paul — isolating the oxymoronic tumors of his religious dogma and excising these malignant tissues from the body of Christ's original message.

But unfortunately for Jesus, I thought, Constantine had won the battle of history in AD 312, and Paul's books had been attached to the canon to contaminate the rest of the batch. And then it was all over, what with the patriarchal Catholic priesthood taking charge in the fourth century and all the testosterone that subsequently pulsed its way down through history. Testosterone seemed the culprit responsible for more than sixteen hundred years of grief, and I was happy to keep a safe distance from the menacing hormone.

Then, during the winter quarter, my worldview received a decided jolt. That morning, I hurried toward UW's Kane Hall in a rotten mood. Christmas break had been too short, and I'd made a real blunder. During vacation I had decided to get my hair permed, and during the procedure I'd forgotten to tell the beautician how quickly it curled; as a result, the rods stayed in too long, and I left the salon looking like Shirley Temple. The first day of class, I pulled the ringlets back and consoled myself — at least I wouldn't have to worry about any of my male classmates getting too friendly. My hibernating heart was contented to stay that way.

That I'd signed up for American History 201 irritated me even more than my awful hairdo. Survey classes were inevitably packed with whispering freshmen, although they did have some advantages. At the 200 level they were usually easier, so if you could put up with the swarm of underclassmen, it was a painless A. I entered the top of the amphitheater lecture hall and started down the stairs amid a throng of young bodies. As the new mob entered, several hundred twenty-year-olds squeezed up the steps to get out, while others milled around below for a chance to talk to the professor.

Then I saw him, walking below on the ground level of the auditorium. Long gray hair fell down his back in a ponytail of soft curls; khakis hugged his exquisite thighs as he moved between sorority beauties and looming athletes, looking for something. This handsome old hippie appeared completely misplaced in the sea of academia. I stopped dead in my tracks; a freshman crashed into my back. "What a beautiful janitor," I whispered. My heart slapped wildly against my chest. *Amazing — it still works!* I thought.

Some people have an acute sixth sense, while others are hope-less failures at anything vaguely intuitive. There are rare times when I feel it. It doesn't happen often, but when it does, *zap!* — I know that I'm walking into something that's about to shake up the whole present direction of things. I felt it the moment I saw the stunning, longhaired custodian standing there. An uncontrollable trembling ran along my skin, traveling up my spine and down each limb, bouncing off my fingertips and toes. In those instances, the body knows you're in deep trouble a long time before your brain catches up. At that moment I was wondering what my body knew that it hadn't yet conveyed to my mind.

I reached up and tugged at my hair, trying to straighten out little tufts of it before slipping into a desk behind a football player. *Okay,* I thought, *it doesn't really matter if this stunning specimen spots me or not.* But remaining incognito was a matter of pride — I didn't want a gorgeous man like him to see me resembling a poodle. If I slumped down long enough, surely he would find his broom and leave. At that moment he discovered what he was looking for: a piece of chalk. He grabbed it and began writing the outline for our first lecture on the board. When he finished and turned to face us, his hazel eyes pierced the crowd with a kind intensity. The older woman next to me gasped and sat up. I leaned toward her and whispered, "Is this guy a babe, or what?"

"My God, tomorrow I'm sitting closer," she said, sighing.

Dr. Taylor turned out to be an expert in his field of American history. He'd earned a national reputation as a rigorous scholar and a superb teacher, with theories as unconventional as his appearance. Even more impressive, he had a teaching style that made History 201 intellectually challenging. When Dr. Taylor entered the lecture hall, there wasn't a whispering freshman in the room. He spoke with passion, yet he often paused to ask if there were any questions, let-ting even academic peons like us know that he thought we could reason. I started reading my textbooks over and over so that I could come up with good comments to make in class. For a week I washed my hair twice a night and smothered it with enough conditioner to caulk the bathtub. Then I began making excuses to visit Dr. Taylor during his office hours. He was shy but attentive and kind, with a quiet, gentle voice that made me tingle inside every time he spoke. I conveniently assumed that since he didn't wear a wedding ring or mention his wife in class, he didn't have one. I made it a point not to ask. When I heard his graduate students talking about him in the halls, I'd linger, noting that they always repeated a variation on the same story: besides being a brilliant historian, he also went out of his way to help anyone in need of assistance.

After class I would go down to the front and question him about the New Deal, the California Doctrine, or the Kansas-Nebraska Act. While he answered, I'd stand as close as I respectfully dared, to memorize his face and the wild gray ringlets of his hair, smell the scent of his skin, letting the details of him breathe life back into my body. I started to wallow in an ocean of desire for Dr. Taylor, luxu-riating in his words and mannerisms like a fixated teenager. I felt as if he stood at the center of the universe and that the most important things the world had to offer fell from his lips. I read all the books he had written (which were plenty) and felt warm and happy inside, even in the middle of a dreary Seattle February.

Within three weeks of the start of winter quarter I began awak-ing each dawn, when even the most extraordinary things seem pos-sible, to the vision of making love with Dr. Taylor on a silk bed, in a warm beach house suffused with summer sea air. White curtains wrestled in the breeze as his long gray curls fell loose around his shoulders. His skin felt damp and hot and tasted of the ocean . . . Then I'd jump out of bed and into a tepid shower to shock myself out of such a foolish fantasy. I'd seen more than one woman become infatuated with my husband merely from watching him speak. I even knew the clinical name for the phenomenon: transference. The malady was just as potent in higher education; I was sure women fell in love with the exciting Dr. Taylor every quarter. I'd always considered myself miles above such shameless behavior.

At the end of the term, I slipped a note under his office door, telling him that he was the most intriguing man I had ever known and suggesting that we become lovers. To my wild disappointment, Dr. Taylor didn't answer my letter. Instead of interpreting his silence as a humane attempt to save me from well-earned humiliation, I stumbled headlong into disaster, telling myself that he must not have gotten the note. Several months later I returned to his office to ask him to sign my copy of his latest book.

You know the kind of decision people make in badly written horror films, when they are determined to go alone into the empty nineteenth-century three-story mansion where weird screaming noises are heard at night? The entire audience is whistling and throwing popcorn at the screen, hollering, "Don't go! For the love of God, don't go!" But the poor deluded souls charge forward, straight into their own version of *The Texas Chainsaw Massacre*.

When I walked through Dr. Taylor's door, the gravity of my folly didn't hit me until the moment he quietly said, "I'm sorry I wasn't able to respond to your letter, but I am happily married." The fact that Dr. Taylor found it necessary to say "happily" revealed plenty. He must have figured that a wild-haired woman like me wouldn't be dissuaded by the word "married" alone. I would have struck a bargain with the devil to be dead in a ditch rather than standing in Professor Taylor's office at that moment.

"Oh, I'm sorry," I gasped, turning my horror-stricken face toward the wall lined with volumes of erudite history. Dr. Taylor signed my book, "Best wishes to an excellent student." I stumbled to my car wondering what, in the name of Jesus, had I just done.

Thirteen

Micael: One Who Is Like God

M Y HEART FELT irreparably broken. Besides the shock of such unfamiliar pain, I was astonished at my behavior. Had I completely lost my mind? How could I feel such passion for a man I didn't even know? On top of my misplaced affection, my impertinence stunned me. Even the positive outcome to my recklessness didn't seem at all comforting: my actions juxtaposed with Dr. Taylor's integrity made me realize that predatory behavior wasn't gender exclusive. Testosterone couldn't be blamed for all my woes.

Although the experience helped renew my faith in men and resurrect my lifeless heart, it also reinforced the growing feeling that I'd ceased to hold an honorable place in society. I had become reckless, disenfranchised, unmoored: a single mother on welfare, brazen and foolish enough to throw herself at a married man. In my angst, I began to question whether life held any meaning. Although I agreed with Nietzsche's assessment of Christianity, I could not bring myself to adopt his nihilistic worldview. I was not willing to equate strength with a Machiavellian show of force or loss of conscience. Although Nietzsche's existentialism did not appeal to me, I began to appreciate Albert Camus. Like Nietzsche, Camus believed that we'd randomly appeared in an empty universe, with no God or absolutes to guide us. However, unlike Nietzsche, he advocated that humans could cultivate purpose without intruding on the existence of others. Most of Camus' characters ended up doing right even though they believed that no moral mandate demanded they do so. I decided that by choosing to be kind I could give direction to my life. Though I saw no real reason to be compassionate, for me it was simply better than being a shit. I also felt akin to Camus' outsider wandering on the fringes of society: "In a universe suddenly divested of illusions and lights, man feels alien, a stranger. His exile is without remedy since he is deprived of the hope of a Promised Land."

I decided that I simply needed to muster the guts to embrace life's emptiness. I would have to face the fact that I was alone and figure out how to raise my children in such a world. Shackling them with the biblical God just to keep them in line was out of the question. Jehovah was a tyrant and not a deity anyway. One evening, while reading Camus, I came across the lines, "I do not want to believe that death is the gateway to another life. For me, it is a closed door." I'd heard one of my professors refer to the philosophy as skeptical realism, which sounded good to me. Yes, I was an existential skeptical realist. Even if God did exist, He certainly wasn't going to pay my light bill. This harsh reality meant that I would have to seek every form of public assistance that I could, every welfare check and food stamp, every free counseling session provided by state aid, every scholarship and student loan — and not just the basic government loans, but every penny I could squeeze from PLUS, an unsubsidized loan program contingent on the borrower's good credit. And so far my plan was working, even though it felt like something held together with pipe cleaners and paste — the work of leprechauns and elves, and all hinging on Doris, who could call at any time and put an end to the whole grand adventure.

The one thing that kept me from going insane with worry was

running. I ran for hours every day. I would set out for a run in the drenching coastal rain, in the wilting, humid heat, at six in the morning, at two in the afternoon, eight at night. I ran because it repressed my anxieties and eased my loneliness, or maybe my hypothermic toes offered the perfect form of physical torture I needed to release my fear. So no matter what the weather, I ran. It was a rush of pure exhilaration when the frigid air burned my lungs with each breath, when the heat bathed my limbs in sheets of perspiration, pumping endorphins into each capillary. I ran as if something were chasing me, just about to catch me and devour me, like the crazed bear in *The Night of the Grizzly,* which had scared the daylights out of me when I was a kid. There were times when the wind blew me sideways or backward into a ditch or the freezing rain soaked my face until my ears ached and turned bright red, but still I didn't miss a day. One afternoon in March, the grizzly seemed just at my heels, so I started to chant a new, calming mantra: *There is nothing to fear, nothing to fear but fear itself.* I ran into the house, and the phone was ringing. I shook myself off like a wet dog. "Hello," I answered in my relaxed, just-in-from-a-good-run voice.

"It's Dawn down at the bank. It seems that there's a glitch in your credit, and I am so very sorry, but we're going to have to turn down your PLUS loan application this time."

"I can't believe it, Dawn; I know my credit is good," I said.

"I am really sorry. The best thing you can do is get your credit report cleared up and then resubmit the loan application."

I let the phone drop as the sweat and rain dripped off my face onto the kitchen linoleum. *Surely there's some crazy mistake,* I told myself. I got on the phone and immediately ordered a copy of my credit report. When it arrived a few days later, it showed defaulted debts on both a Visa and a Sears account. In disbelief, I called the companies. Sears informed me that a few months before the divorce, David had obtained a credit card and charged it to the maximum, then walked away from the debt. Although he'd acquired the card without my knowledge, since we were married when he received it, I was liable for the payments. David had also defaulted on his personal Visa. But I felt confident that I could shake that bill because the divorce decree stated that the account was solely his to pay. I called Visa.

"I'm sorry, Mrs. Brant; even though the divorce decree states it's his card, since you were married to him when the card was issued, you are still liable for the charges."

"But isn't a divorce document legally binding?"

"Not in this circumstance. Unless you pay it or get David to pay it, it will remain on your report."

My credit was ruined. I still had a year to go before receiving my bachelor's degree, and the money available from welfare and government loans wasn't enough. Without the benefit of the PLUS loan, it would be nearly impossible to continue school. I fought back the tears and set the phone down. Walking upstairs, my feet felt heavy, like wearing galoshes filled with water. I pulled my clothes off and stepped into the shower, where I cried with my head under the stream. After the hot water ran out, I climbed out and sat naked on the lid of the closed toilet, letting the cold water run to hide the sound of my weeping. When I was finally all cried out, I put on my robe and went downstairs to fix dinner.

That night, after the kids went to bed, I grabbed the Bombay Sapphire from the back of the freezer and walked into the living room where I stared out the picture window at a constellation of stars tangled in the bare black limbs of the Japanese maple. I held the bottle in one hand and a glass in the other. The moon was

smothered behind a great, shapeless chalky vapor of clouds. The
night seemed darker and longer than at any time in the distant and
dismal story of the world. I poured a long drink. *I'll be goddamned,*
I thought, *here I am, watching for a left hook from the Washington
State Legislature, and David delivers a blindside knockout in the
tenth round.* I began emptying the gin, gulp by gulp.

So what was my new plan? Okay, maybe I should just try and
marry myself a Microsoft millionaire. The idea wasn't so bad. I
could give my kids everything they wanted — multiple pairs of Doc
Martens, unlimited Little League uniforms, and tuition for Prince-
ton — and for me, European facials, body wraps, Crystal Peel treat-
ments, Fendi handbags, and loads of perennials from Molback's
Nursery. I took another drink. I wondered if this was how cowards
felt, or men lost at sea who had given up their struggles and agreed
to let the waves take them. Okay, no Microsoft magnate. Maybe I
would have a gigantic garage sale and then leave for a faraway island
like Minorca, teach English as a second language. I could do transla-
tions for money, have tourists stay in the extra rooms of my white-
washed flat surrounded by red geraniums, oleander, and fragrant
jasmine — another drink — lie in the sun for days and weeks on end,
read Camus and Sartre, and Heidegger. But the kids couldn't even
speak Italian, or whatever it was they spoke on Minorca: French?
Spanish? Catalan? Come to think of it, neither could I. Wasn't that
just the way life goes? It was like swimming against a riptide — you
hope you're making progress as you struggle, unable to feel the current pulling you inexorably away. Then you pause to look up at the
shore and realize you're in a place you never intended to be, with no
way to get back and no place to go but under.

At that point the alcohol had completely saturated my limbs,
and I could feel myself collapsing into the carpet. I sank into the sor-

row as though I were stepping into a pool of the calmest, darkest waters, the surface reaching to my knees, my stomach, the point of my chin — the weight of my body drifting into a great sea of desperation. Each detail of my physical existence was dissolving into a void of hopelessness. I curled into a ball and put my head on my knees.

Then I suddenly felt Micael's warm body encircling me, her small face peering into mine. She had come downstairs and found me in a puddle on the floor; now her gentle breath was kissing the tears on my cheeks. "It's okay, Mom. We're going to be okay." Her eyes were awash with love, her face shining with the pure confidence of a child who still believes the world is a place full of hope, full of wonder. Micael stretched her arms around me to hug me tighter, knowing that her mother needed saving and that she was the one to do it. I looked up and saw the darkness around her glowing, moon shaped face. It was a celestial look, the look of grace. My mind said back to me, "This is your evidence of the divine." In my little daughter's indomitable spirit was mirrored the Hebrew meaning of her name, Micael: one who is like God.

I remembered her birth and the births of her siblings: the pink that bloomed onto their pallid lips and ashen cheeks as they squalled out their first breath, the spiritual energy that filled the room as they lay on my still rubbery stomach, the perfect capsules of wonder they were as David cradled them to his chest. At that moment I knew that if the world contained any certainty, it was that my children began and continued as miracles. It was the only faith I held, the only truth that remained, the only sign of God I trusted. My job was to finish the journey for them.

The next morning I could feel the frantic scramble that pumped too much blood through my heart, inflating the veins in my neck as David's phone rang and rang. Once he answered it, I simply told him that if he didn't pay his delinquent bills, after I kicked his ass between his ears, I would sue him for back child support. It took him several months, but he set up a payment schedule with Sears and Visa, and the bank released my PLUS loan.

I began to realize that something inside me could not close off the universe, reducing all truth to a narrow string of empirical operations, cold as a razor's edge. Something about life demanded the wild chaos of possibility. The miracle of human existence and our ability to love made me hesitate to abandon all hope of the divine. I could not ignore the spark of light that seemed to dwell deep inside humanity, an ember of something greater than empty flesh and bones. If we evolved from sterile happenstance driven solely by our survival-of-the-fittest instincts, then why do we perform acts of compassion or heroism? What makes a soldier risk his life to save a comrade or causes a child to love unconditionally? The human ability to think in the abstract also suggested to me that we were capable of elevated thought. We could create and admire art, music, and architecture, write and ponder love and the meaning of the universe. That an existentialist could even contemplate life's folly pointed to the miraculous gift of the imagination — the inexplicable phenomenon of personal consciousness. Dead matter alone seemed unable to account for man's intellectual creativity and passion. Although I certainly wasn't ready to embrace religion, I had to acknowledge that stubbornly rejecting all possibility of God displayed the same intolerance I had found in Fundamentalism. Dogma, religious or empirical, ended the pilgrimage of discovery. But I set such daunting thoughts aside — midterms were coming, and I had plenty to worry about just trying to pass chemistry.

The process became easier the next time Doris sent me scrambling to the university to retrieve more documents, and a new counselor stepped up to the desk. "This information is completely unnecessary," he said. "Does she do this every six months?"

"Yes," I answered, and then gave him a brief account of Doris's behavior.

He picked up the phone and dialed the welfare office. "Can I speak to your director?"

In the discussion that followed, he used the word "harassment" more than once, and after that I was assigned a new caseworker, and no one at the welfare office mentioned the doom of impending legislation ever again. My heart felt as if someone had taken it down from the ledge it had been teetering on since Doris threw it up there.

That spring I was accepted to do graduate work at the University of Washington's Department of Communications, and once I started the program I felt relaxed and at home. Instead of attending class with frat brothers and sorority sisters, I was studying with adults my age — a few were even parents, and one was a single mom. A group of us began to meet once a week for dinner at the Big Time Brewery, where the in-house microbrews were as varied as my classmates. Jennifer had taken her undergraduate degree at Stanford, Kyle at Iowa State, Carol came from Florida State, Beth from Dartmouth, Brad from USC, Donna from UCLA, and a whole slew of us from the U of W.

August had tapered off into the brisk days of September. After classes we'd gather at the pub, around a sticky table in the soft, layered light that filtered through the windows. Breathing the crisp smell of hard apple cider and hops, we would drink our Bhagwan's Best IPA and discuss Spike Lee, *Pulp Fiction,* which professors we wanted on our graduate committees, our class readings of Marshall McLuhan and Michel Foucault, and whether we had lovers. A new exuberance overtook me. It felt like moving into a new house — first you paint the living room a fresh cream color, watching the roller smooth across old dirt and gashes, eradicating the past into clean oblivion; you carry in the boxes of books and decide where you will put them. You position the furniture, fill the pantry with cans and jars and sacks of flour, and the newly lined drawers with brand-new kitchen towels. You make a batch of bread and pull it, fresh and warm, from the oven to fill the house with its smell.

I relished my new life, attending evening lectures or the theater, expressing my opinions on movies, elected officials, historical events, religion, sex, and the time of day with no concern about who might object, knowing that other than my children, I didn't have to take care of anyone. Instead of seeing the future as a black tangle of thread, I felt it was starting to weave into a hopeful pattern. I didn't know what that pattern was going to look like, but it *was* a pattern. I thought about Rachael, who years before had left the Hutterite colony and moved into town. I remembered seeing in her face the pure joy of liberation; it was breathtaking, almost intoxicating. I now understood what I had seen in her eyes so many years before: once a mind has been set free, it would rather be destroyed than return to captivity.

I chose a fine communications historian named Richard Kielbowicz as chair of my graduate committee and began doing research for my master's thesis on Teddy Roosevelt and the newspaper press. During the next two years Dr. Kielbowicz spent hours critiquing my work and teaching me the rules of rigorous historical research, sending me back to the library over and over to dig deeper and read more, forcing me to scrutinize the details of turn-of-the-century journalism and T.R. Before I knew it, I had spent two years in the university library, scouring newspapers, magazine articles, microfiche, and journals, taking notes among the dusty stacks of books. Although

I loved every tedious minute of it, I was nonetheless relieved when my final semester arrived. As I placed my completed thesis in the mailboxes of the five professors on my graduate committee, joy overwhelmed me — tempered by the fact that within a few days I would be sitting before them, defending my research.

The next week Dr. Kielbowicz was waiting outside the conference room when I arrived. "Hey, don't look so scared," he said. "You're ready."

We walked into the stuffy room, and I took my place at the huge rectangular table opposite five stern faces. My mind raced, memorizing every detail of my surroundings: the bowl shaped cover over the huge ceiling light, the glass bookshelf filled with communications theory journals that ran the length of the wall, the plum colored coffee mug next to Dr. Pember, Dr. Bassett's unruly eyebrows sprouting out like a jumble of spider legs, Dr. Kielbowicz's frozen half smile.

For almost two hours the committee grilled me on the details of Roosevelt's life and his relationship with the press. They asked about turn-of-the-century economic and social conditions, the history of modern journalism, and the Progressive movement. When I answered those questions, they broadened the circle to William McKinley and William Taft, the Spanish-American War, and the railroads. I felt sweat drops forming on my forehead, yet in a strange rush of masochistic madness, I was relishing the inquisition. After spending two years immersed in the world of the rough riding, trust busting Roosevelt, I was going to share what I had learned with anyone who was interested. As the inquiry wound down, Dr. Pember raised his index finger. The professor was infamous for coming up with one last question, typically one that the battered graduate student could not answer. Legend held that he combed the literature of your subject and almost always discovered one obscure theory you couldn't address. No one ever failed the defense because of it — it was just to let you know that you weren't such a smarty-pants after all. When Pember opened his mouth, the committee knew my time was at hand.

"What name did Roosevelt give his foreign policy and why? Then give me an example of how he carried this philosophy out."

Dr. Kielbowicz's jaw tightened, and he looked down. Luckily I had just finished *The Age of Reform,* Richard Hofstadter's superb treatment of T.R.'s international relations. Taking a deep breath, I waded in. I explained Roosevelt's Jackson-Lincoln theory of the presidency — that he demanded absolute prerogative to make independent decisions concerning foreign policy. I gave examples from 1905, 1906, and 1907, when Roosevelt single-handedly ratified the Santo Domingo Agreement, Root-Takahira Agreement, and Gentlemen's Agreement without the approval of Congress. As I spoke, I saw the lines in Dr. Kielbowicz's face loosen. When I stopped, he looked up at me and smiled.

The graduate committee recommended that I continue in the department and do a PhD on the subject. Although I felt proud of my thesis defense, I also realized that there was plenty about Teddy Roosevelt that I didn't know, and that my ability to answer Dr. Pember's question was luck, pure and simple. I'd jammed my head full of information but still knew only snippets of the T.R. story. The true value of my education was that I had learned enough to know how little I really knew. My time in college had given me the tools to investigate, to attempt to seek knowledge with an open but critical mind, yet also the perspective to know that no matter what the subject, I would never possess all the pieces to any particular puzzle.

On a sun filled morning in June 1995, my parents and my sister,

Melanie, arrived from Montana to attend my graduation. Dan and his wife, Mary, came as well, having just returned from leading a Christian tour though the Holy Land. As I put on my blue robe, the kids gathered around me. They laughed and hugged me, and Jason said, "Mom, your ears stick out from that weird hat. Let's tuck them in."

That afternoon my graduate school pals and I gathered outside Hec Edmundson Pavilion in our bright robes and cords. There was a disturbance above us like a sudden rainsquall, and we looked up to see a flock of birds lighting in the cherry tree overhead, quick and random in their movements, skipping delicately from branch to branch, trading places — a mass of shimmering gray with here and there a glint of gold, a flash of scarlet. We could hear them at it, a continuous winged rustling like the tuneless murmur of crickets in tall grass. Their sheen was bright and lustrous against the afternoon sun, and then suddenly they were up and away in a flurry, dissolving into thin air on a fading burst of skittering wings, as we soon would be, dispersed across the nation.

A flood of happiness overwhelmed me, and I bit my lip to fight back the lump of emotion lodged in my throat as the University of Washington Wind Ensemble started "Pomp and Circumstance" and we were ushered to start our march inside. Tom Brokaw spoke to us about the importance of education and what we'd all accomplished, and once his commencement address was finished we stood to receive our degrees. Dr. Dale Johnson, dean of the graduate school, took the stage, and when he called my name out over the loudspeaker, I suddenly remembered the times in the welfare office when I had been ashamed to hear it. *Thank God those days are over,* I thought. *This is my new start.*

Fourteen

Going Home

URING THE LAST QUARTER of graduate school I began working as an academic counselor at the university. After years of learning how to access financial aid, locate scholarship money, and plan my own class schedule, helping single moms and intimidated teenagers maneuver through the system gave me a sense of great satisfaction. They would come into the office looking as frightened and at sea as I had felt the first day I ran onto the Shoreline Community College campus. I pictured the single moms cramming sixteen hours of madness into every day, getting up at five to get the household percolating, an eight-hour day of classes and maybe a part-time job, home by six to start supper, grocery shop, do errands, wash laundry, attend soccer games, and then bedtime — four people in line to use a single bathroom. Any relief that I could provide with scholarship applications or schedule planning made me feel like Bill Gates adding another floor onto the Suzzallo Library.

I felt content with my life and hoped that David would eventually pull himself together, despite all the sad dead weight of evidence to the contrary. He had been through two detox programs, yet still spent several terms in jail for driving while intoxicated. He no longer had a driver's license and was currently without a job. I said nothing to the kids about their dad's plight, but the night Micael came home and told me about the book he had asked her to read, I was livid.

I was in the kitchen, counting ingredients into a bowl for quiche crust: 1 cup flour, 3 tablespoons butter, 1 tablespoon salt. I had grabbed the rolling pin and was pressing out the dough when she said, "Mom, Dad gave me an interesting book to read," sitting the bright red hardback on the kitchen counter. It was entitled *Is Alcoholism Hereditary?* I'd heard of the book, which claimed that drinking problems were primarily genetic.

"Dad said that he inherited his alcoholism from Grandpa, and since he, Uncle Freddie, and Aunt Sally are all alcoholics, we probably will be too."

"He *what?*" I shrieked.

"Oh, he's been telling Jason, Carise, and me that for a long time," she said casually.

I could feel a red rage burst from my throat to my ears in one heartbeat. Here was a guy who couldn't pay child support or even buy his kids birthday gifts, but still somehow found time to lecture them on their inevitable alcoholism. I hadn't seen David in months but at that moment I wanted to run him down, wherever he was, and hit him up alongside the head with the rolling pin I held in my hand.

Instead I swallowed hard. "Hey, guys, everyone down here; let's have a talk."

As they sat on the couch, I marveled at their likeness, all with their father's olive skin and willowy height, his dark brown, almond shaped eyes. Carise had become a tenderhearted young woman of seventeen with a shy radiance that made teenage boys crane their necks as she walked past them in the mall. She didn't seem to notice the attention and was more interested in filling out college

applications for the fall and shopping with her girlfriends. She was
an optimist concerning every issue I'd ever heard her discuss — all
but one: the topic of God, a subject Micael would occasionally raise
at dinner.

"So who here believes in God?" she'd say.

"Who knows?" Jason would answer with a shrug.

"I'm an agnostic. I don't think there is any way we can know
if there is a God," Carise would invariably say.

"I believe that some kind of divine spirit courses through the
universe but that the energy isn't necessarily male. In fact, after reading *The Mists of Avalon,* I think God is probably a goddess," Micael
would say in return.

Strong opinions affected Micael's theology as well as every other
topic in her life. The year before, at age fifteen, she had decided to become a vegetarian because, "For every sixteen pounds of grain fed to
cattle, we only get a pound back in meat. With all that wasted grain,
we could feed the world." Then she would hasten to add that she was
keeping the conviction secret from her cattle ranching grandparents.

At thirteen, Jason never discussed his feelings about God — or
much else, for that matter. He spent most of his time alone in his
room, playing video games and completely uninterested in the sports
he had formerly loved. I assumed that his apathy toward soccer and
baseball might be a result of David's absence from his games. Even
though Jason tried to act as if he didn't notice, each Saturday his
face dropped when his was the only dad missing again.

That day, sitting on the couch, the kids could see by the color
of my face that the conversation was going to be more than a theo-
retical discussion about God. Something big was up.

"Do you believe you are destined to follow your father's alcoholism?" I asked.

"I think it has more to do with your upbringing," Micael said.

"But Dad says it's in our genes," Jason added.

"I don't know, Mom; it's hard to know what to think. Dad says the latest research says that we are," Carise weighed in.

"Research says that you could have a propensity toward alcoholism. But your dad is wrong to tell you that you are destined to it. To me that's like telling someone they're destined to become a murderer because their father was. And no one makes anyone take the first drink. I want you kids to remember that you have just as much heritage in strong pioneers as you do in alcoholics."

I knew that whatever words I used to combat David's fatalism, they would never be as effective as strongly rooting my children in their Montana heritage. The irony of my sudden ancestral pride didn't escape me. I had spent much of my life keeping my rural roots a secret, yet now, in a time of trouble, I was turning to them without hesitation. Since the divorce, I had taken the kids back to Montana every chance I got, like a migrating bird returning to nest, the four of us slingshotting across the plains and grain fields of eastern Washington. We'd pack the aging 1978 Ford and head out in the predawn darkness when the stars were still blinking across the horizon. By that afternoon, we were climbing up into the Idaho Rockies, zipping past the Cataldo Mission that Jesuit priests built in the mid-1800s, through the silver- and coal-mining towns where whiskered men still patronized crumbling, brick-fronted bars as they had for well over a century.

Once we hit Montana, I worried less about the speedometer — an infraction, no matter how egregious, cost five dollars. The law mirrored the territory, a place where most things were untamed, independent, and more than likely reckless. We'd speed past the Ten Thousand Dollar Bar into St. Regis, getting off the freeway for a last leg of dirt road, across a land that seemed out of step with the rest of the world. Over the sage and shortgrass a red-tailed hawk might emerge from a line of cottonwoods, assailed by a pair of magpies, diving and pecking at their eternal enemy. As we wound deeper into the hills onto the Flathead Indian Reservation, silence encompassed the entire landscape.

One year Carise's friend Amanda joined our adventure. Amanda had never experienced the rural West. By evening, as we had made our final crossing over the Clark Fork River on a highway with no streetlamps or passing cars, her small voice, tinged with alarm, sounded from the backseat, "It's so . . . *lonely* out here."

It was the same calm loneliness that renewed my soul. It had taken me nearly half a lifetime to recognize the healing quality of the West's silence, how its stillness could infuse people from the inside out, creating patience and endurance that grows even in the face of life's grinding disappointments. Its quiet coaxes the mind to wait, trusting that the rains will come in time to water the grain and wash away the grasshopper eggs, so they won't become a swarm of locusts and turn the alfalfa into a crop of toothpicks in the hardpan.

Seeing my children embrace the wide-open stillness of the West gave me confidence that they would learn the value of patience and endurance. During mild summer mornings we would hike to the crumbling homesteads I had explored as a young girl, and I would repeat the tales my father told me as a child as if they traveled across oceans of time to reach me, even from beyond the memory of his voice. I'd see in the kids' stunned faces the dawning realization that people had survived in shacks with no running water or electricity, or that Grandpa had been born in one such hovel without the help of a doctor. We'd walk along the Flathead River to marvel at the prehistoric Indian paintings or out into the fields to check the hay and mint crops. In the evenings we'd head for the Corn Hole, an ancient mineral mud bath permeating the air with the earthy, soothing smell of sulfur. Since time immemorial, Montana's Indians had considered it a magical curing place. My dad would wedge himself in up to his waist, letting the mud envelop his wrecked knees and ruined hip, injuries sustained from throwing himself in front of bolting cattle and falling off the barn roof during a long hard lifetime of ranching. His grandchildren would climb into the warm muck, their silky brows creased with alarm over Grandpa's crippled body.

Even at seventy-two my father's massive arms and barrel chest bulged with muscle, though his weathered skin was brown and eroded like the western landscape around him. Decades of tireless farmwork had broken him down like an old McCormick tractor, and I watched him with the same concern and love as his grandchildren did. After I had my own kids, I had made my peace with my father, for only then had I realized how much I must have terrified him — my bullheadedness and wanderlust dreams had no doubt made him aware that I was not prepared for the harsh, cold realities of life.

During these visits, Dad and I would jump in the pickup and head out to fix fence or water cows, and I would roll down the window to let the smell of ripe, sweet alfalfa fill my head. The years of our silent animosity had vanished into the high-country air, replaced by comfortable chatter, the same kind I had heard years before, when Dad's cronies came by our house to eat huckleberry pie and cuss. Our conversation would move on to the particulars of NAFTA, GATT, and the WTO as we'd step out of the pickup to check the creek level — brimming with water murky as chocolate milk, swirling around the roots of the cottonwoods and filling the irrigation ditch.

We'd walk out into the budding field and smell the sun warming the hay into maturity.

"Some folks find God in a church," Dad would say, "but I find Him here on this prairie, all around me, everywhere."

These retreats to the farm helped me rediscover my own spiritual footing. I felt the enduring geography that had nurtured me as a child come alive again. After the kids were in bed, I would sit on the porch and watch the wind sweep across the valley like a mother's hand combing her baby's hair at bedtime. The same breeze that had touched my face decades before, now reconnected me again to its rhythms and smells, its patience and tranquility. Coming back was like a prodigal's return: only by having abandoned my heritage could I now appreciate its wealth.

I remembered those long-ago hot summer days when I would rush into the land's swelling embrace, feeling the foxtails brush against my bare legs and smelling the grassy musk rising up from the earth. The breeze would caress the vast prairie, coaxing the meadow chickadees out to join it, rising and swirling in a soft gale. I'd stand and listen dreamily to the meadowlarks serenading one another, trading beautiful stanzas carried on the wind. Before long, from across the valley, another small creature, and another, would answer with their own unique songs. I'd look across a land that in ages past had been grooved by buffalo herds and veined with winding Indian trails. The U.S. Army had marched across it, surveying and mapping, jotting notes full of longitudes and latitudes, and now Herefords nibbled at their shadows along its swooping hillsides. And still it was as it had been since ages past, as I had found it when a child, as I had come back to rest in it when an adult: hushed and sacred and filled with a magical presence. Slowly I was beginning to feel a quiet peace emerge in my life.

Fifteen

The Gun

J UST ABOUT THE TIME I was making peace with my
   past, David seemed to be headed in the opposite direction. Considering his capability for violence, I had
never aggressively pursued child support payments over the years.
But once I began collecting welfare, the state stepped in and began attempting to garnish whatever wages David made so that they
could reimburse the system. They had not been successful in the
past, however, because even though he had been making money
over the years preaching in a Religious Science church in Seattle,
the wages were not being reported to the state and so they could not
be traced. Now, however, David had begun construction work and
so the Division of Support Enforcement and Recovery had a track-
able wage to go after.

The case had landed in the Family Support Division of the King
County Prosecuting Attorney's Office, and the prosecuting attorney immediately subpoenaed David. When he appeared before the
court, the commissioner ordered him to pay four hundred dollars
each month in child support and informed him that if he failed
to do so the state would imprison him. When David didn't make
his payment the following month, he was arrested. When he could
not raise the two-thousand-dollar bond, he was incarcerated in the
King County Jail. Several months earlier David had lost his job as a

minister, as well as his driver's license, because of numerous DUIs. He told the commissioners he was desperate to make a new start but needed help in beating his alcoholism. When a space opened up, he was admitted into a government detoxification program.

I could tell that David's absence from Jason's life was starting to take a severe toll on him. Now, at fourteen, he seemed like a boiling cauldron. Considering Jason's mental state, I thought about the gun I had hidden underneath my pillow and went to retrieve it one afternoon, to hide it in a more secure location. It was gone. I instinctively knew who had taken it. My knuckles were white on the steering wheel, as I sped toward the house of his buddy Brian, with images playing in my mind's eye of my son accidentally shooting someone. I felt as if Jason was within seconds of changing everyone's life forever. Regrets buzzed around my mind, as ineffectual as houseflies. I rolled the window down and let the crisp November air hit my face.

The car screeched into Brian's driveway, and I jumped out onto a thin crust of frost that cracked under my shoes. Leaping up the front steps, I knocked on the door. I could see Brian's father, a husky Vietnam vet, ambling up to the door with a beer in one hand. "Well come on in, lady, have a sit-down," he said.

"Keith, I think the boys have my gun," I said, my legs turning to putty as I collapsed into the red velour easy chair. He looked at me as if he needed a moment to contemplate the idea.

"I'm sure if the boys have your gun, they'll know how to respect it" — a hopeful notion that didn't calm my internal hysteria one little bit.

Just about then we could hear Jason, Brian, and three other teenage boys laughing and hooting as they charged through the back door.

"Do you have my gun, Jason?" I hollered.

"Mom, slow down. Don't freak out. We were just down at the river, target practicing on ducks — we didn't kill any of them."

I was ready to nail his pelt to the side of a barn and brand it with gun control slogans. But I knew that if there were any pelts to be flayed, it should be my own. So ended the illusion I had taken shelter in: that we were all safer with a gun under my pillow. The next day I took the pistol back down Highway 99. As I walked into the same gun shop at which I'd bought it several years before, the aged proprietor lifted his eyes from his workbench. He rose and limped toward me, fixing me with the same unflinching gaze. He acted as if he didn't recognize me, but I suspected that he did. "I usually don't take guns back, but I'll do it this time," he said without hesitation. I had a feeling that he knew I would return someday: the woman he figured wouldn't have the disposition to kill her ex. A gun in such a woman's house was no help to anyone — just a danger to the kids.

One afternoon not too much later the principal called to tell me that Jason had been expelled from school. During a surprise inspection they had found marijuana in his locker. When I questioned his sisters that evening, they told me that Jason had been selling it to his classmates. Many of his friends had dropped out of school; several had been sent to juvenile detention; one would soon be sentenced to prison for stealing a car. Nothing I did seemed to help: counselors, books, sports, pleading, threatening — he still continued to slip away from his family, his life, his potential. All I could think to do was uproot him and force him to make a fresh start, so I packed our belongings and moved us onto an island off the Seattle coastline.

The next fall Jason enrolled as a sophomore at Bainbridge High. He was eager to give his new life a chance, trying out for soccer and making the high school team. I was overjoyed and would sneak out to the sidelines after work at the university and watch the squad practice. I loved seeing Jason playing sports again, his quick, agile body racing down the field, in complete control of the ball. The coach was happy with his good fortune, and Jason even said he liked his classes. Relief enveloped me.

Then one day Jason called and in a muffled voice asked me to come and pick him up. I pulled into the Safeway parking lot to find him sitting on the pavement, his hair hanging down over his face, his arms hugging his long, gangly legs to his chest. When he stood up, I was horrified. His face was swollen like an overripe pumpkin, his eyes already reduced to twin slits between blue-black lids; his shirt was torn down the side, and his face was bleeding. He had gotten into a fight with one of his teammates, and a group of other boys said they were going to beat the living tar out of him as soon as they caught him alone.

The next day the assistant principal, Mr. Davis, a watchful, kind-faced man with thick black glasses, phoned and asked me to come and see him in his office. Once I sat in the chair opposite his desk, he closed the door and said, "The kids at Bainbridge High School don't like outsiders. Most of them are from very wealthy families and have been in school together since the first grade. The fact that Jason came in and immediately made the soccer team got some of them really mad. He took a slot away from a kid who grew up on the island. I have to tell you, I'm sick of watching this kind of thing happen. I'll help Jason in any way I can."

"Do you think they'll really gang together and beat him up?" I asked.

"Yes, I do. But tell Jason I'll try to protect him as much as I can."

I went home and told Jason about the conversation.

"What, is Mr. Davis going to follow me around all day with a billy club in his hand?" Jason said. After that he wanted nothing to do with Bainbridge High School, and when he stepped off the school bus in the morning, instead of going to school he would walk to Safeway and hang out there all day.

I decided that being the parent of a teenage boy was like being a test rat in an experiment intended to induce psychosis. Researchers teach the rat that by simply pushing a lever, it will get a nice serving of grain, making it feel relaxed and comforted. Then one day, instead of a succulent treat the scientist shocks the hell out of the poor little rodent. The next time, a satisfying delicacy . . . maybe several times a delicacy . . . then, *zap*. The researcher switches this routine back and forth indiscriminately until the rat breaks down and goes completely mad. Vacillating between hope and ruin sends the beleaguered creature over the edge into insanity.

I was following the rat psychosis routine when an acquaintance whose son had a similar experience during high school told me about Job Corps, a government program designed for kids like Jason who didn't fit into a traditional school yet wanted to get an education or learn a trade. I talked to Jason about the program, and he said that he would go. When the time came, we loaded his things in the car, took a ferry to the mainland, then drove north to Sedro-Woolley, Washington. Soon we were speeding up Interstate 5, past stands of pine trees and thickets of Scotch broom. Fifty miles north of Seattle we turned off into farm country, past wide red barns and rolling wheat fields ripe with harvest, snaking along on a narrow two-lane through the backcountry of Washington State. The last leg of the drive, we turned down a dirt lane that curved peacefully through the countryside, bordered by enormous poplar trees, six feet across the trunk and at least a hundred feet high, their branches shimmering with gray-green leaves. After a bend in the road, a large group

of brick buildings came into view — a high-security compound for-
tified with guard posts and fences — and suddenly my heart felt as
if it were being cinched tight with barbed wire. The complex had
been built early in the century as the state's first mental institution,
so famous for its look of madness that Milos Forman had filmed
segments of *One Flew Over the Cuckoo's Nest* there. Enormous security buildings, uniformed sentries, and guard dogs combined to give
the scene a nightmarish, gulagesque feel.

As we approached the front gate, an armed officer stopped us.
"Absolutely no vehicles beyond this point," he barked. "You'll have
to get out and register before entering. No one in or out without
security clearance."

"Why do you need such heavy security?" I asked, feeling as
though I were delivering Jason to San Quentin rather than the Job
Corps.

"We've got former gang members living here, ma'am. Can't take
the chance their rivals won't come looking for 'em," he answered.

As we walked onto the campus, I immediately realized that
most of the students appeared closer to twenty than my son's sixteen
years — a pack of young men so brimming with agitation that being
in their presence was like standing beside some turbulant spectacle
of nature, a geyser blowing its top or a swarming hive of bees. Next
to them Jason looked immature and awkward — no match for the
streetwise men sporting tattoos and bandannas leaning against the
corners of the buildings. I felt physically ill. Living with me, Jason
would become a high school dropout; on the other hand, leaving
him here seemed like a Faustian bargain. Although Jason acted
tough, I knew he was as frightened as I was. I left him waving from
the huge front door of his dorm with veiled terror in his eyes. As I
drove away, I hesitated several times, my shirt stuck to my back wet

with sweat, fighting the urge to return and rescue him. How could I possibly leave him in such a place?

I pushed on the gas and sped down the curved lane, past the stands of poplar. Once the chilling institution was out of sight, I hit the brakes and opened my door vomiting while the car was still moving. I fumbled around under the seat and brought out a bottle of water. The plastic container was hot, and its contents warm as tea. I rinsed out my mouth and spit onto the damp ground smelling of moss and humus. Sitting in silence, I felt a heavy blast of cool air hit my face, and a quiet maternal intuition urged me to drive away — this difficult place was where Jason needed to be. Tears blurred the road as I drove out of Sedro-Woolley.

In my mind Jason was a newborn again, bundled in the fold of his father's arm as we brought him home from a Chicago hospital, his sisters examining his fingers and toes with enthusiasm, and kissing his bald head and fat cheeks. From that point on, he had become the repository of their unbridled affection, and they had become the only two people on earth he shared his real feelings with. He had tumbled through life, bantering with his sisters — the youngest, the only son, the least able to deal with the absence of a father. I bit my lip and tried to hold the images in my mind before they sank back into the past, but they shrank from my grasp as if I were trying to pluck moonlight off the water.

Jason's face was still before me an hour later as I continued down the interstate, when suddenly I saw the exit to Calvary Baptist Church. Without thinking, I veered off the freeway onto an overpass I hadn't traveled for ten years. It was Saturday, and I knew that the churchyard would be teeming with church gardeners, so I put on my sunglasses and pulled down the visor. I imagined them: Mrs. Daniels bending over a solitary weed that was trying desperately to push its way through a cluster of bright purple irises; Mr. Plye, in a feat of painstaking grace, delicately trimming the burgundy, and butter-cream colored roses; Mrs. Bligh sweeping grass off the sidewalk. As I crested the hill, I saw it: the tall white building still jutting into that open sky, as it had looked sixteen years before, when David and I first laid eyes on it. But now its appearance made me inhale a sudden ragged breath. My heart dropped, and a black emptiness opened in my gut.

The rust of time and neglect had faded the previously vibrant sign, CALVARY BAPTIST, A MEMBER OF THE INDEPENDENT BAPTIST CHURCHES OF AMERICA, into illegibility. The once colorful rhododendrons blooming in fuchsia and white were now lifeless, parched and wilted, much like Calvary Baptist itself. Weeds, filling what had been immaculate flowerbeds, now crept up past broken basement windows. White paint hung from the clapboard siding like ragged strips of clothing from a third-world beggar. I pulled into the deserted parking lot and stared at the desolation.

Getting out of the car, I moved down the sidewalk, disturbing the dead leaves with my feet. As I peeked into a cracked and dirty window, memories of the people who had attended Calvary materialized like apparitions from the past. I could hear the click of their footsteps, the laughter, see their bright and curious faces that filled the room with expectation. The hymns that once rang inside the white walls came alive again. I began humming one softly, a song by Fanny Crosby, the words as comforting as the melody:

> He hideth my soul in the cleft of the rock
> That shadows a dry, thirsty land;
> He hideth my life with the depths of His love,
> And covers me there with His hand.

That was all I could remember; the years had erased the lyrics from my mind. But the melodies had imprinted themselves inside me even if the words had vanished. Now the faces of the people came into focus, fine-hearted, decent people who had come to find God — people I had forgotten too easily. Instead I had chosen to remember the extremists: the Davids, the Roberts, the Jerry Falwells. I had lumped them together and evicted them all from my life. Some of the sincere souls at Calvary Baptist had reached out to me after the divorce; I had never returned their phone calls. Susan had continued to try and keep in touch, but I had habitually made excuses not to meet her for lunch. The good Christians in my life had not abandoned me as much as I had abandoned them.

At that moment the great mystery that hides behind our tears, behind our exhausted, browbeaten days, seemed to shine through the clouds and let me know that grace had always been there, watching over me, watching over my children. I cried over my own bitterness — the anger that I'd clung to like a tattered blanket for years. It was time to let it go. It was time to separate the concept of spirituality from the aberration of Fundamentalism.

Sixteen

The Absence of Dogma

THE PIGEONS SCATTERED as I walked onto the University of Washington campus, crossing the snow skifted plaza of Red Square with an important document tucked under my arm. The magnificent Suzzallo Library loomed before me. Built in 1926 and not much disturbed by renovation, its sandstone walls rose six stories into the silent, overcast sky. A platoon of terra-cotta heroes jutted out from its facade a hundred feet over my head, peering down from their niches: Dante, Shakespeare, Plato, Sir Isaac Newton, Leonardo da Vinci, Goethe, and Darwin, symbolizing—and protecting—the pursuit of truth.

Stepping into the warm entryway, I was greeted with the pleasant smell of old books. I wound up the staircase into the library's sixty-foot-high Gothic reading room, a space set apart from the commonplace elements of this world. Sandstone rafters meet at a pitched angle above the floor-to-ceiling windows that line both sides of the grand hall. Immense brass chandeliers cast a buttery glow onto the frescoed ceiling, ornamented with rich colors and gilded stenciling, the closest thing the Pacific Northwest can compare to the Sistine Chapel. Panels along the far wall bear the names of explorers: Marco Polo, Christopher Columbus, Ferdinand Magellan, and Vasco da Gama in the south; and in the north, Juan Ponce de Leon, Hernando Cortés, Vasco Balboa, and Hernando de Soto. Oak

bookcases topped with intricate hand carvings, ribbed wood paneling, and Gothic ironwork fill the room with ornamentation and the
sort of symbolic messages that one might expect to find in the great
hall of a secret society.

As if oblivious of the grandeur surrounding them, a scattering of people sat at the wooden desks, engrossed in their irregu-
lar French verbs and integral theorems — or fast asleep, dreaming
of spring break in Florida. I picked out a cozy alcove under a beam
of warm light, nestled in, and opened the book I had carried in with
me. I could feel my heart quicken as I started my fascinating journey
into the gnostic gospels, the translation of a two-thousand-year-old
codex that had been discovered in 1945. That year, near the town
of Nag Hammadi, on an Egyptian mountainside honeycombed
with ancient gravesites, an Arab peasant named Mohammad Ali al-
Samman was digging for *sabakh,* a soft soil used to fertilize crops,
when his mattock clunked against something. It proved to be an
earthenware jar. Although he was reluctant to break it, fearing that
he might release a spirit that lived inside, he also hoped it might
contain gold, so he raised his shovel and smashed the jar. Thirteen
leatherbound papyri fell out. Mohammad Ali had stumbled upon
the Secret Books of Jesus — the gnostic gospels. All but fragments
of them had disappeared in the fourth century when the Roman
Catholic Church banned them as heretical; merely possessing them
had been decreed a criminal offense. While the church's minions ma-
rauded the countryside, finding the manuscripts and burning them,
someone, possibly a monk from the nearby St. Pachomius monas-
tery, had saved these copies from destruction by rolling them up and
sealing them in the terra-cotta jar, where they remained for almost
sixteen hundred years. There was little debate about the date of their
origin. Scholars placed the writings between AD 350 and 400.

They were copies of earlier documents written in the second half of the first century AD — as early as, or even earlier than, the Gospels of Matthew, Mark, Luke, and John.

From earlier reading I already knew that the gnostics had been a mystical sect of Christians, who afforded women equality with men and refused to create a priesthood, casting lots at each service to determine a new leader. They believed that God was both male and female and viewed the Scripture as metaphor and not law. I had read about the gnostic gospels but never actually studied the writings; now I felt light-headed as I began to explore the ancient texts.

In the silence of the reading room, the words of the secret gospels filled my head, summoning up a world of vineyards and fig trees flanking dusty, winding roads into rock-walled cities. Out of the pages I saw Mary Magdalene walking in leather sandals worn thin by the rocky hillside. She stopped to take refuge from the searing heat in an olive grove outside Judea. In the next moment, the gnostic Jesus appeared beside her. He had the same calm eyes I remembered in paintings from my childhood, but his face was stronger and more intelligent, with chiseled Semitic features and dark skin. Standing before Mary, he spoke quietly about the road to enlightenment. He told her she must let her soul peer through the mind, past the bonds of this material world; only then would it be free to dwell in the eternal gnosis, the knowledge of spiritual truth. Her illuminated spirit would see the interconnectedness of all things: "All natures, all formations, all creatures exist as one . . . Go then and preach the gospel . . . Do not lay down any rules beyond what I appoint . . . do not give a law like the lawgiver." Next, Jesus kissed her on the mouth, as, according to the text, he did often.

Then a young, fresh-skinned Thomas Didymus appeared, sitting at a wooden table in a dirt-floored home in Caesarea, locks of dark curls falling into his eyes. He held his quill to weathered parchment. "Tell me of your secret teachings," he coaxed Jesus.

"Whoever finds the interpretation of these sayings will not experience death," the gnostic Christ began. "If you bring forth what is within you, what you bring forth will save you . . . He who has known himself has simultaneously achieved knowledge about the depth of all things."

As his eyes rose from the manuscript he was writing, Thomas finally understood the esoteric message Jesus had been delivering in parables and symbols — that the same divinity that Christ possesses dwells inside us all. Jesus looked at Thomas and said, "I am no longer your master."

Suddenly Christ's words harmonized with those from all of the great mystical traditions: "Look within yourself and find God," said the Buddha. "The Lord is enshrined in the hearts of all," states the Isha Upanishad. The Islamic Sufi mystic Rumi declared, "Deep in our hearts the light of heaven is shining." Confucius said, "What the undeveloped man seeks is outside; what the advanced man seeks is within himself."

I imagined the rocky shores of the Jordan, where a small group of gnostic followers shivered, the cold whipping their garments. Their leader, Valentinus, standing in the current, called for them to enter and be awakened. "As you lower into the water and are resurrected out, you will be reborn to the knowledge of your own divinity," he said.

The clock chimed outside in the plaza, and I sat up. I thought about the similarities between Christian gnosticism and other mystical faiths I had read about, those that shunned religious dogma and taught inner enlightenment. For years I had assiduously avoided Christianity, but now I wondered if the gnostic Christ might have been onto something: inner knowing rather than outward doctrine. The thought reminded me of a small Buddhist temple in the woods, where people meditated on Sunday mornings for ninety minutes at a time. When I first heard about the place, I'd thought, *That sounds crazy, sitting for an hour and a half—I'd go mad.* But that afternoon in the Suzzallo Library, I decided that I was ready to give the experience a try.

On a bright spring morning in May, I pulled up the driveway and parked next to an immaculate Japanese-style home. Behind it a finely raked gravel path disappeared into a lush garden. Following the trail, I let it direct me into another world as it wandered past silent ponds reflecting the garden hush, lotus-white lilies, and carved stone pots pouring tranquility from bamboo waterfalls. The perfume of cedar and juniper permeated the morning sunshine beaming through the Japanese maples. Violet moss flowers lined the path as a thicket of thin bamboo reeds brushed their emerald smoothness against my legs. The garden was redolent of rain moistened earth warming to life. Then, at a turn in the clearing, a lovely cedar structure emerged, a small but exquisite wooden temple.

Symbolism inspires the Buddhist temple's design. The foundation stands on a square base representing the earth, crowned by a winged roof, emblematic of water. The flight of stairs ascending the temple represents the steps of illumination, and its stylized peak recalls the wind. Earth, water, fire, and air: simply contemplating the structure is said to draw the observer closer to enlightenment — the realization that all is one.

As I walked up the creaking cedar steps, they emanated a warm, lingering sweetness. A huge keisu gong protected the doorway, while oriental lanterns danced in the soft summer breeze. I took off my shoes and set them next to others placed neatly in a row. Incense greeted me as I stepped into a room where purple cushions lined either side of a long aisle. Up front, a shrine encasing the Buddha was surrounded with offerings of fruit and flowers, white candles, and clear water in ritual bowls. Since I had never attended such a service, I kept my eyes on the people seated on the purple cushions, cross-legged, holding their hands in a circle, thumbs to thumbs, left palm cradled in the right. A beautiful woman entered and lit the candles, signaling the ceremony to begin. She retreated, and the gong sounded as a large man in a black and white robe entered. He did not look at us, but walked down the aisle toward the shrine, where he lit the center candle, offering its incense to the Buddha, and then made three full prostrations on the floor.

The meditation began. The books I'd read on the subject suggested that I let my thoughts pass without judgment, observing each idea as a transitory event, not identifying with it but letting it rise and pass like a cloud in the sky. I didn't find the exercise an easy task. I kept thinking, *This is lunacy, such a waste of time, just sitting for an hour and a half . . . I'd better cook those vegetables in the fridge before they turn into fungus . . . Speaking of fungus, there's enough of it around my bathroom sink right now to harvest penicillin . . . Oh, my God, my legs are falling asleep . . . Maybe I'll move my toes just a hair to wake them up, but shit, not a soul around me is so much as twitching, and it would be a dead giveaway that I'm a total amateur . . . By the end of this, my legs will have gangrene, and they'll have to carry me out of this place on a stretcher like Gandhi.*

Finally I remembered to concentrate on my breath — in and out, in and out — and an odd thing happened. The rising and falling events in my flighty brain began to fade as faces in a dream. I felt waves washing over my mind, like a tide raking the beach, caressing my naked feet. I was a solitary gull between heaven and earth, embarking on a thousand-mile journey, beyond the sound and reach of the everyday world. For what seemed a mere moment, the leg aching and mind chattering stopped. The sunlight was like the water, the water like the sky, and the sky like the soul. The gong outside sounded, and the meditation was over. *Amazing,* I thought. *That was ninety minutes, and my legs are still with me.*

The woman passed out song booklets and then hit a huge bowl shaped gong with a padded stick. The note rang out, and everyone began to sing in the same monotone, *Tendaai Shomyooo kyooo-ku.* In the open vowel tones I heard a universal resonance reminding me of the elongated chants of the mystical sects of all major religions. The Muslim Sufis chant *Allaahh,* Buddhists and Hindus call out *Ommmm,* Jews who follow the kabbalah recite *Daai Daai ya-dle-Daai,* and Christians sing *Ah-men* and *Alleluia.* Gregorian and other Christian chants are based on these vowel tones, drawn out across notes in extended musical phrases. As we chanted, it seemed to me that at their heart, religions had more to unify them than to fight over. After we finished, the Zen master, still motionless in the lotus position, made a few observations about the interdependence of things, and that the awareness of this truth leads to *ahimsa,* a desire for nonviolence and respect for all life.

We had tea, and the ceremony was over.

A few weeks later, Susan called and left a message on my answering machine: "Please say you'll meet me for dinner. I have something very important to tell you."

Susan had booked a table at Maximilien in the Pike Place Market. The night was dry and mild, and I jumped out of my car and walked the four blocks down to the waterfront. Between the old brick and stucco buildings that bordered Virginia Street, a departing ferry moved toward Vashon Island like a drifting jack-o'-lantern.

On the corner of Post Alley, four Hispanic boys in oversized parkas and matching Lakers caps stood leaning against the wall blowing cigarette smoke into the air. I thought of Jason.

I entered the dark restaurant and saw Susan sitting in a corner booth. She looked as beautiful as ever with her coal black hair cut into a hip new do, messy and spiked on top, her lips still red and shining. As I reached the table she jumped up and threw her arms around me. I could smell the same expensive Halston perfume that she had worn for years, and I felt my body relax into her. Good friends never change, I thought.

"God, why did we let ourselves get out of touch?" she asked.

"I don't know," I said, but I did know of course. I had let it happen, willed it to happen, so busy trying to create a new life for me and my kids, unable to deal with so many parts of my past, unwilling to look back, even at old friends.

The waiter arrived at the table just then — a handsome black-tied man with white teeth and a compact smile. "Would you ladies care for a drink?"

"I'll have a martini," Susan said, "Bombay Sapphire, up with two olives, please."

"The same for me."

"So, I'm separated from Robert," she blurted out. "After all this time I know it's hard to believe, but things were simply getting unbearable."

"My God, what happened?"

"Well you know that evangelical church we've been attending for years?"

"Overlake Temple?"

"Yes. Robert decided it was just too liberal for him, so he found this totally right-wing Fundamentalist group out in Monroe and told me that we were going to start attending it. So I went, Sunday after Sunday, even though I was uncomfortable with the pastor's condemnation of *everything*. After a while I really began to miss our friends at Overlake, so I asked Robert if I couldn't attend the Saturday evening service if I continued to go to Monroe on Sunday mornings. He said no. No discussion — that was it."

"Unbelievable."

"Yeah, and it gets worse. I started attending the Saturday evening service anyway, so Robert talked to his new pastor who said I was in a state of rebellion, and if I continued attending the service at Overlake, the church would have to discipline me."

"What the hell did that entail?"

"Get this, one Sunday morning the pastor informed me that I wouldn't be allowed to take communion that day, and that he was going to call me up in front of the parish to address my rebellion toward Robert's authority. I walked out of the church. During the service he informed the congregation that the members were bound by Second Thessalonians to discipline me for disobedience to my husband — I wouldn't be able to take communion, and I was in danger of being excommunicated. I wasn't even there to defend myself, and my kids were sitting right in the service."

"What a crock of bull."

The finely dressed waiters glanced our way.

"When Robert got home that day, I took the kids and moved out of the house."

"Thank God you are free from that hypocrisy," I whispered.

"Yes, but you have to remember, Carlene, that not all Christians are like Robert and not all churches are like the one in Monroe."

"You're right," I said.

I was elated that Susan had broken away from the tyrant Robert, and that she was back in my life again. For months I considered what she'd said about religion; I knew that there was plenty of wisdom in her remarks. Each spiritual gathering had a different personality and couldn't be prejudged as unhealthy. So when a friend on my block asked me to join her for services one Sunday, I found myself, for the first time in years, packed into a Baptist church foyer. As we jostled toward the sanctuary, a sea of bodies enclosed me, and suddenly eight months of Zen calm, stored up from countless hours of meditating, evaporated in one rapid heartbeat, and I had the overwhelming urge to emulate the demon possessed man in Mark, screeching and tearing his hair from his head, bolting from the tombs of the Gadarenes. We pressed through into an enormous sanctuary. Up front an elaborate orchestra played updated hymns: "Fairest Lord Jesus" remixed in pop fashion, "The Old Rugged Cross" driven by a rock-and-roll pulse, and "How Great Thou Art" in symphonic medley. I sat down in a burgundy upholstered pew, feeling like a Yankees fan in the middle of the Seattle Mariners' home section. The worship area looked like a combination of lush mortuary and sports stadium. A huge balcony overlooked the main floor, from which clean-cut parishioners waved to their friends and made plans to meet at their favorite restaurant afterward for Sunday brunch.

An immaculate fellow with a megawatt smile stepped to the pulpit. He was tall, sinewy, and narrow shouldered, with a bald forehead that wrinkled deeply when he smiled. Pastor Ted opened his sermon with a joke. As the sermon progressed, however, he turned grave and began to shout that the Bible demanded that God's people be set apart from sin, and then he praised the current president of the United States for taking a stand against evil in the world. "It's good to know we finally have a friend in the White House," he said, "a man who lets the God of the Bible tell him what decisions to make. A man who consults his *heavenly Father,* rather than his earthly father, when he wants to make a big decision like going to war." I shifted uneasily in my seat as "Amens!" exploded around me.

"We can also be comforted by the fact that our current House majority leader believes that God has anointed him to bring a biblical worldview to American politics. Senator DeLay has *publicly* testified to the fact that 'only Christianity offers the real truth and gives the proper answers to a lost and sinful world.'"

"Amen!" erupted around me again like hoots at an NBA tournament match, while the words of theologian Hans Küng ran through my head: "When we believe that ours is the only faith that contains the truth, violence and suffering will surely be the result."

As I listened to Pastor Ted, I wondered where such a "biblical worldview in government" would lead America. If we were going to consult the Bible on government decisions, the logical conclusion would be to create a theocracy. If the document is God-breathed, we must embrace the entire text and stop picking out only the verses we like — every sentence is fair game for our biblical America. But be afraid for your daughters if Jehovah takes over. The government could find itself in the business of stoning girls who turn out not to be virgins on their wedding night.

But didn't entangling holy law with national law set up a state religion and violate the free rights of all? Didn't such religion, whether taken from the Bible or the Koran, isolate and entrench us, destroying any hope of achieving harmony with one another? Instead of viewing the world as a collaborative, interconnected whole, such a "faith" divides us along doctrinal and religious preferences, tempting us to believe that God has taken our side. It seemed to me that Jesus — the gnostic and the canonical Christ — said that when we show kindness to others, we show kindness to ourselves, and that when we judge others, we judge ourselves. If we were at war with our "unsaved" family, neighbors, or a "godless" society, a war was surely raging inside us. It made me suspect that our capacity to make peace with the world and those around us depended primarily on our capacity to make peace with ourselves.

I HADN'T SEEN David in ages when Micael asked if we could give him a ride to the airport on the day she was leaving for the Middle East. My heart sank. "Sure, that would be fine," I said, feigning nonchalance. I already had enough to be worried about. Micael would be among the first group of Peace Corps volunteers ever sent into Azerbaijan, a country bordering Iran, where she would be stationed alone in a remote village somewhere near the Caspian Sea. I wouldn't see her for two years. She had graduated from Willamette University in Oregon in the spring of 2003 and decided to serve in the Peace Corps before going on to graduate school. I was thankful that Carise, at least, was staying on "safe" soil. She had graduated from Western Washington University that same year and was now working at a public relations firm in Seattle. But Jason was about to depart for a destination even more disturbing than Micael's. He had flourished in the Job Corps; the tattooed young men there had turned out to be good-hearted and generous, offering Jason friendship and camaraderie. After graduating, he had joined the Washington State National Guard. He had grown into a fine young man, strong and thoughtful. Several days before Micael's departure, I received his phone call: "Mom, they've just called us up for active duty. I'm training in urban warfare, and I'll be in Baghdad on street patrol within a few months."

So I was in no mood to exchange small talk with David.

Immediately my mind began picking through scraps of the past, digging in the upturned dirt of blame. As I felt a wave of resentment toward him, I chastised myself. I shouldn't be holding a grudge against David. My life was good. I had been fortunate in meeting a wonderful man, someone who had become an important part of my new life, a kind and gentle person whom my kids also adored. I had been blessed in my career as well. An entry-level job at the local public television station had led to a position as coordinating producer on an exciting new PBS series. Best of all, Carise, Micael, and Jason had grown into happy, adventurous adults.

David's life seemed on solid ground as well. Since finishing his detox program, he had stayed sober and was now an apartment manager in south Seattle, and a part-time minister and teacher at a local Unity church. In classes and sermons, David frequently discussed his former life as a conservative pastor, describing his descent into pornography and alcoholism, warning the congregation against self-righteousness and religious arrogance and using the Bible as a weapon of judgment. He was turning his life around, and even though I knew I should let go of my anger, part of me still shook a silent fist at him.

When he got into the car that evening, I was stunned by his appearance. His gray hair was thinning, and his eyes looked red and weary — sunburned by the glare of life. "Hello, David," I said with counterfeit cheeriness. But after that words abandoned me. For several seconds the air was stone still. Then Carise, ever the diplomat, jumped in with a question about her father's new girlfriend, and Micael followed up by asking about his latest sermon. I kept my gaze fixed on the road and avoided eye contact.

At the airport, as we lugged Micael's baggage to the check-in counter, I glanced at him and remembered how he had looked almost thirty years before, boarding an international flight to West Germany, off to smuggle Bibles into Communist countries — strong, idealistic, and unafraid. He had been much like his beautiful daughter was this evening: glowing with excitement and confidence.

That summer of 1976, I had flown to France with the same Bible smuggling fervor. We had been soldiers together, he and I, setting out to save the world, testifying to all who would listen. Now the words had become ghosts in our mouths. It was then I noticed that David was weeping, tears streaming down his cheeks and onto his jacket. It was not like him to show such unchecked emotion in public. I knew him — probably better than anyone — and as I looked at his face, I could feel his heartbreak. He ached for the loss of years, the time he had foolishly squandered, absent from his children's lives — the evening when Carise descended the staircase, radiant in her first prom dress, or the afternoon Micael burst in to announce that she had landed the lead role in the school play, Jason's championship soccer game — these could never be recaptured.

As we walked Micael to the departure gate, I wept as well. I cried because I would miss her terribly, but I also wept for David. I suddenly understood that his burden was more than I had imagined. In a rush of tears, I forgave him for the past, releasing my bitterness toward him, casting it far into a dark abyss. In an odd irony of events, David and I had traveled along much the same path: youthful zealotry, a loss of faith, and finally, belief that spiritual growth is a road of discovery — not of submission to a rulebook. It is all we have, the ability to forgive and find common ground, the only means of turning our battered lives into song.

Epilogue

NOT LONG AFTER Jean and Doug returned to the mission field in 1992, Doug started seeing prostitutes again and reinfected Jean with venereal disease without her knowing it. They returned to America in 1996, and during a routine pap smear Jean discovered she had not only venereal disease but also uterine cancer. Her doctor told her the cancer was a direct result of being infected for so long. Jean fought her cancer and won, divorced Doug, and is now married to a Washington State patrolman.

Susan has filed for divorce from Robert and is now a successful real estate agent in Seattle.

Dan has hired a woman to expand his ministerial staff of fourteen associate pastors.

A little over a year ago my father died, with the Camas Prairie grassland beneath his feet. Like his own father before him, he dropped instantly dead of a heart attack, onto the soil that he loved.

Mom has moved off the ranch and now lives near Spokane, Washington.

Carise is a sales manager for a Seattle mortgage firm. Micael returned from the Peace Corps and will attend American University as a graduate student in International Studies next fall. Jason served eighteen months in Baghdad, was promoted in rank several times, and reenlisted at the end of his term. He is now building roads in Afghanistan.

David is back in the ministry, filling churches to capacity as he gives Christian living seminars up and down the West Coast.

Acknowledgments

CARISE, MICAEL, AND JASON have been delightful companions on this journey. From childhood, they have always been kind, loving individuals. Each one read the manuscript before it was ever submitted for publication, offering insight, critique, and encouragement. Although they are first and foremost my children, now as adults they are also my cherished friends.

Rupert Macnee has been my steady ally on this path.

Bonnie Solow has shown me unwavering support and friendship. Bonnie is the perfect agent: brilliant, warm, and resolutely tenacious.

Chuck Adams has been a great honor to work with. He is a superb editor, always motivated by deep wisdom and a warm heart.

Robert Jones, my copyeditor, has exhibited astonishing knowledge of all things human and divine.

And finally, everyone at Algonquin Books has been utterly gracious and a true pleasure to work with.

About the Author

CARLENE CROSS EARNED A DEGREE in Religious Studies from Big Sky Bible College before marrying the minister of a thriving Fundamentalist church near Seattle, Washington. As a minister's wife she was a popular feature soloist — both vocal and flautist — performing for conferences and retreats throughout Washington. She also taught Bible studies, family life seminars, and counseled scores of women in the movement.

In 1990 she divorced and returned to school to complete a BA in history and an MA in communications history from the University of Washington. She lives in Seattle, where she has worked as a college counselor and a public television producer.

She is author of a previous nonfiction work entitled *The Undying West: A Chronicle of Montana's Camas Prairie,* published in 1999.